Back Lanes and Muddy Pitches

Rob

Published by Zymurgy Publishing

A CIP catalogue record for this book is available from the
British Library

Cover design by Nick Ridley

10 9 8 7 6 5 4 3 2 1

Printed and bound by Bookmarque Limited, Croydon. U.K.

ISBN 1 903506 12 3

Published by Zymurgy Publishing, Newcastle upon Tyne
© 2004 Zymurgy Publishing

About The Author

Robert Rowell was born and brought up in Gateshead.
He studied accountancy in Sheffield before moving to Italy
in his early twenties.
He now lives near Montpellier in France, with his wife,
Marie-Anne, and two young daughters, Isabella and
Charlotte.
He is 45.

"It's almost seven in the morning when we make it back to our bedrooms, after one last glass of champagne. My room, number 15, is on the ground floor, along the corridor on the right. Theatre of so much discussion and so many difficult, often painful decisions, I enter it now like I have never entered it before, with my wife on one arm, and the World Cup under the other!"

Aimé Jacquet,
French national coach, 1998

"Football… bloody hell."

Sir Alex Ferguson,
Manchester United Manager, 1999

Robert Rowell vs. Rest of the World
49 Whitehouse Crescent, Springwell Estate, Gateshead
7 August, 1959

Wet And Slippery

Push!

And again, Mrs. Rowell. Puuuush!

With the scores level after nine months, we were now well into extra time. Legend has it that when I finally reared my ugly head, I was already six weeks late, and the ten and three-quarter pounds at which I was officially recorded add weight to that story. Quite a lot of weight come to think of it.

Six weeks! You'd think I'd be kicking to get out, but what Doctor Arthur didn't know was that it wasn't so much my mother who wasn't pushing (did you ever hear of a mother *pulling* during childbirth?), it was more a case of me desperately hanging on in there.

Why was I so afraid of making my very first tackle, that of entering the world? Maybe it was the thought of leaving the cosy thirty-seven degrees of the womb – where I had been happily chewing away on the placenta of the twin that never was – for the wet and windy north-east of England. A more likely reason is that when I was pulling on my genes in preparation for the big jump, I noticed they were completely covered in ginger hair and freckles, and the thought of how painful my youth would be as a result made me adamant that I would not be going anywhere. How would you fancy being laughed at and having your head kicked in by all those rough Geordies?

Finally, though, after many hours of labour and several near-death experiences, Robert Louis (Henry by the time Dad had managed to crawl out of the pub and into the registry office) Rowell was born. The doctor said I was a fighter to have come out alive, which is funny when you think I've been as soft as clarts ever since.

There are no photographs to prove it, but the simple fact that I have never been what you would call "bonny" at any stage of my life that I can remember, leads me to the conclusion that I was most probably not a "bonny baby". This theory of mine is confirmed by my sisters almost throwing up when they first saw me. As expected, the ginger hair and freckles were there in abundance, accompanying me throughout my childhood right up to my late teens, when, thankfully, I started to lose both. I was also "blessed" from the off with Dad's chicken-legs, an excuse for a chest, and milky-white skin – the sort of bluey whiteness you cannot get with cheaper washing powders. These "assets" have remained with me ever since, if anything becoming accentuated with the passing of the years, and nowadays tend to keep me away from beaches populated by Italians.

Mam and Dad, legendary couple. Mam was born a McGregor, a name once banned from Britain for a hundred years, thanks to Rob Roy and his clan's (unfair) reputation for robbing the rich to give to themselves. She met Dad during the Second World War while he was stationed in Scotland. Dad just found time to get shot in the chest during the Battle of Normandy – quite a feat when you think he was running away from the Germans at the time – before recovering to be "gently persuaded" by my mother's twenty or so brothers to do the decent thing. They married on the very last day of the war, which was a case of out of the frying pan and into the fire as far as Dad was concerned, since that's when the real war started. Dad sums up his sixty year love-hate relationship with Mam and her family in a way only he can: "The McGregors are a wonderful family", he says, "but I was just unlucky."

That's Dad for you. To the outside world he was Harry, full-time office clerk, part-time pianist, always the joker and one of the lads. To his wife Margaret, however, he was a bloody old flamer, a bloody old waster and a bloody-old-goat-if-ever-there-was-one. "Yer a big man", she would mock, "but a wee jacket fits yer." In public she might have played along to the lady-in-the-shadows image, but between the (literally) four walls of number 49 Whitehouse Crescent, she was, quite simply, the boss. And the boss she always remained, even though we all grew to be about twice her size.

Thinking back, I shouldn't have been so afraid of going in for that first tackle, since all the ingredients were there to make of me the greatest footballer that ever lived. First, this was Gateshead, manufacturer of fine footballers since the last century, and the perfect place to learn the footballing trade. Second, this was Springwell Estate – *tough* Gateshead – and as we all know, the tougher the area, the better the player. Third, this was already quite a sporting family, there being three elder guinea pigs to show the way: Gloria the gymnast bounced up, down and off school trampolines; Ellen the athlete huffed and puffed her way around the half mile; and Audrey the netballer had elbowed half of Gateshead's girls into submission by the time I arrived on the scene. Fourth, I had football in the blood. Dad had been a bit of a Stanley Matthews in his day, and rumour has it that Saint Mirren came knocking on his door just after the war (I never really found out why he didn't open it). Finally, there was a fair chance of my inheriting what I would call the low centres of gravity of my parents – Tom Sharpe would be less polite and say they were PORGs – Persons Of Restricted Growth. What I'm getting at is that Maradona wouldn't have been Maradona had he been six feet tall. (As it turned out, probably due to having porridge forced down my throat every morning for fifteen years, I comfortably outgrew my parents, and nowadays they have to take the stepladders out to consult me.) The only visible flaw in the DNA make-up was a (by then late) French grandmother, who apparently claimed that football was a lot of fuss over "running after a balloon" (which I suppose it was in those days). There again, what did the French ever know about football?

Anyway, once out, there was no going back. But let me just say one thing: for the sake of future generations of children afflicted, like me, by the orange syndrome, I strongly recommend that a chunk of national lottery takings be set aside to find a prevention of the disease – one that is a bit more scientifically sound than the old wives' tale about pouring the milk in before the tea during pregnancy. They could call the campaign the Fight Against Carrot Curls And Widespread Freckles. In short, FACCAWF. It could save a lot of heartbreak, I can tell you.

Whether this early handicap was the sole reason I never "made it" as a professional footballer is questionable – no doubt considerable shortages of talent and determination also played their part. Either way, though I still dream of scoring a hat-trick in the World Cup Final, in my more rational moments I am gradually beginning to accept that not only will I fail in my ambition to become the greatest footballer that ever lived, it is highly unlikely that I will come even remotely close. And so I am left wondering what went wrong. Whatever happened to all that greatness thrust upon me at birth?

To read this book, then, is to look in on the life of the one that got away. The failed footballer. Those he played with, those he played against, those he watched. And like all the other also-rans, there are a few tales to tell of great goals, great dribbles, great passes, great footballing moments, missed boats, catastrophes and bad luck.

But most of all just bad excuses.

Robert Rowell 1   Rest of the World 0
(after extra time)

Son-shine

> *Green grass was my first love –*
> *And it will be my last.*

Our Gloria threw the ball out. I dribbled it round Dad, ran up and excitedly slotted it between the post and my strangely immobile sister. Goal! One-nil!

Gloria ran off to fetch the ball, threw it out once more, and the same thing happened again. Two-nil. And again. Three-nil. Four-nil. Five-nil. Then, like the puppy that suddenly realises it doesn't have the energy to chase around any more, my lungs gave up on me. No matter. I'd won easily, and my prize of a succulent penny ice-pop was well-deserved. I was right on course to becoming the greatest footballer that ever lived!

My best guess is that this match took place some time around my fourth birthday, in the summer of 1963, but this date is about as reliable as my shooting. For a start, the fact that I was wearing only a T-shirt is no proof that it was summer-time, since the day you pull on a jumper in Geordieland is the day you enter middle age (go into Newcastle on a frosty Friday night and you'll see what I mean: all the lads are in short sleeves, and the lasses are no wiser, wearing nothing but flimsy, lobster-revealing dresses, their hunched shoulders the only indication of the sub-zero temperatures). As for the year, it could have been any time between 1960, when I learned to walk, and 1966, by which time Gloria was in her teens and had better things to do than keep goal – like wearing flimsy, lobster-revealing dresses and hunching her shoulders.

As a child, I was always, as Mam put it, "in the wars", and the few memories I have of the toddler years confirm this: falling head-first into the North Sea on my debut outing to Whitley Bay provided me with lots of nightmares and an incurable phobia for water (I still can't swim unless it's got hops in it); the scar in the middle of my forehead – clearly visible now that there's no fringe to hide it – is from when I nutted next door's antique sewing machine; and knocking over a pot of freshly-brewed tea left me with a piece of meat for a left arm that not even the butcher would try to sell you.

But the ten-minutes-of-footie-with-Dad memory stands out for being the only one of my early childhood which doesn't make me wince every time it comes to mind. It is fitting that football, my life-long obsession, is in there, but the reason I think I remember it so well is for its surreal, blissful nature.

I say surreal because it was the only time in my entire life that I recall Dad letting me win; in fact sometimes I wonder whether it actually happened at all. For as long as I can remember, life with Dad was one, long father-versus-son contest. Whether it be football or Scrabble, Margaret Thatcher's politics or who Mam had dished out the most potatoes to, you name it, we battled and argued over it.

And there was no getting the better of him, either. For Dad hated losing, even to his own kids, and would rather see us in tears than admit defeat. He tried so hard that during play his cheeks would go all beetroot, and the intense concentration made his lips shrivel up. It didn't help that he happened to be the world's biggest – and I'm struggling to find a kinder word for it – cheat (the French blood, no doubt). He also played the sort of wicked mind games that would make Alex Ferguson look like a saint.

Take snooker. Just as I might be about to pot the unmissable black to win the frame, right on cue would come "watch the white doesn't go in-off into the bottom pocket". Hand-on-the-shoulder, fatherly advice? Not a chance. It was all designed to get my neurons in a twist, and it worked too. The bottom pocket in question would suddenly take on the size of the entrance to the Channel Tunnel, the shot was inevitably messed up, and before you could say wily wizard of the green baize, Dad had potted the black and was singing *Oh I do like to be beside the seaside* – which is what he always sang to rub salt into the wound. Even at chess, where my fifteen books on the subject (some of which I'd even opened) plus three "A"-levels to his none, were surely guaranteed to triumph over his decaying old brain, he would still manage to have me sweating from start to finish. And just when I knew I had him, and could feel the childish grin creep uncontrollably across my face in view of Rook to H8 and checkmate, mate, Dad would bring out plan B for Blatant, accidentally on purpose give the table a kick, and the board and all its players went flying across the carpet.

There was a time, during the twenty years or so between adolescence and my mid-thirties, when merely walking into the room in which Dad was sitting was enough to get the adrenalin going, but nowadays, thankfully, that's all behind me. Not because Dad can't kick a ball any more (he can) or has lost his win-at-all-costs fighting spirit (quite the contrary, old age has made him into a worse loser and bigger cheat than ever), but simply because I refuse to play him. I just can't stomach the thought of letting him see, now that he's an ageing great granddad and I'm a seen-it-all, high-flying big nob, how his psychological tricks are still worth ten points at table tennis, or how upset I can become when he kicks his golf ball a few yards further up the fairway, and sings that stupid bloody song of his about the seaside.

Dad's out-of-character behaviour aside, the memory remains above all a blissfully happy one, not because of the scoreline (though no doubt it helps) but because that was the day I fell in love for the first time – with the feel, colour and smell of grass, my footballing aphrodisiac. And unlike all my later love affairs with girls, Newcastle United centre-forwards, that kind of thing, this one was to be for ever.

Indeed many of my life's rare, utterly peaceful moments have involved nothing more than lying down in a field – usually following all-afternoon games of football – while sipping on penny ice-pops, and dreaming lovely dreams about one day having my very own football pitch. It is fitting, then, that I write this on a lovely, early Spring day in our little house in Normandy. There outside is my very own, freshly mown (if rather uneven) half-acre, with home-made goal, complete with net. If my luck is in, my wife will agree to leave her roses alone, and swap her gardening gloves for the goalkeeping variety, *fingas adidas*. That way I'll be able to spend the rest of the afternoon caressing Platini-style free-kicks into the top corner, before collapsing in a luxurious sea of sun, sweat and chlorophyl. The penny ice-pops are on me!

My love of grass is such that if ever I die (and it is looking increasingly likely that some day I will), please: no flowers. Cover my tomb instead with the green stuff – its beautiful scent will be enough to send me w-a-a-a-y-y-y up into the heavens.

Me 5   Dad 0

Sunderland vs. Newcastle United (first leg)
Dean Street, Gateshead
Autumn 1965

Rain At First…

I was two when we moved down hill and up market to 21 Dean Street in Low Fell, and a year older when they pushed Dad's piano up through the snow to number 58. There we even had our very own front garden. It was admittedly no bigger than a five-pound note, but it was a garden all the same, and to us it was like living in the countryside. Unfortunately, Dad's fingers were greyer than they were green, and I was shocked to come in one day to find that he'd cemented the whole thing over, thus blotting out nature from our lives altogether.

It took a while to get going seriously with the football. There was simply nobody to play with. My first ever friend was "Decksie" Robinson, with whom I shared an interest in cutting hands on broken glass to see what blood looked like. But never football. When his family moved away there was Larry Pitman, with whom I had daily "barnies" and climbed walls. Until the day he brought half the car park wall of the Black Horse down on my big toe – the first of many incidents in my life involving public houses. Then there was Jim Bratton, but all he ever wanted to do was play with his Dinkys. And the McGuinness sisters down the street weren't much use either, somewhat distancing themselves when I nearly put one of their eyes out with an arrow. And still no football.

With half of Low Fell out through suspension or injury, I often had to make my own amusement. This basically consisted of driving an invisible car up and down the sides of the pavements of Dean Street. It was big-time enjoyment, too, what with all the gears, the horn, the left- and right-hand indicators. And unlike Dad's Ford Zephyr, my car went for ages without breaking down. Who needs football when you can drive your own car at six years old?

One early evening, just as I was pulling in to fill up at the lamp-post at the top of Dean Street, two mean-looking older boys came up to me. They had "we're gonna knack your head in" written all over their faces, and for once I wished I'd had Dad's car windows to wind up – at least his were real. I instinctively cowered down and braced myself for the inevitable stranglehold, but nothing came, and when I finally drew up the courage to look up from behind my steering wheel it was a question, not a fist, they hit me with.

"Hey kid, who do yer support, Newcastle or Sunderland?"

As any Geordie will tell you, getting the answer to this question right has a bigger influence on your chances in life than all the university degrees in the world. Not only that, in Gateshead, supporting the wrong team was considered sufficient justification for the big and tough to beat up the little and feeble (Ian Peters, for example, spent half his childhood doing me in for not supporting Manchester United, and when I look at all the trophies they've won since, sometimes I wish I'd seen the sense he was trying to knock into me). But at that precise moment I didn't have a clue about the relative merits of the two clubs. And there being no time to do a fifty-page feasibility study the way I probably would nowadays, I simply plumped for the team with the longest name.

"Sunderland?"

"OK kid. See you around." And off they went. No stranglehold, nothing. It seemed that I'd got it right. Relieved, I filled up and drove off.

A day or two later, I was just parking outside our front door when a very strange thing happened. A ball came bouncing down the hill. Then all of a sudden boys I'd never seen before appeared from nowhere, and in an instant football took over as the one and only pastime in our neighbourhood. All things considered, I was quite happy to say good-bye to playing with the traffic. Robert Rowell, Sunderland supporter, had parked his invisible car for good.

Sunderland 1   Newcastle United 0

Newcastle United vs. Sunderland (second leg)
58 Dean Street, Gateshead
Autumn 1965

...Brighter Spells Later

Just a few days after avoiding being filled in while filling up, we were paid a visit by Auntie Ellen, Uncle Gordon, and their two teenage sons, David and Ian. I was in awe of this family, for it seemed to differ from our own in almost every respect. First, they lived in stinking rich Gosforth, where they had a house that didn't need to lean on the next one along to stop it from falling down, with luxurious bay windows and grass both front and back. Second, the parents were capable of speaking to each other without raising their voices, in what sounded to me at the time like the Queen's English (bear in mind I hadn't yet been south of Durham) – a remarkable achievement when you remember that being born a Geordie doesn't exactly provide you with the tight lips of royalty. Finally – and most impressively – the two boys were able to sit quite contentedly on the sofa without shuffling their feet, picking their noses or wrestling with each other. They wore the sort of perm-pressed smiles that don't budge even when you punch them in the teeth, and it was clearly just a question of time before they'd be running successful scout groups, successful marriages and successful careers. The only possible blemish on their characters was a latent fondness for philately, otherwise they were perfect, and quite naturally I looked up to them. In summary, this was the kind of family you see on the cover of life assurance pamphlets, where everyone has grey hair, cardigans with all their buttons, and happy families smiles all round – this in the knowledge that were they all to be killed in a train crash tomorrow, they'd become very rich indeed.

I looked forward to the visits of my cousins, mainly because I was the sole beneficiary of the toys they'd grown out of. Train sets, model aeroplanes and Meccano were all solemnly handed over in their original boxes in pristine condition; by the end of the day I'd smashed them to bits. So when I saw their car pull up on the Sunday afternoon in question, I came dashing in from the street to see what Santa had brought.

"Just wait and see what the boys have got for you", said Auntie Ellen, and the most important gift I have ever received was ceremoniously held up in front of me.

What? A Newcastle United shirt? I struggled to hide my disappointment.

"What's the matter? Don't you like it?"

"Er, it's just that I think I'm a Sunderland supporter."

"Sunderland? You support Sunderland? But they're rubbish!"

Who was little I to argue with the Osmond brothers? The shirt's V-shaped neck might have been from the late fifties and consequently unwearable on Dean Street, but one thing was for sure: I had seen the black-and-white light.

A question often asked of professional footballers in soccer magazines is: who was the greatest influence on your career? I know what my answer would be: David and Ian. For in rescuing me from the clutches of Sunderland Association Football Club, they didn't so much influence my career as save my bloody life. I don't need a psychologist to explain to me that those few days of being a Sunderland fan were responsible for many a boyhood nightmare about having two heads and wagging a tail. And I shudder to think what would have become of me had my cousins not paid us a visit that day. For once you are a Newcastle United supporter, trying to picture being a Sunderland fan is like a man trying to imagine being a woman. You can't – and in this case even cross-dressing isn't an option. For the instant you become a Magpie, you have no choice but to hate everything about the "mackems". You can't control it, it's in the air you breathe, the food you eat (incidentally, the worst hamburger I ever had was at the only Sunderland home game I ever attended). You loathe the club and its supporters, the town and its people. Not forgetting that dreadful wee-wee-wee Wearside accent. Just imagine standing through ninety minutes of that!

The neutrals say, isn't it great for north-east football when both Newcastle and Sunderland are in the Premier League. I say, frankly, no, it's not. Sunderland have arguably been a better run club than Newcastle for most of the last hundred or so years (six league titles to our four), but as far as I'm concerned, they could win the league ten times on the trot and it wouldn't change a thing. They'd still be Sunderland, and that to me means they will always be second division.

This said, having left Geordieside many years ago, I must say I no longer sense the bitter rivalry that those who live there assure me still exists. Indeed as I enter my middle ages, I feel a certain amount of shame at having spent so much of my life hating Sunderland, and am becoming more and more compassionate towards that (surprisingly high) number of unfortunate people who didn't have life-saving cousins like mine. Rather like my feelings towards Brussels sprouts, I know I'll never love them, but I'm working damned hard on not throwing up every time I see one. So much so that whenever I'm back on Geordieside nowadays and come across a red-and-white jersey in the street, no longer do I sneer and do a U-turn. I ask instead whether one of its heads wouldn't like a sweet, or offer to hold its tail as it crosses the road. After all, the poor beggars need all the help they can get.

Newcastle United 1   Sunderland gone.

England vs. West Germany
58 Dean Street, Gateshead
30 July, 1966

Clouded

It's the final minute of extra time. England captain Bobby Moore clears his lines by playing an inch-perfect ball out to centre-forward Geoff Hurst, ten yards inside the German half.

Just then, there's a knock at the front door. Instinctively all the farting stops in case Mam lets them in. Dad's eyes and ears are too busy concentrating on the events at Wembley, though, and he hears nothing.

Neither does Geoff Hurst. Exhausted, he slowly advances towards Tilkowski's goal.

Another knock. Louder this time. Dad jumps through the roof. "Who the bloody hell is that at this time of day?" Mam takes a break in her baking to show Mrs. Carson, an elderly lady from down the street, into the front room. We should have known it was her all along, since she always turns up during important football games: "My husband's watching some daft football match so I thought I'd pop in." She then assures us that's she's "not stoppin'", which is Geordie for I'll be here all afternoon, and takes off her coat.

Dad sighs. He doesn't have time for Mrs. Carson at the best of times. His face struggles to produce a smile for the nosiest person on Dean Street, and his attention immediately returns to the television set.

Hurst's unchallenged run takes him to the edge of the German penalty area. And commentator Kenneth Wolstenholme begins what will become the most memorable sentence ever uttered in the history of English football. "Some people are on the pitch…"

Mrs. Carson is now cosily installed on the sofa, quite unaware that history is about to be made just a few feet across the room. Instead she is going through her warm-up routine, preparing her chops for action. But with England seconds away from victory, there is only one thing on Dad's mind, and the mind of every Englishman in the land. "Kick the bugger! Kick it out of the bloody ground for God's sake!"

"…They think it's all over…"

Mrs. Carson takes a deep breath and comes lunging in. "And I says to her bla bla bla and you know what she goes and says back bla bla bla and I said well you cheeky devil you bla bla bla and – yes milk no sugar please Margaret – so I says I'm not having any of this bla bla bla and I walked out the shop and eeeeeeeee you should have seen her face."

But Dad rides the challenge like a man who has endured Mrs. Carson's late tackles before. "Wallop the bugger man! Wallop it!"

Geoff Hurst must have heard him this time. Ignoring Alan Ball's call to pass it across the area, he pulls back his left leg in preparation for one, final, almighty swipe at the ball. Its intended destination: the moon.

Mrs. Carson isn't happy. In normal circumstances she'd have control of the midfield and ninety per cent of the possession, but today she just can't seem to get a kick. So she prepares her vocal cords for a last-gasp, studs-down-the-shins tackle. "Harry Rowell, you're a rude man and you're not listening to a word I'm saying!"

"Schhhh man! Can't you see it's the World Cup Final!"

BOOOMPH. The German goal jumps off its hinges. Wolstenholme's timing is perfect "…It is now!"

Jackie Charlton falls to the ground in tears. Bobby Moore, the Jules Rimet trophy held aloft, is hoisted up by his team-mates. And Nobby Stiles does a toothless jig. England are world champions.

"Well thank you very much, I must say!" But for once in her life, Mrs. Carson is drowned out. She is the only person in the whole of England who isn't jumping around their front room with joy.

Except, that is, for me. For the most striking thing about England's only ever World Cup triumph is that, unlike all my other friends of the same age, I have no recollection of it whatsoever. Which is strange when you consider that I was already football daft at the time. I have the written records to prove it, too. Just weeks after the World Cup Final, our schoolteacher, Mrs. Wilkinson, had us write a diary every morning. In mine all I ever seemed to talk about was football ("Yesterday I played with Jim. First he scored no goals and then he scored three goals."). But there is no mention of the World Cup Final. No mention of Geoff Hurst. Not even of Mrs. Carson. Nothing.

The reason is quite simple. I loved playing football too much to ever watch it on television. I wasn't yet interested in what England were up to, nor for that matter Newcastle United – I don't even recall our losing 3-0 home and away to Sunderland in the 66-67 season, two defeats that had I known or cared about, would have otherwise haunted me for years. So I have always had to rely on Dad to tell me about the '66 final. He of course remembers it well, partly for Mrs. Carson's unsuccessful pitch invasion, which he can laugh about now, but mainly because – he says – it was the greatest game of all time.

Then one day I saw it on video, only to nod off halfway through. The game was played at about the same pace as Dad's other favourite classic, Gone With The Wind – sporadic moments of excitement being lost amongst long periods where nothing happens at all. It is amazing how much time the players were given to receive the ball, miscontrol it, have another go, advance a couple of yards, lift their heads, then kick it into the crowd. With no disrespect intended to what are among the greatest sporting heroes in English history, by modern standards the '66 Final is like watching a game of table-top football, where the only player allowed to move is the one nearest the ball.

The main problem, though, is that the only people in the world who believe England won it are the English themselves. This I discovered when I moved abroad in my early twenties. During a vicious attack on the English game by some Italian colleagues, in defence of my country I pointed out that we too had won a World Cup. But before I could say *pappardelle all'amatricciana* I had four Italians down my throat, all excitedly informing me that England didn't win the World Cup, they stole it. That "ze referee heez paid mach manny for Heengland to ween", since, for England's controversial third goal, "ze ball heez never crosseeng ze line".

Rubbish! Of course the ball crossed the line, it nearly burst the net. It was clear from the radio commentary, anybody could see that – couldn't they, ref? I went on to point out that England scored a (to we English) much more memorable fourth goal, so where was the big deal? But my arguments fell on deaf ears. At first I put this down to sour grappa on the part of the Italians – wasn't 1966, after all, the year when the North Koreans sent them home with their noodles between their legs? – but I later found out during my travels that it wasn't just the Italians, it was the whole world against us. Whether I was going through passport control in Denmark, or checking out at a village store in France, the passport controller or the cashier, seeing I was English, would mutter something ever so faintly in my ear as I passed.

"The ball never crossed the line."

England 4   West Germany 2
(after extra time)

Jessell Street Rangers vs. Dean Street Rovers
Low Fell, Gateshead
Autumn 1967

Warming Up

The greatest eight-year-old footballers that ever lived – Di Stefano, Pele, Maradona, myself – all had one thing in common: they learned the game the hard way, in the company of lads much bigger than themselves. On Dean Street, my footballing elders were Bradders, Curly, and Tubby, who were all three years older. Then came a few others, most of whose names and faces I can no longer remember, and there were even a couple of girls, too, who quite naturally played in goal. They weren't particulary good at it either.

Our little world must have been no bigger than a half-mile square, yet it contained all of the three things we needed to live happily ever after: corner-shops at which to spend our pocket money; back lanes in which to play our football; and twenty-four hours a day in which to do it all. We never crossed the outer boundaries (except to go to school, and even then only with the help of Mr. Black the lollipop man). We didn't see the need. To us, beyond Beacon Street to the north was where old people did a spot of gardening before going to Heaven; over the back lane at the top was Hell, where you were likely to have your head kicked in if ever you went there; then there was Church Road, everything beyond which was quite simply "down south"; finally, the other side of Kells Lane was where Mam and Dad went to "see a man about a dog" – their way of referring to adult activities that were none of our business, like going for a drink or to buy our Christmas presents (I crossed Kells Lane just once, the day I watched on in horror as Neil Amos got run over by a lorry on Durham Road, and after that I was quite happy to leave the dangerous business of seeing men about dogs to grown-ups).

Nowadays even the parents would think twice before roaming the back lanes the way we did back then, but in those days there simply weren't the risks. Motor cars weren't a real threat, there were so few of them, and paedophilia was a type of cheese. When a car did come along, it was simply a case of grabbing the ball and pressing your body against the back lane wall until the danger had passed. Sometimes the ball had to be sacrificed, though, usually to Low Fell's answer to James Dean, who, having just passed his test, had nothing better to do than fly around Low Fell seeing how many revs he could squeeze out of his fourth-hand Ford Rustang before it burst into flames. We found a way of putting an end to his tricks, though. One day as we watched our ball disappear under his front bumper for the umpteenth time, one of the older boys kicked out at the side of his car, connected perfectly, then fell to the ground clutching his knee as if he'd been knocked over. All I can say is that if the skid-marks in the bloke's underpants were anything like the ones he left on the Tarmac, he must have all but cacked himself. (If you are watching, Stewart Stanger, and ever wondered who put the dent in the wing of your car, it was Bradders; and by the way, if you fancy your chances, come and meet us at the school gates at four o'clock.)

Like all back lanes, ours more closely resembled open-ended squash courts than football pitches, making them the ideal place for developing close control and fracturing your skull. Looking back, they probably gave me ninety per cent of all the football skills I ever picked up, the most notable of which I still cite at job interviews when they ask me what my greatest strengths are: dribbling. I loved dribbling so much that I didn't make a single pass to a team-mate until the age of thirteen. This earned me a bit of a reputation among my mates for being "greedy", but to me they were just being jealous, since it seemed obvious to me that passing was something poor players did so that the good players – like me – could have the ball back.

I became so proficient at my art that in the end my feet were reacting to situations long before the rest of me even had a chance to weigh up whether dropping the left shoulder (trick number 15) was preferable to say, the right-foot, left-foot ball shift (number 56). And all my brain could ever do was stand and watch and say "wow, that was clever". I must say, the tricks I picked up as a child have served me well over the years, getting me out of many a sticky situation on a football field, as some feint I last performed at the age of ten suddenly reappears to leave my gob-smacked opponent flat on his backside, and both me and my team-mates pleasantly surprised.

Any coach worth his weight in training manuals will tell you that the kind of excessive dribbling I used to get up to was a total waste of energy, on the basis that passing the ball to a team-mate is nearly always a much more effective way of getting it round an opponent than trying to put it through his legs. This is true, I know it is, but the problem is that even now, all those years on, there is still a part of me that just can't help it. Nowadays my attempted dribbles usually end up with me going splat like a carrot in a food-mixer, but at least once in every match I will allow the boyhood instincts to ignore the calls of my team-mates to pass it, FOR CHRIST'S SAKE PASS IT, and off I go, catch me if you can, the more the merrier. Sometimes I get so carried away I even end up dribbling in the wrong direction, or taking on my own team-mates, but who cares? What matters isn't whether we're getting any closer to goal. It is purely a question of artistic beauty, and the sheer kick that comes from making it round the other side of two grown legs with the ball still at your feet.

Dribble, dribble, tackle, dribble, shoot, dribble, dribble, shoot, it was the same every evening and every weekend, ten kids running after a ball in a back lane. Then one day someone had the bright idea of forming a team, and from then on, whenever Bradders and Curly came to knock on my front door, it was no longer to ask if I fancied a kick-about in the back lane, it was to have a trial for Dean Street Rovers. All very impressive, though I must say I didn't really see the difference, since it still looked like ten kids running after a ball to me. Dean Street Rovers went undefeated for weeks and months, simply because there was nobody to play against. In fact the only competitive match we ever succeeded in organising was against a team from down over the other side of Durham Road, which meant venturing into seeing-men-about-dogs land. With no Mr. Black the lollipop man to show us the way, we weren't even sure we'd make it there and back alive.

That this game was going to mark a very special moment in my football career – it was after all my world debut – didn't strike me until we emerged from a hole in a hedge onto a magnificent football pitch that must have been at least twice as wide as our back lane. There was grass, admittedly long and untended, but grass all the same. And there had been no need to take our jumpers along, since our opponents had their own, home-made goals: empty oil drums for posts, and an iron rod looping round for the bar. Perhaps what intimidated me the most, though, was that they were all sparklingly clad in their favourite football teams' colours. Blimey, they must be good.

But they weren't, they were crap. As I have observed so many times since, brand new boots aren't much use when it's two left feet that fill them. And in those days at least, if your parents could afford to buy you a new set of black-and-white stripes before the previous ones had gone grey-and-grey, the chances were they could also afford to avoid living in the sort of rough-and-tough neighbourhood normally required to produce good footballers. Sure enough, our back lane technique proved far too much for our clumsy opponents, and we thrashed the pants off them.

As for me, half the size and two-thirds the age of everyone else, I spent the whole game on the wing out of the way, occasionally kicking out at thin air as the bigger boys dribbled amongst themselves. However, I did manage a larger say in the proceedings than my poor positional sense and two touches of the ball would normally have allowed. Late in the game Bradders, suddenly remembering that I was there, told me to go and stand next to the goal for a throw-in, and I watched on in joyful amazement as the ball bounced off my ginger mop before sneaking inside the post.

I succeeded in repeating the act a couple of minutes later, and the trip home afterwards was like all trips home when you've contributed two goals and your team has won. Lovely. As the older boys sang my praises, I thought forward to the day when I would be better than all of them, by which time the Newcastle United scouts would be knocking on our door, begging for me to sign up in time for the following Saturday.

I didn't have to wait long. One day, I was kicking about with Mickey Goodacre in the back lane when a man dressed in a raincoat came up and offered us sweets. Now Mam had always warned us against speaking to strangers, but this man wasn't just any old stranger, he said he was a scout for Newcastle United! Not only that, he promised he'd get us a trial if we did him a favour in return – something about him scratching ours if we scratched his. But just then, racing around the corner came good old Jimmie Dean in his Ford Rustang, we all ran for cover, and when the danger had passed the man and his raincoat were nowhere to be seen.

Needless to say, we never came across the Newcastle United scout again. Equally needless to say, I'm still waiting for that trial. I could kick that Stewart Stanger's head in.

Jessell Street Rangers 3   Dean Street Rovers 8

Newcastle United vs. Sunderland
St. James' Park, Newcastle
Boxing Day, 1967

Wyn-swept

Despite all the mouths to feed, our parents gave us wonderful family Christmases. This year, the real Santa Claus brought me a bicycle, a solid steel thing that looked much the worse for its trip down the chimney, and which Dad had re-painted red to hide the rust. I didn't yet know how to ride a bike, and it was too cold outside to try, so I took it to bits instead. And all the king's horses and all the king's men couldn't put Humpty together again.

I had to wait for the next morning's visit to Auntie Ellen's house in posh Gosforth to see what the other Santa Clauses in my life had to offer. I wasn't disappointed, either. Cousins David and Ian were going to see the derby match against Sunderland (which was always played on Boxing Day in those days), so Dad gave them enough money for ground admission and return bus fares to convince them that I was going with them. Wow! What a Christmas present! Here I was, just eight years old, I didn't even know what a proper football match looked like, yet I was about to go and see the biggest game of the season.

Dad himself wouldn't be coming with us. In the late fifties he had become disgusted by Newcastle's amateurish approach, and did something very bold, something no true supporter would ever contemplate. He divorced. To the rational mind, this split was entirely justified. With its huge supporter base, you could have been forgiven for expecting the club to be among the most successful. Not so. Boardroom squabbles and crazy decisions faithfully followed the team home and away, and if the Magpies won anything at all (three F.A. Cups in the early fifties), this was purely thanks to an F.A. ruling that prohibited directors from coming onto the pitch during games. There then followed a long, barren period during which television neutrals referred to us as "sleeping giants", this to keep our spirits up and make sure we kept turning up every week. "Coming soon to a football club near you: Silverware."

They were lying, of course. They had forgotten that one of the major problems with football directors is they insist on carrying on long after the legs have gone, on the basis that it's their ball so they can do what they like with it. Little did I know it at the time, but in accepting to go along to Saint James' Park that afternoon I was about to inherit the same bunch of geriatrics (and lack of success) that had brought about the rift with Dad. I was doomed.

But that was the last thing on my mind as we crossed Leazes Park towards the ground. Instead my eight-year-old thoughts were focused on not being an embarrassment on this my big day, and I was soon given the chance to show my cousins how big and tough I was: about a hundred yards away I spotted the red and white colours of Sunderland wrapped around the neck of a lad about my size, and immediately ran off in the scarf's direction, confidently announcing that I was going to "knack" its owner's head in. Only for my cousins to speedily call me back, thus thwarting my only ever attempt at football hooliganism. Good job, too. My true colours being gooey brown, I'd have chickened out of a fight with a girl half my age, never mind a boy my own. But David and Ian weren't to know that, and I was looking very impressive going into my first derby.

Ten minutes later I was bawling my head off. My early show of street-wisdom had obviously convinced my cousins that pushing me through a tiny gap in the corrugated iron fencing, thus saving on ground admission, would be something hard boy Robert Rowell could handle no problem. As the queue for the turnstiles slowly moved forward, they had a quick look to check there were no bobbies about, lifted me up, squeezed me through, and the cry-baby tears for which I'd become famous on Dean Street came flooding through. How could they do this to me? Hadn't Dad said there was enough money to pay for all of us? How very unGosforthlike.

David and Ian came through the legal way a full fifteen minutes later, and I was promptly led off towards traumatic experience number two: the lion's cage known locally as the Leazes End. In those days you had to be in the ground before everybody else if you wanted a spot with decent views of both goalmouths. The trouble was, everybody else usually had the same idea, and today everybody else had got there before us. I had a choice: allow myself to be passed down over everybody's heads to the front like all the other toddlers, thus allowing a clearer view of the action and with it the risk of never seeing my family again; or stay put – which understandably I did. The result was a perfect view of a dozen Geordie backsides, and the only thing to keep my morale up during the two hours to kick-off was a promise that "we'll lift you up onto our shoulders when the match starts." This and a packet of tasteless peanuts hurled up to us from the touchline in return for some pennies thrown the other way (what with all the flying objects, the linesmen had a hard job concentrating on offsides at Newcastle).

For all I saw of the game, I might just as well have stayed home and listened to the commentary on the radio. On one, maybe two occasions, David and Ian honoured their pre-match promise, lifting me up for just about long enough to track down the whereabouts of the ball, before deciding I was too heavy and gently lowering me back down into my hole. Otherwise it was a nightmare. As Nick Hornby put it, when you can't see what's going on you always imagine that the ball is flying towards the top corner of your team's goal. There again Nick Hornby is an Arsenal supporter and can afford to make jokes like that. I on the other hand am a Newcastle United supporter, so the ball usually does spend most of its time on its way towards our top corner!

On an alarmingly frequent basis we would all be uprooted and transported to another section of the ground as a result of the massive crowd shifts that accompanied intense moments of excitement, and which were part and parcel of the "enjoyment" before seats replaced standing terraces. Back then, Saint James' Park more closely resembled an overcrowded public lavatory than a football ground, and surely my kids will never believe the stories of crushed ribs, ripped-off shoes, and the trauma – on at least one occasion – of finding myself lying prostrate in the Gallowgate End, desperately trying to avoid being trampled on by all those above – and failing miserably. Aye, times were tough, but we were happy!

Thirty years later, I can still "smell" the atmosphere of that match (not to mention the soupy stench of hops from the brewery next door). The constant hum of nervous excitement, the spontaneous outbursts of chanting, and surely no sporting public will ever match a football crowd for its ability to communicate to anyone within half a mile of the ground the goings-on within: the great tidal wave of a roar when Newcastle attacked; the collective "oohs" when a shot was fired just wide, and groans when it ended up in the rafters; loud applause for a well-timed tackle or a play-switching, forty yard pass; high-pitched squeals when Sunderland's centre-forward found himself one-on-one with our 'keeper; and the occasional lull that accompanied throw-ins and goal-kicks, broken only by a solitary shout of "come on Newcastle, get stuck into them man!"

About mid-way through the first half, a brief but loud cheer gave way to enthusiastic clapping and everyone chanted *Ooh it's a corner, Ooh it's a corner.*

Corner to Newcastle, I figured.

Then in quick succession came the familiar thump of a ball being kicked, a short silence as it sailed through the air, another thump – leather against head? – then an almighty intake of breath as fifty-eight thousand, three hundred and eighty-one people leant on the bloke in front in anticipation.

Chance, I figured.

Then a bigger thump, and in an instant my ear-drums exploded and the whole of Saint James' Park started pogo-dancing on my feet.

Goal, I figured.

It was several seconds before David remembered that I was somewhere down below, so he briefly bent down to shout the good news into my ear. "Wyn Davies! What a centre-forward!" Before returning to the surface to join in the singing:

Come on without, come on within

You ain't seen nothing like the mighty Wyn.

Now I didn't know who this Wyn Davies was, but if when he scored a goal everybody – Osmond brothers from Gosforth included – went mad and sang songs about him, then I thought he must be special and that was good enough for me. From now on Wyn Davies was going to be my hero.

Wyn Davies was about the only positive to emerge from an otherwise highly distressing afternoon. By the time Newcastle scored their second – the winner – I was far too drained to savour the moment. All I wanted was for the referee to blow his final whistle so I could go home to Mam and Dad.

I have always had that feeling during Newcastle games, of wanting the referee to blow his final whistle so I can go home to Mam and Dad – even when I was old enough to go to games on my own, and tall enough to see at least one of the goalmouths. The simple fact of the matter is that I hate going to Newcastle matches. From the very moment I squeezed between those two loose sheets of corrugated iron into the

Saint James' House of Worship, Newcastle United weren't just my team any more, they were a religious faith. Even before we arrived at the spot from which I wasn't going to be able to see anything anyway, I discovered that the nice feeling I normally had when I went anywhere to be entertained, such as the pictures on Saturday mornings with our Gloria, had been replaced by a knot in my stomach. I somehow knew that what went on out there, depending on the outcome, was going to determine whether I would spend the next seven days strutting about the streets of Low Fell with my head held high, or keeping to the back lanes in order to avoid the Sunderland supporters.

To me, watching the Magpies has always been like going to the dentist's: there is a significant chance the experience will be much more painful than pleasant, and you spend the whole time wondering where the next attack on your nerve-ends is going to come from. Take the Kamikaze match at Anfield in 1996 when Newcastle lost four-three, live on Sky, with Stan Collymore scoring the winner for Liverpool in the dying seconds. Everybody was going on afterwards about what a game, the "game of the decade". Stuff that, we lost, our best ever attempt at the championship slipped further from our grasp, and I nearly had a heart attack. Not even my fridge's entire supply of "anaesthetic" was enough to dull the pain. Oh how I would have loved instead to have hidden myself away in a soundproof room, to learn afterwards that we'd sneaked a defensively-perfect, Arsenal-like, one-nil win. And judging by the expressions on the faces of those Newcastle fans Sky zoomed in on afterwards, no doubt they would have opted for the same – they certainly weren't crying because they'd missed the last train back to Newcastle!

If possessing a brain and following Newcastle United are two things that clearly don't go together, why on earth, then, do I feel compelled to support them? The answer is: the same reason I used to feel compelled to go on the Big Dipper – everyone would call me chicken if I didn't. And there's the solidarity: I watch and suffer because other Newcastle fans are watching and suffering. Sure, there were times as a boy when I would come charging out of Saint James' Park promising never to return, but by the time the bus had dropped me off at the bottom of our street, I was already looking to see whether there wasn't another one coming the other way to take me back. As Jackie Milburn put it, "we Geordies are a resilient race", and nowadays I totally accept that I am lumbered with Newcastle United for the rest of my days, to honour and to hold, to love and to cherish, till death us do part. Surely all the sacrifice will be rewarded in the next life: on reaching heaven, all being well Saint Peter will be watching over a golden turnstile, this to make sure that followers of the Red Devils and other evil sects don't try sneaking in the home end. "Robert Rowell? Newcastle United supporter? Poor soul. You deserve bliss after what you've been through. Go straight on in, my son." And click-click-click I will go into the great Leazes End in the sky.

Yes, of course I can look back at memorable wins like the five-nil thrashing of Man. United and think, hey, what a game. But how many of those ninety minutes did I actually enjoy at the time? Perhaps one, the last, by which time it was too late even for Alex Ferguson to contrive a comeback. Because you see the other thing about Newcastle is they can be four-nil up at QPR at half-time (which they once were), five-three up with just five minutes to go (which they also once were), only to end up drawing five-each – which they bloody well did!

Newcastle United 2   Sunderland 1

Robert the Bruce vs. Robert the Brave
Kilmaurs, Ayrshire, Scotland
Summer 1968

Biting

You take the high road
And I'll take the low road,
And I'll be in Scotland
Afore yee…

Like many people in our street, we had a telephone but
rarely used it. It cost too much. Old people died off, babies
were born, girls got married, but still it didn't budge. And
the only time we ever made a long-distance phone call was
just after England had beaten Scotland in the annual home
international fixture, when Dad would decide it was high
time he got in touch with his Scottish brothers-in-law, just
to see "how they were keeping". Oh I do like to be beside the
seaside and all that.

At the time I just couldn't understand this uncharacteristic
two-hours-a-year ill-feeling towards the Scots. In fact I
felt closer to them than to the English. By birth my blood
was twice as Scottish as it was English, and London, where
England was, was twice as far as Scotland. Most important of
all, Newcastle United had a number of Scots, Irish and Welsh
players in their team, but not one from "down south". Indeed
had it not been for Welshman Wyn Davies, when the Home
Internationals came along I would probably have supported
Scotland instead of Wales, but never England.

Even when we went on holiday, it was always north, never south. The summer of '68, like every summer before it, saw us exchange one set of clouds for another, and set off on an eight hundred mile trek to the village of Kilmaurs, near Kilmarnock in Scotland. That was where Robert and Grace McGregor lived, and where their first daughter – my Mam – had spent the first nineteen years of her life before being whisked off by Dad to be "educated", as he put it, in the land of milk and honey that she had been led to believe was Gateshead, England.

Did I say eight hundred miles? Well, that's what it seemed like to us. If Dad saw a car being towed to the scrap-heap, he would give the bloke a fiver and it ended up in our back yard. So when we all piled into his latest bargain for the journey into the unknown, we crossed our fingers, closed our eyes and prayed, as Dad stood out front, sleeves rolled up, frantically trying to crank the motor into action.

Only when our bones started shaking did our Audrey know it was safe to send word through to the kitchen that it was OK to pack the egg sandwiches. Years of experience had taught Mam that three weeks' worth and enough bananas to feed the Leazes End was by no means overdoing it. In fact we got through half of them just bidding farewell to the neighbours – in vintage Laurel and Hardy style, we waved oh goodbye-aye, they waved oh goodbye-aye back, and then the engine would drop out or we'd run out of petrol and we were back to square one. This went on for so long that in the end it wasn't so much oh goodbye-aye as oh get stuff-uffed.

After reaching the other side of Newcastle without incident – no exhaust-pipes trailing underneath, no fights in the back, no divorces in the front – at Heddon-on-the-Wall it all started to go wrong. There were two choices of road for the westward stretch towards Carlisle: the A69, a relatively quick, modern road which meandered forgivingly through the rolling hills; and the military road, which we called the Roman Road because it ran parallel to Hadrian's Wall and was originally designed for chariots. It went straight as a die, up-and-down, up-and-down over the hills, the biggest roller-coaster in the world. That's the one Dad always took.

Now I was quite a queasy little boy, so very soon it wasn't just the Roman Road that was going up-and-down, up-and-down. If my fellow passengers were lucky, I would give Dad ample notice that I wasn't feeling very well, allowing him to pull over and open the back door just in time for me to spew into the gap. This was all very well when we had gravity behind us, but if my advance warning happened to come halfway up a steep climb it was a different matter altogether. Dad would be too busy double-declutching his way down through the gears trying to keep the wheels turning to worry about me, and stopping would only mean having to roll all the way back down to take another run at it. So while everyone else leant forward to help nudge the car over the brow, I had no choice but to take matters – more specifically the first plastic bag I could lay my hands on – into my own hands.

For when we were up we were up,

And when we were down we were down,

And when we were only halfway up ...

BYEEEEERRRRCK!

I couldn't keep it down.

(Oh the grand old puke of yoke...)

If there's one thing I've noticed during a lifetime of cookie-popping, it's that during that wretched, retching split-second before volcanic eruption, nothing, but nothing else matters. Not weapons of mass destruction. Not Newcastle United's chances of avoiding relegation. Not whether there was anything in the plastic bag before I spewed into it. So when a few minutes later we were safely over the top and Mam asked for the bag of egg sandwiches, and when my sisters looked everywhere but couldn't find it, and when it was finally located beneath my feet, and when I looked out of the window as if nothing had happened and they all cried out together "Ugggggggh, no! Robert!" I thought it serves you right for not stopping.

"Never mind", chirped Mam, ever the optimist, "we're nearly there", which was what she always said when she sensed rebellion brewing in the back one hundred and twenty miles from destination. My sisters spent the rest of the journey looking at me as if they'd just seen a bad road accident, and nobody seemed to fancy a banana any more.

As if the sick-stops weren't enough, we also pit-stopped regularly to resuscitate the car (Dad was a genius at bringing the dead back to life), or to unravel the tangled ball of children in the back. There were no seat-belts in those days of course, but at the speed we were going the chances of an accident were minimal – sometimes we could only watch on in embarrassment as old ladies out walking their dogs mirror-signal-manœuvred before overtaking.

After leaving a trail of regurgitated egg sandwiches all the way to Scotland, just after nightfall Mam said "we're nearly there" for the hundred and fiftieth time, we turned a corner, and lo and behold this time we were there. My grandparents came running out to greet us, we all ran in to shelter from the rain, and granddad solemnly placed a lump of coal on the fire by way of celebration. May the holidays commence.

It rained solid for two weeks, of course, so we spent most of our time indoors. We passed our days trying to avoid the tight marking of grandma's pet mongrel, which took great pleasure in gnawing away at our ankles. When a hole in the sky did finally appear, Dad was about as glad to get out of the house as I was, and off we went to the local park for a kickabout.

There we were, happily knocking the ball to each other across the sticky surface, when a gang of youths suddenly appeared from nowhere to ambush the English. As if knowing something about the Scots that I obviously didn't, Dad ran off like a whippet, leaving me and my ball to fend for ourselves.

Unlike today, when we see teams like Rangers suffer huge, humiliating home defeats at the hands of unknown foreign teams like Paris Saint-Germain, this was a time when Scottish football was a force to be reckoned with, and on paper at least I was on a hiding to nothing. On the other hand, after such a long lay-off I was feeling "up for it", so despite being one against ten, I dribbled and dribbled and the Scottish kids didn't manage a single kick at the ball. Kicks at my shins and kicks at my ankles, but never the ball. Battered and bruised, I somehow worked my way out through the park gates, looking over my shoulder briefly to see that they were jumping up and down as if they were the ones who'd won, then dashed off up the main street, round the corner, and back to the relative safety of grandma's dog's mouth. There I joined up the dots two weeks of Scotland had left on my tattered shins, and the resulting picture confirmed what Dad had been trying to get through to me for years: you can like the Scots all you want, but there's no guarantee they'll like you back in return. Now, just in case I hadn't already realised it, I was *English*.

I spewed up all the way back to Gateshead the next day, for the last time as it turned out. Sadly, my grandparents passed away within a few months of each other, and to all intents and purposes Scotland and the Scots became a thing of the past. I did of course come across Scottish people again over the years, indeed I am yet to meet a Scot I haven't taken an instant liking to. Scotland is still my second favourite national team, and I have never let this be influenced by overheard references to the "b****** English", or by being present when they've jumped onto their chairs to sing – and amazingly know all the words to – their anti-English anthems.

I don't know about you, but I have always felt more impressed than intimidated by the ability of Scottish people to reel off the dates of historic battles with the "auld enemy" (hissing through grated teeth as they do so): Bannockburn 1314, Culloden 1746, Wembley 1928. This is partly because I didn't know those battles had ever taken place, but mainly I think it is to do with a certain sympathy I feel for the Scottish cause. After centuries of conflict, it is we English that have ended up with all the best bits: the political power, the good beer, the roads wide enough for two cars. Other than their pride, all we have left the Scots are the heather, the pleated skirts, the haggis and that terrible, droning bagpipe music.

I am also a great admirer of the Scottish appetite for enjoyment, something I witnessed at first hand some twenty-two years later in Turin, when Scotland took on Brazil in a sort of *joie de vivre* World Cup Final. What made the Scots different from the South Americans was why they were so happy: the Brazilians were banging drums because they'd brought their gorgeous girlfriends with them and had a great team; the Scots were singing because they'd left their women at home and their team was crap – so let's have a great time while our sporrans are full of the wife's food money! No matter what time of day it was, they seemed to be celebrating: in the streets of Turin beforehand, while singing *Oh Flower of Scotland, de-dee de-dee* before the match, at corners and throw-ins, when an aeroplane flew over, even when the Brazilians scored the winner! And when the referee blew his final whistle to inform them their country was out, that it was now time to go home, the Scottish fans stayed put, scarves waving, laughing and joking, singing and dancing, as if the party was just beginning. And judging from the snoring pile of tartan I came across on a bench in a Milan underground station two days after (the smelly puddle below which was proof at last that the Scots do not wear nappies under their kilts), it seemed to me that they took an extraordinarily long time to make their way home. Some of them probably never made it at all!

If at first you don't succeed, try, try and try again. Well, it was years before I drew up the courage to chance my limbs against the Scots on a football pitch again. And you know what? Despite my telling them that I was half Scottish by blood. Despite, for the sake of Auld Lang Syne, going round and shaking each player's hand beforehand. Despite the game being played on neutral soil with a neutral referee, a thousand miles south of Bannockburn.

And despite being on the same side, none of it seemed to count for much – as soon as the whistle went, to them I was just another sassenach. And like Grandma's pet mongrel a third of a century before, all they seemed to be interested in was my ankles.

Robert the Bruce 10 Robert the Brave 1

Newcastle United vs. Sunderland
Dean Street, Gateshead
Then and now

Rainy Days

I was an exceedingly sad little child. I don't mean melancholy sad, I mean sad in the way that I allowed football, and Newcastle United, to totally consume my life.

To begin with, the ball followed me everywhere. I took it to bed (and still would if my wife wasn't such a jealous silly-billy), and played keepy-up all the way to the bottom shop when Mam sent me for corned beef. Every available hour was spent in its company. School and meal-times were merely half-time breaks.

Even when it was pouring down outside, which was often the case in Gateshead, I would think up ways of "staying involved" with the game from indoors. For example, I would spend hours remembering and writing down the names, in alphabetical order, of the ninety-two teams that made up the football league (with this knack of mine for recalling accurate yet useless information, no wonder I ended up as an accountant!). Or I would pass the time drawing my hero Wyn Davies. The portraits were good enough to impress Mr. Durham in art class, though he did point out that in real life people's faces weren't pink, nor were their ears so high up the side of their heads (there again, Mr. Durham probably wasn't aware that Wyn Davies was Welsh). As for the action shots, big Wyn would always be smashing the ball past Jim Montgomery in the Sunderland goal. Right foot, left foot, with his head, over-head kicks, you name it, it was drawn. I took great pains to get the folds in the players' jerseys right, the swooooosh as the ball made contact with the net, as well as drawing the smiling faces and outstretched arms of the fifty thousand people lucky enough to be there to see it. Wyn Davies scored more goals in just one week of my drawings than he did in five seasons for Newcastle.

And then there were all the silly games I made up. The first game I invented required nothing more than an ordinary set of playing cards, in which the blacks were Newcastle and the reds were Sunderland. If I told you how it worked, you'd no doubt agree with Dad that it was a stupid bloody game, so I won't. What made it especially sad, though, and which had Dad pleading from behind his Evening Chronicle to "give it a break will you!", was the running commentary I kept up for the benefit of the imaginary listeners of Radio Dean Street Five Eight. "Dramatic news just in from Saint James' Park! The Queen of Diamonds has scored a last-minute equaliser for Sunderland!"

I still have that pack of cards. They may be tatty now, and somewhere along the line one of the jokers has had to substitute the missing nine of spades that was once Wyn Davies (one joker for another, many might say), but otherwise they're all there. And I have to admit, like a faithful old friend, I do turn to them now and again in times of need. After a miserable day at the office, other people might read poetry or go for a long jog to get their anxieties out of their systems. Not me. I get the cards out. Newcastle versus Sunderland, just like when I was a kid. Except that nowadays I'm not quite as fairplay as I was then, so to increase Newcastle's chances of winning I remove half the red ones first. Yes, I know what you're thinking: sad, very sad.

Newcastle United 4   Sunderland 0

Ujpest Dozsa vs. Newcastle United
Dean Street, Gateshead
11 June, 1969

Fogg-On The Tyne

Some people have all the luck. Take our Gloria. She only ever supported Newcastle United for one full season, and chanced upon the glorious Inter-Cities Fairs Cup campaign of 1968-69, the only season of triumph success-starved children like myself ever knew.

That Newcastle had been allowed to enter the Fairs Cup at all was down to a crazy ruling dreamt up by oak-panelled men in oak-panelled offices. Normally, finishing tenth in Division One the season before wouldn't have got us as far as Durham, never mind Europe, but UEFA's "only one club per city" rule pushed the Magpies up the pecking order, ahead of Everton, Tottenham and Arsenal, who, despite having all finished above us, were ineligible simply because other clubs from their respective cities had finished higher still.

Naturally, we were odds-on favourites to exit the competition at each hurdle, and yet somehow we soldiered on. Our secret weapon was my hero Wyn Davies, the heading machine. English teams knew all about Wyn "The Leap", and more importantly how to stop him, so much so that they had succeeded in reducing his flow of domestic goals to a drip. Dad kidded me on that they only called him "The Leap" because he scored one goal every four years, and the statistics aren't much kinder – it was one in every four games. But in Europe, at least, Wyn Davies was dynamite. Time and again the ball was simply pumped as high up into the sky as possible, and while big Wyn's five-foot-two continental marker clung on to one of his knees, he simply nodded it past the keeper, or into the path of "Pop" Robson so that he in turn could volley it home. The slick, play-the-ball-along-the-bottom foreign teams got the frights of their lives every time Wyn Davies ran out onto the pitch.

I was too young to attend evening matches in those days, but Gloria saw them all, including the first leg of the final against the crack Hungarian side, Ujpest Dozsa. As always we knew nothing about our opponents, other than that we were in for "another" thrashing. And judging from the first half (which I have since seen on video), it certainly looked as though we were in for a pasting. The boys from Budapest passed and moved, passed and moved, and the ball never rose to anywhere near Wyn Davies' altitude, except on those rare occasions when a Newcastle defender clogged it out of the penalty area so that the Hungarians could have it back and carry on where they had left off.

But it was to be, in football-speak, "a game of two halves". After the interval, Bobby Moncur, Newcastle's captain, scored his first two goals of the season to help Newcastle claim an impressive three-nil victory. Yet such was the general disbelief that a team as crap as Newcastle could ever bring home some decent silverware, that many people still expected us to throw it all away in Hungary.

Bringing us the game live from Budapest was one of those huge old radios that took up half our front room. It was more complicated to operate than an RAF bomber and had just as many lethal buttons – press the wrong one and you blew up the house. With just our Audrey and myself in at the time, it was she who sat in the cockpit. What an ordeal! You'd think with a machine that size you'd at least pick up a decent reception, but no matter how much Audrey tweaked the buttons, air traffic control was having none of it. With all the bangs, crackles and pops we'd have had more joy putting our ears to a bowl of Rice Crispies, so with half the match gone, and still no idea of the score, I went out to sit on the back steps, head in hands, and pleaded with Audrey to switch off the engines and crash-land.

But just then she had a brainwave. If she tuned into BBC Radio Newcastle instead of Radio Budapest, not only might we obtain a better reception, we could also listen to the commentary in English! In an instant the crackling was replaced by audible voices, which were discussing Ujpest's two-nil half-time lead and a difficult second forty-five minutes for Newcastle in prospect. Maybe we should have stuck with Radio Budapest after all!

Meanwhile, a thousand miles away and unknown to us Geordies back home, the United players were looking dejectedly at the dressing room floor in search for inspiration, when in walked manager Joe Harvey. What were Joe's historic words that were to change the course of history? Was it "Let's switch it from 4-3-3 to 4-4-2; Robson, you drop back into the gap behind Davies; Foggon, come in tight when we're defending and push out wide when we attack…?"

Nope. Joe Harvey was a no-nonsense Yorkshireman whose idea of tactics was when in doubt, lump it. All he said was "Get an early goal and they'll be dead and buried". Quite brilliant in its simplicity, and eleven drooped heads perked up in the realisation that oh, yes, scoring a goal would indeed improve our chances.

It was to be another one of those games of two halves, making four in total if you count the first leg. That man Bob Moncur scored the early goal that had been so carefully mapped out on the dressing room blackboard, and Ujpest collapsed as Joe had promised.

And where was our Gloria during those ninety minutes of suffering? Out with her mates, that's where. In typical glory-hunting style, she picked five minutes to go – with Newcastle home and dry – as the moment to waltz in through the front door and join in the celebrations. The thing was, if Gloria was fanatical, it wasn't about Newcastle United at all (if I were to ask her today what she can remember of the 1968-69 season, she probably wouldn't recall a single detail). No, her interest extended exclusively to their dishy young left-winger, Alan "eee, eez lovely man!" Foggon. She was so besotted that the whole of Low Fell knew about their "relationship", mostly thanks to her having scrawled "Glo loves Foggo" in black felt-tip on every public bench in the area.

Two days after the final, it was Gloria and her mate Christine who took me along to cheer Foggon and the other players when they returned home with the cup in an open-top bus. Hundreds of thousands of people crammed into Saint James' Park that day. At one point, Foggon, standing up in the old stand all of three hundred yards away, looked in our general direction and smiled. Well, he had a right to be pleased with himself, after all he'd just won a major cup-medal and was still only nineteen years of age. Our Gloria nearly fainted. "Eeeeeeeeeee!" she drooled, "Ee smiled at me!". I could see from the dreamy look in her eyes that she had taken this distant tweak of the lips to be a sign that Alan Foggon was madly in love with her, and that in no time at all she'd be showing off her engagement ring to all her mates. Eeeeeeeeeeeeeeeeeeeeeeeee!

Needless to say, she never got her man. Then one day Foggon, who only had to think of chocolate to put weight on, became too podgy for the first division, and rolled across the Welsh border to Cardiff City. And that's when Gloria decided to turn her attentions away from football and concentrate instead on sewing and other women's sports. And when other, less glamorous but more accessible names started taking Alan Foggon's place on Low Fell's park benches.

Ujpest Dozsa 2   Newcastle United 3

Newcastle United vs. Sunderland
Sparrow's Newsagents, Low Fell, Gateshead
Saturday evening at six

Pink Sky At Night

If some day I end up shipwrecked on a desert island, the three things I would like to have with me are: a voluptuous French actress by the name of Laetitia Casta; a lifetime's supply of bread and Marmite sandwiches; and a bundle of old copies of The Pink.

The Pink? For the unfamiliar, this is Geordieside's Saturday evening sports newspaper, containing all the results and reports on the day's football action. It has always been my football bible, so much so that despite having left the area a quarter of a century ago, Mam and Dad still send it on to me every week.

I am still amazed at how they do it (the people at The Pink, that is, not Mam and Dad). I mean, the games kick off at three, they end at around ten to five, and an hour later it's on the counter of every newsagent in the north-east so you can Read All About It.

Admittedly, this leaves very little time for the journalists to edit their accounts of the afternoon's proceedings. For example, you will find whole paragraphs dedicated to the most insignificant of incidents ("Newcastle won a throw-in on the right. Hibbitt took it but the ball went straight to an Ipswich player, who headed it out for another throw-in. Craig took it this time and found Robson, who played a neat one-two with Davies before losing possession...") whereas the events of the last quarter of an hour or so – with head office screaming at the journalists to submit their copy in time for printing – will often be reduced to just a couple of lines ("With twenty minutes to go and Ipswich looking good value for their lead, the visitors won a dangerous free-kick on the edge of the United area. Then DAVIES, ROBSON and SCOTT scored to make it four-two to Newcastle."). Blink and you'd miss it.

I am yet to come across anyone who actually read those match reports, but that wasn't why we bought The Pink in the first place. Inside those rose-tinted pages was a feast of other information that would keep you happy until bedtime: interesting articles, snippets on the behind-the-scenes events at Saint James' Park, the "Let Off Steam" page (where Newcastle and Sunderland supporters basically insulted each other). And I'm sure even Miss Casta would be curious to see how Winlaton Vulcans got on against J.T. Dove in Division E of the North-East Sunday League. The question is, does she like Marmite?

THE PINK

Some days are good days
And some days are bad,
But I'll always remember
When I was a lad.

I'd nip down to Sparrow's
Of a Saturday night,
A tanner in my pocket
– Had a hold of it tight.

The shop was like like Saint James's
When it's absolutely heavin',
Magpies versus Rokerites
Our numbers roughly even.

Little me just listened in
But never said a word,
For children (Mam had said)
Should be seen and never heard.

Health was topic number one
With "How's your Uncle Terry?"
"He leaves the clinic Monday…
                    (oh good)
…Aye, for Saltwell ceme-tery".

Money chat was close behind
If somebody'd found a job;
"You're coming out wi' fifteen quid?
Haway, lend us a few bob!"

As for man meets woman talk
It wasn't that romantic:
"She snogged me, I snogged her back
And now we're courtin' frantic."

For sex and drugs and rock and roll
Were in their infancy,
Like curried rice and pancake roll
A distant fantasy.

Suddenly all ears pricked up
When toot-toot came the van,
Its door swung open wide with a
"Here, there ye gan".

Out rolled the bundle
Tied up with a string;
"Pick it up, hinny
And bring the beggar in!"

The big blokes were at the front,
Their tanners at the ready;
Much too small to argue, me
I took it steady-eddy.

Mr. Sparrow drew his knife,
The string went with a tweak;
Each man got his copy with a
"See yezzall next week".

When at last I got my prize
For waiting patiently,
I just about tripped over
– It was twice the size o' me!

Total concentration now,
I didn't feel the rain,
And nearly got knocked over
As I crossed the Kell's Lane.

All the day's results were there
And who scored when for who,
Plus every league table
Down to Scots Division Two;

MAGPIES LOSE AT HOME
- SUNDERLAND GO DOWN -
And a picture of Wyn Davies
Versus Ipswich Town.

Davies? Pop Robson?
They couldn't kick back doors
– Just how we won the Fairs Cup,
Mine's as good as yours.

Aye, winning was a rare event
– A sort of weekend bonus –
But what really had us tickled Pink
Was Sunderland down below us!

....

Thirty seasons down the road,
A thousand miles away,
In the land of cordon bleu
And "Parlez-vous français?"

We dine in fancy restaurants,
We read Le Figaro,
We wear silk ties
And we sip Bordeaux;

But when I make it home at night
To my Ikea flat,
And see that Wor René's been
- That's French for Postman Pat -

Out rolls the bundle,
I recognise its shape,
Wrapped up in brown paper
And stuck with sellotape;

Now I do like my red wines:
Pomerol, Gamay…
But the best thing for your pallet's
This particular rosé.

So when I settle down
And put my slippers on,
I cannot wait to read
Just how The Lads got on:

MAGPIES LOSE AT HOME
- SUNDERLAND FLOP AWAY -
Shearer's in full colour now
Just like Match Of The Day.

Shearer? Dyer?
We've never won a thing;
We're a bunch o' flippin' losers, man,
Yet still the Geordies sing.

Aye, Saint James's might have seats now,
And I might have no hair;
A lot of things have changed for good,
But you know what? I really couldn't care.

'Cause many things have stayed the same,
And I'd just like to drink…
To Mam, Dad and The Royal Mail
For sending me The Pink!

Me vs. Jelly-Pants
Dean Street, Gateshead
Summer 1969

Rock Hard

On summer weekends, while other lads were driven to Whitley Bay and other exotic resorts by their mams and dads, often the only thing to keep me company was my ball. Sometimes I would make my own goal-net out of Mam's old wool, and attach it to two posts that a century earlier had supported a front gate. Then, imagining that I was my hero Wyn Davies (I even had my ginger mop cut in exactly the same way as his), I would set about smashing shots in from all angles. After a few minutes, all that was left of the net were a few dangling strands, and with the paint now peeling off the front door, Mam would run out, tea-towel in hand, screaming at me to stop.

Another favourite was "keepy-up". Feet, knees, head, chest (if you had one), everything but hands and arms were used to juggle the ball and keep it from touching the ground. Indeed Dean Street was where I would set my personal best-ever of one thousand, one hundred and seventy-seven. In those days you could get into Newcastle's first team with a score like that.

Then there was the big blue garage door that faced downhill from the top of Dean Street. If my childhood had a centre, the big blue garage door was it. It was both the start and finish of our running races in summer, and where our two main football pitches – both back lanes – met up in the middle. It was where we played "F.A. Cups" and "Spot", football games you will recognise if you've played them, and not want to hear about if you haven't. Finally, one afternoon in the summer of '69, the big blue garage door was where I made a permanent change to the contents of my mouth.

My grave mistake that day was in calling upon Jelly-Pants. Now Jelly-Pants was a nice lad, but he was unhealthily tall for his age and extremely awkward with it. He wore these baggy, knee-length shorts (didn't we all? Yes we did, only you could take a whole scout group camping in his), which wobbled one way while his legs moved the other – hence the absurdly cruel nickname. As a kid I used to have terrible nightmares about crashing into cars while sledging down Dean Street, or clattering head-first into brick walls on Tubby's brand new bike. But for Jelly-Pants such nightmares were everyday reality. His bodily components were in such violent disagreement with each other that he spent much of his childhood being rushed off in ambulances to the Queen Elizabeth Hospital.

The inability of his limbs to do what his brain asked of them made Jelly-Pants a bit of an all-rounder when it came to sporting hopelessness (he was, quite naturally, a Sunderland supporter). He was such a danger unto himself that in the end his parents decided that the indoor activity of schoolwork was the safest option for him. Whenever we knocked on his front door – there was no excuse for missing a Dean Street Rovers training session – he, his pencil and his ruler would watch forlornly from an upstairs window as his mother answered with a categoric "No, Jelly-Pants is not coming out to play today." Only to re-open the door a few seconds later with "And stop calling him Jelly-Pants!" Once, unbelievably, we even threw pieces of coal at their front door in protest, and a whole lot of fun it was too. But to no avail. The only place Jelly-Pants was going was top of the class.

Except that today, for some reason, his mother said yes, he *could* come out to play, the sack of loosely-connected arms and legs that constituted Jelly-Pants came eagerly tumbling down the stairs, and in no time at all we were knocking about at the big blue garage door.

I went in goal first and Jelly-Pants, true to form, couldn't score to save his life. Shots at goal: twenty. Shots on target: none. My turn now, I said. One last shot, said Jelly-Pants, and from all of three yards out he blasted the ball as hard as he could towards my bottom right-hand corner.

What entered my head in that split second I am not totally sure. As the ball made its way towards a certain goal, instinctively I dived like a Kamikaze pilot and pulled off the exact same world-class save Gordon Banks would make against Pele at the Mexico World Cup.

Admittedly, Jelly-Pants was no Pele. But there again Gordon Banks wasn't playing on tarmac either. At the very moment my outstretched hand scooped the ball round the post, the ground met my chin with such force as to send one of my lower front teeth flying, and the tooth fairy was the last thing on my mind as I screamed all the way to the doctor's.

What remained of that tooth wasn't finally capped until I was in my twenties, and its neglect during the intervening years caused its owner (me) some unimaginable grief. The Easter following the Jelly-Pants incident, for example, the tooth became infected and the resulting abscess spread throughout my lower jaw. Every morning I looked in the mirror to observe that my chin was twice as big as it had been the night before, but with all the dentists on holiday my Easter eggs would just have to wait. The pain became so unbearable that my parents, looking on helplessly at their son's sudden transformation from cheeky-chops to jelly-jaw, tried to soothe my misery by producing the Newcastle United strip originally intended for my eleventh birthday. It didn't work, though. My only wish in life was for an end to the drum-beat in my mouth, yet here I was sporting black-and-white stripes and a huge, distorted chin – a sort of cross between Wyn Davies and Elephant Man.

The lower half of my face still squirms at the memory whenever I drive past the still blue – but not as big as I used to think it was – garage door. Only to break out into a smile of satisfaction, this at the thought that I may be a couple of teeth short, but I tipped Jelly-Pants's shot round the post all the same. Gordon Banks would have been proud.

Me 0   Jelly-Pants 0
(match abandoned)

Dad vs. Dean Street Rovers
Dean Street, Gateshead
Summer 1969

Lightning and Thunder

If Dad never went to watch *my* Newcastle United, it never
stopped him from saying how useless they were. Wyn Davies
"couldn't kick back doors", and as far as he was concerned his
own yesteryear favourites, from Hughie Gallacher through to
"Wor Jackie" Milburn, would wipe the dressing room floor
with the current squad.

Dad's reasoning was absurdly simple: when he was a
young man, he claimed, there were two possible choices of
career path: the lucky ones made it as professional footballers,
everyone else went down the pits. The fight to keep your head
above ground was consequently so fierce that it was bound to
ensure – Dad reckoned – a much higher standard of football
than in the "you lot never had it so good" swinging sixties. I
shouldn't worry, he said. It was only natural. He was better
than me, his Dad had been better than him, his Dad's Dad
had been better still, etc. etc. Blimey, I thought, Charles
Dickens must have been one hell of a player.

Then one day we were playing pitch-and-putt over near
Newcastle Racecourse, and in the clubhouse afterwards we
bumped into none other than "Wor Jackie" himself. Milburn
was no ordinary hero on Geordieside, he was a legend. He'd
won three F.A. Cups, scored 199 goals in 395 games for
Newcastle, and would later be made a Freeman of the City.
I must admit I didn't recognise the great man myself, but I

knew immediately he must be some sort of a god from the way Dad's mouth drooled as he bent down on one knee to pay homage.

"Jackie, do you have any tips for my young lad here?"

"Aye, kick a ball off a wall until your legs drop off."

Dad almost fainted at the wisdom, but I bet Milburn said that to all the boys. Either way, his advice turned out to be totally useless. I spent hours and hours pounding the top house wall, and after a couple of days its owners were all but screaming for the men in white coats – kick a ball off a wall until Mr. Hill knocks your block off.

It must be said that even before the Milburn incident I'd had my doubts about Dad's opinions on football and indeed life in general. His fondness for the likes of George Formby and Bing Crosby was clear evidence he wasn't all there, and his personal recommendation for sore throats – Black Bullets in vinegar – was old wives' at its best. But what of his own soccer pedigree? By the time I'd begun to trespass on his territory, he had already bought enough drinks for enough people in Low Fell to ensure that he would always be glowingly described as having been a "very canny footballer". At New Years Eve knees-ups at our house, people like Uncle George would pull me aside and tell me, "you might be good, son, but you'll never be as good as your Dad". Too much whisky? Brotherly love? Either way, the widely-held consensus was that he really had been good enough, only he'd turned his back on the game. What a crazy decision. As anyone with tiny footballs running through his blood will tell you, even the most secure, best-paid job in the world is worth giving up just for a trial with a professional football club – Saint Mirren included. That's because compared to the glory that goes with being a professional footballer, everything else really is the pits.

But the coal-mines weren't Dad's only other option. It was his father who urged him to leave his playing days behind and follow his footsteps into Tommy Strang's football pools business instead. Admittedly, this was highly lucrative compared to the pittances paid to miners (and in those days footballers) – the reason why there was only one car parked in the whole of Beacon Street was because Granddad parked the other one behind the big blue garage door at the top of Dean Street. It all went sour, though. Tougher competition came along, forcing Strang's out of business and Dad out of a job. By this time Granddad's fortune had been whittled away – too many "friends" – and Saint Mirren seemed like a million miles away. With numerous mouths to feed, Dad had to start all over again. He went through a couple of tedious jobs as an office clerk before ending up at the Post Office, where his quest for eternal cushiness eventually took him to a position behind the counter on the Team Valley Trading Estate, a stressfree little number he stuck to like sellotape for the rest of his working life.

It was while walking up Dean Street on his way home from the post office one Friday night that Dad's "we were better than you lot" theory was finally laid to rest. Dean Street Rovers was noisily kicking about at the big blue garage door when the ball bounced out of control and down the hill, right into Dad's path. Dad hadn't kicked a ball in years but he couldn't resist the temptation. In no time at all he was floating down the right-wing of Football Past, his folded-up Evening Chronicle hanging from one jacket pocket, my pocket money jingling away in the other. We watched on as he shimmied this way and that through his own version of the Stanley Matthews sword dance:

You put your right leg in,
Your right leg out,
In out, in out,
Shake it all about;
You do the hokey-kokey and you turn around...
... and the ball didn't budge an inch.

Now in Dad's heyday – at least judging from the rare film evidence I've seen of that period – such lightning "skills" would have had the opposing full-back hopelessly sliding along on his backside in the direction of the very first leg-movement, leaving the winger with the embarrassingly simple task of skipping out of the way and setting off on the well-trodden path towards the corner flag. There he would stop to take a ten-yard run-up, and belt the rain-soaked, twice-its-normal-weight, thick leather football as hard and as high as possible towards the six yard box. The sight of this great mass of mud was enough to get the goalkeeper into a terrible flap, and he inevitably fumbled the catch (did you know that not a single cross was caught between 1946 and 1957?). With not a defender in sight, centre-forward Desperate Dan would then come sliding in with the type of lunge that nowadays would see him behind bars. His three-inch nails for studs would connect perfectly with the goalkeeper's front teeth, bundling him and his dentures into one corner of the net while his cloth cap and the ball trickled into the other. The Pathé News commentator would then have the cheek to describe the goal, in his very King of England voice, as "one of the finest ever scored at Wembley."

To be fair to Dad, he did succeed in shoving a couple of three-year olds out of the way when they came dangerously close to spoiling his act in its early stages, but he hadn't bargained for what was to follow. The problem was that at some point between the nineteen-forties and now, somebody somewhere had had the bright idea that if you concentrated on the ball instead of the dazzling feet display, you'd stand a much better chance of making a successful tackle. Consequently, ten would-be Ron Harrises came thundering in, the ball was whipped away, and Dad ran for his life.

Poor Dad. Mam was still nursing his sores when I went in half an hour later, but at least one thing was now clear: the "Dean Street Rovers Woz Here" graffitied all down his shins would remind him he'd best come home the back way in future.

Dad 0   Dean Street Rovers 1

Kells Lane vs. Brighton Avenue
Oakfield School, Gateshead
November 1969

Global Warning

Terrible things used to happen to me during music lessons. Like the day the teacher told me to come out and play the triangle just as I was thinking how maybe I should have gone for a pee during the break.

As we all know, the triangle is a highly-sophisticated musical instrument requiring the deft use of both hands, one to hold it, the other to make piddly-ting-ting-ting noises with a metal rod. Only soon it wasn't just the triangle that was going piddly-ting-ting-ting. With both hands fully occupied, my little old man was left free to cause havoc downstairs, and despite some frantic leg-crossing a couple of drops finally managed to squeeze through. Then a few more, then a steady stream, and the next thing I knew the River Tyne was flowing down my inside-leg. At which an ever so dainty little girl called Julie, who'd been happily watching the busting of the dam from all of two feet away, raised her hand and pointed out that please miss, I think Robert has wee-weed himself.

"Oh Robert! Why didn't you put your hand up?" And I went home that evening wearing a pair of shorts originally designed for Jelly-Pants.

Then there was the time Mr. Durham caught me "larking about" during our singing of Bread And Butter For Your Supper That's All Mother's Got. He stopped tinkling with his ivories, pulled me out to the front, and announced that Rowell was going to sing all by himself. As he played his way through the interminable build-up to my grand entrée, and with fifty schoolchildren all staring at me in anticipation, I felt the blood leave my tongue and rush uncontrollably towards my cheeks, all the better to show the world how much of a twit I was feeling. By the time the intro was over my mouth was as dry as a Jacob's cream cracker, and all I was able to offer was a muffled squeal. The class erupted, the teacher said OK Rowell, you can sit down now, and I've hated karaokes ever since.

I don't think Mr. Durham liked me very much after that. In fact I was convinced he had it in for me. So it came as quite a pleasant surprise when, in my last week at Kells Lane School, he declared in front of the whole class – girls included (wow!) – that Robert Rowell was the best footballer in the school.

And yet I hadn't been selected to play for the school team until well into my final year. The problem was quite simple: Mr. Durham had never seen me play before. Kells Lane being a mixed school, physical education meant rounders with the sissies. And I was unable to attend the after-school training sessions because it coincided with my old friend music. More specifically, violin lessons.

The violin had been introduced to me on possibly the worst day of my life, at the end of the fourth form. Dad came home from parents' day in a rage over my poor academic performance. It wasn't as though I was a particularly stupid boy. It's just that, as Aunt Annie put it, I was a bit of a "dreaming bairn". Unlike Jelly-Pants, I hadn't yet grasped the desirability of finishing closer to the top of the class than the bottom. Nor could I see what working at my spelling was going to do for my dribbling technique. So when I assured Dad that all was going well, I wasn't lying. I was simply referring to my performance in the breaks between lessons, during which I excelled at the three Ts: Tackling, Taking it on and Thumping it.

On parents' day, however, Dad found out that as far as the three Rs were concerned, I had finished second bottom of the class. I must say I was stunned by the fierceness of his attack. He was normally a very calm person (in our family, if the belt had to be swung, it was Mam's job to swing it). Yet today Dad was furious. He went on and on without my listening to a single word, then just as I was beginning to think phew, I'm glad that's over with, maybe I can go out and catch up on some serious footie now, he casually dropped the big one: "And by the way I've put your name down for the violin".

Since I already knew how to play the piano, Dad thought the violin would be no trouble and would add a string to my bow, so to speak. He was wrong. The violin didn't so much rest under my chin as grab at my throat, and went to ridiculous lengths to make me look stupid during lessons.

Until the day I came to blows with the little piece of light wood known as the bridge, whose job it is to keep the violin's strings taut. We were practising Ten Little Indians at the time (or was it Au Clair De La Lune? It didn't really matter – in our case it always sounded as if we were sharpening knives):

All together children, one, two…
Screech screech, scratch scratch,
Screech screech, scratch;
(quick change of fingers)
Scratch scratch, screech…

Kerplonk. The bridge disintegrated into tiny pieces, and twenty children looked at me as if I'd just smashed the violin off the wall Jimi Hendrix style. The teacher said not to worry and hunted around for a new bridge, and in the end borrowed a slightly larger one from a lurking viola instead. That should do the trick, she said.

My temperamental violin strings weren't at all happy about their new playing partner, so if they'd been whining before, they were screaming in agony now. I started sweating at the inevitability of what was to follow, but there was no alternative – we were due to make our first screech in public the following week and the show had to go on.

Now children, once again, from the beginning, one, two…
Screech screech, scratch scratch,
Screech screech…

And this time the kerplonk nearly put one of the windows out.

Dad, having meanwhile seen an improvement in my class results, agreed that the punishment for my earlier sins had gone a bridge too far, so he sent a discreet note to the headmaster and within a couple of days I was the envy of the music class. Out went the violin, in came football training, Mr. Durham asked where I'd been all term and within a week I'd moved from school orchestra to school team.

Kells Lane was a very old school and didn't have its own ground, so all of our home games were played at the more recently-built Oakfield, a half-mile walk down to Chowdene Bank. I was very nervous when we marched out through the school gates on the evening of my debut. I'd been told that with Oakfield being such a long trek, it was like playing away even when we were at home; and that the local hard-boys who hung around the gates after matches certainly weren't there to swap football cards. To raise morale before battle, then, we sang traditional football songs, *There's only one Paul Iley, Malla Smith clap-clap-clap*, and the school anthem,

Kells Lane boys on the hop
Kiss your girls and drink your pop
Wo-oh oh-oh-oh-oh ohhh.

The game itself was of course a nonsense. Other than the two goalkeepers – who stood shivering between their posts waiting for something to happen – the rest of us followed the ball all over the pitch like a swarm of bees, completely ignoring the positions the teacher had given us during the thirty minute pre-match team talk. The big leather ball was far too heavy to be kicked more than a few feet, so if you fancied your chances there was little point hanging around on the wings – you had to go inside and buzz with the rest of them. The swarm gradually worked its way from one part of the pitch to another, oblivious of the events in the world at large, until one of the busier bees emerged, ball at his feet, to pant his way across the fifty or so empty yards that separated him from a one-on-one with the goalkeeper.

Halfway through the second half, the swarm was busy buzzing away in Brighton Avenue's goalmouth. My handed-down Bobby Charltons still hadn't had a kick, but suddenly there was the big medicine ball at my feet. With the huge goal just a few yards away, I took an almighty swing – almost spraining my left ankle in the process – and the ball trickled off towards goal. The 'keeper had all the time in the world to stroll along his goal-line and pick it up, but chose instead to wait until the last moment before making an acrobatic dive that, though faultless in artistic content, nevertheless allowed the ball to slip under his body and crawl over the goal-line. Had there been nets, the ball wouldn't have reached them – a real Jimmy Greaves special.

Pheep! It took a few seconds for it to sink in, and when it did I felt terribly embarrassed. Other than when wetting my pants and smashing my violin to bits, I just wasn't used to standing out in a crowd like that. But then all these boys with big smiles on their faces started patting me on the back and for the first time in my life I felt popular.

Goal!!! I've scored! I've scored! And I set off towards our half, running, jumping and punching the air after the fashion of the time. Mr. Durham punched the air too, which was a trifle embarrassing what with him being match referee.

If scoring for Dean Street Rovers against Jessell Street Rangers had brought a certain thrill, this was like scoring in the World Cup Final by comparison. After all, this game was official: there were proper strips, real posts and a leather ball, and the result would be solemnly read out at school assembly the following day. I was about to become famous.

But most invigorating of all was scoring in front of a crowd. Even had I been a bit luckier with the violin, I doubt very much whether my screeching Ten Little Indians in public would have had Low Fell's mams, dads and older brothers chanting *Rowelly for England* the way my fans did at Oakfield that day. In fact the only disappointment in my moment of glory was the distinct absence of female squeals. I should have learned from our Gloria that the girls were too busy ogling Julian Thomas's curly locks to take any interest in *my* skills.

Ah well, it was perhaps a bit much to expect to become both the world's greatest footballer and its most sexy, so I concentrated on the former. Minutes later I scored a goal my memory tells me was identical to the first, and this time there was no hesitation in my celebration routine. Robert Rowell had arrived. Better late than never.

Kells Lane 4   Brighton Avenue 2

Deluge

Many of our away games took us to the dangerous and dizzy depths of downtown Gateshead. Windy, rough and ugly, it is easy to see why Doctor Samuel Johnson, a chap who wrote dictionaries in the eighteenth century, described the place as "a dirty lane leading to Newcastle". The only thing that had changed two centuries later was the rise in the number of dirty lanes.

I had previously only ever been "down Gateshead" when accompanying Dad to Bensham to collect rent. In Monopoly money, Bensham was the Old Kent Road of the north. Patches of wasteland overgrown with weeds and covered in loose rubble mingled with rows of houses that were begging for the last rites. We wouldn't have gone near the place had it not been for the Rowell family still owning some flats there. These were the last, miserable survivors of the one-time wealth of Granddad Rowell. The tenants were the sort who put in their dentures to look credit-worthy, and as soon as you'd handed over the keys went racing off to gamble the rent money on the 3.30 at Ayr. Dad spent more time in court than Private Eye.

My poor French grandmother. Why she left northern France for downtown Gateshead is a riddle wrapped up in a mystery inside a stotty cake. Having said that, when she arrived just after the First World War she found a friendly, respectable, working-class community – in her heavy French accent, "nice furk". Those were the days when you could leave your front door unlocked without fear of rape and pillage. But by the time I was a boy, they weren't just locking their doors, they were boarding up the windows, and today's bus journey took us to an area of downtown Gateshead where Julius Caesar's famous words of "we came, we saw, we scarpered" were never more appropriate.

It is a well-known fact that in football the away team loses much more often than it wins. In his book The Soccer Tribe, Desmond Morris put this down to what he termed "away-itis" – playing in unfamiliar surroundings, staying in strange hotels, that kind of thing. Well I can tell you, we didn't stay in any hotels before the King Edward's game but we knew all the same that we were going to get hammered. You see, as a youngster you soon learn that winning away from home is the quickest way to a bloody nose. So, unconsciously perhaps, you don't try so hard. On top of that, you tend to spend more of the game looking out for quick escape routes than the opposing centre-forward. This "aggrophobia" – the fear of having your head kicked in after matches at schools like King Edward's – stays with you throughout your career, irrespective of level, so much so that even professionals let it get to them, and understandably so. With several thousand Biffa Bacons waiting outside after your team has just gone and ruined their whole weekend, would you volunteer to be the first to get on the team coach?

It has to be said that in the case of Kells Lane, there was no need to let the other team win, simply because they were usually much better than us anyway. Low Fell and downtown Gateshead might have been on the same page-map in the A-Z of Newcastle & District, but when it came to footballing ability we were a lot more than just a few streets apart. The difference was that the boys from King Edward's had received the kind of upbringing you need to produce successful footballers: a tough, working-class neighbourhood, an abundance of back lanes, and an abundance of kids with nothing else legal to do than play football. And although our school did boast one or two qualified back-laners – "Malla" Smith and myself for example – most of the other boys were reluctant participants, there on teacher's orders to make up the numbers. They had unlikely addresses like Valley Drive and The Plantation, and were better at clipping roses than taking throw-ins. The boys of King Edward's had probably never seen a flower in their entire lives, but they certainly knew how to kick a ball, and the only time we left our penalty area that day was to get changed and go home.

Coincidentally, on the day on which I write this, I went with my pregnant wife to the maternity hospital to find out whether our first child was going to be a boy or a boy. As the doctor moved the scan this way and that, pointing out the baby's head, feet and hands as he did so, I explained to my wife that, if "he" was going to have any chance of becoming another Zinedine Zidane, we were going to have to give up slick Paris for squalid Marseille, the "Gateshead of the south". "He" might turn out to be as thick as two short planks for our troubles, but you can't expect your child to have brains in his feet *and* in his head.

I went on to reminisce about the drubbings we received whenever we played "down Gateshead". Tears in my eyes, I recalled the beating-up we got after the King Edward's game (despite having "let" them win) – and not a teacher in sight to protect us. Then there were the de Coubertin-style comments of Mr. Tate the headmaster at the following day's school assembly, when he reminded us that the important thing in sport was to participate. Bollocks, he hadn't had his head kicked in, so what did he know?

Just then the doctor interrupted my moment of nostalgia. Without so much as offering me a stiff drink or a chair, he pointed to a dark spot on the screen where normally there should have been a willie, and quite unapologetically broke the news. I was devastated, of course, but my wife sighed with relief – we would be staying in Paris after all.

King Edward's 11   Kells Lane 0

England vs. West Germany
58 Dean Street, Gateshead
14 June, 1970

Frozen In Parts

If England versus Scotland was important, it was handbags compared to the heavy artillery of England versus Germany. For these were weapons that hurt, the painful evidence of which was a wound the size of a banana in the middle of Dad's chest. What's more, unlike against the Scots, with the Germans there was no kissing and making up afterwards.

The meeting of the two nations in the 1970 World Cup Quarter-Final in Mexico was our biggest match since 1966, and my biggest ever. The pre-match atmosphere in our living room was so electric that there should really have been a skull and crossbones on our front door: "Danger: area of high voltage." With Mrs. Carson joining us just as the two teams were coming out, there we were: two bags of nerves waiting for kick-off, and one nervous bag waiting for a cup of tea.

Dad had a unique way of demonstrating how wound up he was during England games, which involved sitting on the edge of his armchair, rolling his trouser-legs up to his knees, and nervously rubbing his hands up and down those trademark chicken-legs of his. You just had to glance through our front window to see how England were doing: frantic rubbing for prolonged pressure, three rubs for a free-kick on the edge of the penalty area, two rubs for a corner. If on the other hand England were being run off the park,

Dad would roll his trouser-legs back down into their "off" position, conveniently remember he belonged to a different footballing era, and start cursing every bad pass or shot off-target ("Jackie Milburn could have scored with his backside from there, man!").

Adding to the tension was the high-pitched commentary of David Coleman. Coleman had this special ability of giving life-and-death importance to the most innocuous of throw-ins, of making World Cup Finals out of the likes of Rochdale versus Doncaster. It was bad enough when you could see what was going on, but it became unbearable when the picture froze without warning (due to some problem with the satellite transmission), only for Coleman's hysteria to continue unaffected. After a few seconds a message would come up on the screen saying something like "we apologize for the temporary loss of vision – in the meantime please go completely off your rocker in the company of David Coleman", and Dad and I would flick coins to see whose head should go in the oven first.

Well into the second half, things were going wonderfully well for England, thank you very much. We'd scored once, we'd scored twice, we were on our way to the semi-finals! Dad's trouser-bottoms were up to his knee-balls with excitement, and all that rubbing had reduced his legs to a couple of dangling stumps.

Now I am first and foremost a Newcastle fan – I'd much rather they won the league than England won the World Cup – but what happened during the next half hour has haunted me far more than anything Newcastle ever put me through. Indeed despite my then tender years, I fear that the scars the Germans left me that day, like Dad's war wound, will never heal. Shooting pains still flood through my body when I think back to all the "if onlys". If only Sir Alf Ramsey hadn't taken off Bobby Charlton (presumably so that he could comb the three most famous hairs in football into place in time for the semi-final), surely Franz Beckenbauer wouldn't have had the same freedom to move forward and cause havoc. If only Gordon Banks hadn't fallen sick beforehand (a bottle of bad beer, for the record), surely he wouldn't have flapped at Uwe Seeler's looping header the way his five-foot-nothing replacement Peter Bonetti did. If only this, if only that.

Extra-time was a formality. The sadistic, almost satanic expression on Gerd Müller's face as he smashed in the extra-time winner reduced David Coleman's commentary to a rare whisper, and the way Dad silently rolled down his trouser-legs to half-mast was all the confirmation I needed that we were all but dead and buried. The funereal air even "rubbed off" on the normally insensitive Mrs. Carson, who for once sat quietly out of respect.

I think it was after that match that some famous person – I don't know who – tried to cheer up English spirits by quipping, "We shouldn't mind so much if the Germans beat us once at our national sport, after all, we have beaten them twice at theirs". No doubt he felt pretty pleased with himself at having thought that little witticism up, but I personally wish he had kept his fat gob tightly shut instead. For in life there are two things that should be avoided at all costs. One is dying. The other is taking the mick out of the Germans. It's as suicidal as poking fun at the school bully: one of these days you know he'll get you back. And big time.

Sure enough, those thirty minutes in Mexico were but a foretaste of the thirty years of purgatory that followed: Wembley 1972, Madrid 1982, Turin 1990, Wembley 1996 – our misery at last coming to an end at Euro 2000. As for old clever-clogs, his little ditty now reads something like this: "we shouldn't mind so much if the Germans beat us, erm, *five* times at our national sport, etc. etc." Doesn't quite sound so funny any more, does it? That's what you get for rubbing the Germans up the wrong leg.

England 2   West Germany 3
(after extra rubs)

Breckendene Athletic vs. High Fell United
Team Valley Trading Estate, Gateshead
Summer 1970

Nippy

Dean Street Rovers saw two important changes to its constitution at the start of the seventies, reflecting its development from the original, scattered bunch of toddlers into an organized group of teenagers or nearly-teenagers. For the convenience of parents, we now fell into the "old enough to know better" age group. Old enough to know better than pick your nose; old enough to know better than cry over losing Fred the rubber crocodile; old enough to know better than have the light on at night, for fear of Dracula flying in to suck blood from your throat.

Since only three of us actually lived on Dean Street itself, and having signed up Sharpy from over Durham Road way, a vote of the committee decided in favour of a change in name to "High Fell United", thus implying domination of a much larger area of Gateshead than two rows of terraced houses. Had we continued expanding at the same rate, today we'd probably be called Newcastle United.

The other, more significant change, was the move away from the back lanes, after one, long, wrangling match with the local residents. The building society surveys may well have warned would-be house buyers of the rising damp, but nobody had told them about the much bigger drain on resources that was High Fell United, Public Enemy Number One. "Doler" – the man in the top house who made a living out of avoiding work – couldn't get any sleep; the big blue door was becoming less and less blue by the day; and when the ball bounced off the Sergeants' metal garage door, it recorded five on the Richter scale, sending tremors down the spines of all those living within a ten-mile radius.

In the early days, when the ball miscued into somebody's back yard, it would come back like a boomerang, accompanied by nothing stronger than a "mind how you go with that ball!". But as time wore on, the warnings became rather more aggressive, and were peppered with words like "kitchen knife", or worse still, "polly sontya" (as in "you'd better watch out or I'll get the polly sontya"). And sometimes when the ball did come back – if it came back at all – curiously it had lost all of its bounce. Phhhhhhh. Something was up.

"Click-clack" was the unofficial spokesman for Neighbourhood Watch. He hated us and we hated him, and things really came to a head about nine months after he and his wife had made the almighty mistake of rubbing belly-buttons. Strategically, their house at the top of Robson Street was the last place in the world to live if you wanted babies, since three of our football "pitches" all happened to converge just outside their front door. We might have been a bit more understanding had Click-clack's problem been our playing at eleven o'clock at night, but he was unhappy no matter what time of day it was. Anyway, as far as we were concerned, we were there long before him and his family, so we had no intention of moving – if baby fancied a siesta she should try Spain, they did that sort of thing over there.

Click-clack spent most of his free time peeping at us from behind the upstairs curtains. And this wasn't because he had a thing about pubescent little boys, either. One day, while we were "kicking in" at the bottom of Louis Terrace, just five yards and one rattling window-pane away from his little darling's right ear and screaming gob, he decided he could stand no more. He came running out in a rage, grabbed a hold of the ball, pulled out a notepad and pencil from his back pocket, and began asking for names and addresses. He started with Curly who, being twice his size, just stood there in silence. And when he got similar reactions out of Bradders and Tubby, he glanced around in desperation for someone his own size to pick on. Me. His manliness was about to be saved.

"Right! You! What's your name?"

"Robert."

"Robert what?"

"Robert Rowell."

"Rowell? Is that Rowell of Rowell's fish and chip shop?"

Rowell's was more of an institution than a chippie. It was on the corner of Kells Lane and Wesley Street, opposite the Black Horse, and when I was a lad, it was a grumpy, snotty little old woman called Vera who dished out the chips. "Greasy Vera" wasn't a Rowell, she was a Growl. If you dared ask for something *hors menu* like extra batter, she fiffed and faffed and huffed and puffed as if you'd just asked her to go down Bensham to collect rent. What was standard fare, though, even if you didn't ask for it, was a lavish wipe of the back of her hand under her nose, thereby adding a certain *je ne sais quoi* to the taste of the chips. On the one hand, I was embarrassed to admit any sort of connection to the most feared, most notorious woman in Low Fell, but on the other I hadn't yet learned how to lie.

"Yes."

"Well you're old enough to know better – just you wait until I tell Greasy Vera!" My name went into the referee's notebook, and a jubilant Click-clack ran home to his wife announcing "peace in our time".

The thought of me being thrown into Greasy Vera's fat-pan had even the older boys shaking in their boots, and an urgent committee meeting was convened to decide what to do. Someone submitted the idea of moving to the playing field down on Kells Lane. On the negative side, the "player" (as we later called the playing field) was at least three hundred yards away and therefore a bit of a run (we never actually walked anywhere – did you?), and unlike the back lanes, we wouldn't have exclusive territorial rights. On the other hand, the grass surface would give us the chance to attempt overhead kicks and other acrobatics that the Tarmac had warned my mouth never to try again. So we had a vote, and the "ayes" had it. As did the teeth.

The "player" turned out to be a revelation, and became the centre of our footballing activity for years to come. Unfortunately, though, it was no good for official matches: it was far too bumpy, there were no goal-posts, and you usually went home covered in dung – ironically left there by the dogs of those who'd bullied us away from the back lanes in the first place! So when Bradders came home from school one day announcing a match against fresh opponents on the following Saturday, he also informed us that the game would take place not at the "player", but on the hallowed turf of "Little Wembley".

Little Wembley earned its name from the sloping banks of grass that surrounded it, giving it the feel of a proper football stadium. One of tens of regulation pitches down at the Team Valley Trading Estate, like all the others it was in a disgraceful state, making it perfect for the Sunday Cloggers League for which it had been intended, but a career-threatener for rising stars like ourselves. The goalmouths hadn't seen grass for centuries and were either mudbaths or rock cakes, depending on the season, but never something in between; the goal-nets were in such a bad state that even the holes needed replacing; and the playing surface was never rolled, so you usually ended the match with your ankles sticking out at right-angles.

Worst of all was the journey home afterwards, especially after defeat. It was a long, steep, uphill-all-the-way drag, and by the time we'd reached the dark and spooky "witch's path", the penny ice-pops had already run out. With our mud-caked bodies and sprained ankles, we wouldn't have stood a chance had the witch's path lived up to its mythical status as devourer of young children.

Playing against Breckendene gave me my first inkling that maybe, just maybe, I wasn't the only eleven-year-old in the world destined to become the greatest footballer that ever lived. It's true, I'd come across some decent players when turning out for Kells Lane, but I can't say I ever saw anyone as good as myself, and I always blamed our dreadful results on the rest of the team being crap. Well, it seemed a pretty reasonable excuse at the time.

But just seconds into our first game against Breckendene, I discovered I had a challenger, a lad called Ket. The first time he received the ball, for a moment it looked as though he didn't quite know what to do with it. But when Tubby – who was always full of bounce in the early stages of a match (up to his collapsing in a heap of lard after five minutes) – was dispatched forth to bulldozer the little squirt to the ground, on arrival he found that both Ket and the ball had disappeared.

This in itself was not as impressive as it sounds, since even Jelly-Pants could circumnavigate Tubby on a good day. But the way Ket went on to nip past the outstretched limbs and gob-smacked expressions of Curly, Sharpy and then – horror of all horrors – the invincible Bradders, came as a real shock to the system. Just where did he learn all that Waltzing Matilda stuff?

It was a miserable walk home. Not only had we lost, but my team-mates enthused about Ket all the way. "Don't get us wrong, Rowelly, you're a good player as well, but Ket is, well, you know…" Good player? As well? Gobble them up, witch's path!

The football pitches down the "valley", Little Wembley included, have all gone now. They gave way long ago to office blocks and businesses – good news for north-east enterprise (and ankles), no doubt, but where do all the footballers go? Not to the "player", that's for sure. Swings and roundabouts now sit bang in the middle of where our imaginary centre circle used to be, and on the rare occasions I actually see kids there, they never have a ball at their feet. Nor do they seem even the slightest bit distraught about it! Whatever happened to High Fell United? Have Gateshead's kids transferred their footie-playing from player to Playstation? (There, at least, they can practise their overhead kicks without the risk of landing in a pile of dog-dirt).

As to who was better, Ket or Rowelly, it turned out not mattering very much, since neither of us made it anyway. I still see Ket occasionally, down at Dad's club. There he drinks pints of India Pale Ale and plays dominoes the same way all the other mere mortals around him drink India Pale Ale and play dominoes. So you would never know, from the way he holds his glass or lays down his double-six, that he was once capable of waltzing past Tubby, Curly, Sharpie and Bradders all thanks to a couple of deft movements of the hips.

Breckendene Athletic 6 High Fell United 5

Hilton vs. Lumley
Greenwell Junior High School, Gateshead
September 1970

Welsh Mist

The summer of 1970 was an apprehensive one, as I contemplated the switch in schools from little old Kells Lane to the lion's den, Greenwell Junior High. There I would come up against rough-and-tough boys from Sheriff Hill, Beacon Lough, and my birthplace, Springwell Estate. I prepared my nose for action.

I was particularly worried about the tradition of "Foggy's Friday", during which rumour had it that big boys flushed the heads of "freshers" down loos. But in the end, all that practising holding my breath under water turned out to be unnecessary. Yes, I was chased, cornered, and grabbed, but in the end suffered nothing worse than being thrown into the sand-pit normally reserved for the high jump.

I would have been better advised spending the summer concentrating on my football. And yet my first games afternoon started off where the last P.E. lesson at Kells Lane had left off. Dedicated to the beautiful game; the six houses, all named after local castles, played each other in a round robin. I was in top form, at least for four-fifths of the afternoon. The Hilton all-whites demolished house after house, I had stormer after stormer, scoring goal after goal. Mr. Brabham put my name down for the school trials. Yes! I was in. This school was turning out to be not so bad after all.

As the afternoon wore on, rumours began to circulate

about how good a team Lumley had – the house we were due to play last – and in particular "this lad called Jonnie Wales". Not that I was worried myself, though. My confidence was sky high and I felt certain even more rumours were going around the place about "this lad called Robert Rowell." Nobody could be better than me on my current form. Not Ket. Not this Jonnie what's-his-face. No one.

I was in for the shock of my life. If I had rather disdainfully been wondering where all the good players were supposed to be, I now discovered that they were all playing for Lumley. What's more, it was true, this lad called Jonnie Wales stood head and shoulders above everyone, me included. He was tall for his age, which helped, and in terms of being able to look after himself he was as hard as a rock, which helped even more. But his skills and tricks were from a different planet. He did things with the ball that I had never seen done before, and danced rings around all of us.

One moment of brilliance stood out in particular. With the ball bouncing towards him, and an opponent running up from behind, Jonnie had a quick glance over his shoulder to see what was what. This was enough in itself to set my brain ticking, since I had never before seen anyone my age look over his shoulder during a football match, except the goalkeeper, and even then only when it was already too late. As far as I was concerned, looking over your shoulder was something you did on Foggy's Friday. This lad had *vision*.

Then, with the outside of his boot, he calmly flicked the ball over his and the other lad's head, waltzed round to the other side, controlled it on the drop, and carried on upfield. As if he did that sort of thing every day of the week. His opponent sat there with the puzzled expression of an orang-utan which has just found a flea in its armpit, and the rest of us stopped dead in our tracks, watching on in a mix of envy, admiration, and – let's be honest – loathing.

Being a canny little trickster myself, there have been precious few times in my life when I have been truly knocked out by moments of such sheer skill, where I say to myself, hey, that was brilliant, I wish I could do that. These include some gob-stopping stuff from Tommy Craig, the Newcastle midfielder during the seventies, from Georgi Kinkladze, Manchester City's prince of dribblers in the nineties; and Tino Asprilla's debut drag-back nutmeg for Newcastle against Middlesbrough had me checking the T.V. aerial. But Jonnie stands out above all of them simply because he was the first. He performed those tricks at an age when we still believed Batman really could run up the sides of Gotham City's buildings. What's more, I was standing just five yards away at the time, close enough to see that there had been no use of mirrors or sleight of foot. Without question, what he had just done was pure magic.

Jonnie Wales took away my breath, my legs, my stomach. Worst of all, he took away my self-belief. Why hadn't some one had the guts to tell me earlier that there was no chance of me becoming the greatest footballer that ever lived? That the position had already been filled? That way I could have concentrated my energies on tiddly winks or marbles instead.

From that moment on Jonnie Wales became my reference, my bible of footballing perfection. Everything I did on a soccer pitch was now going to be evaluated in terms of "what would Jonnie have done?" Platini, Maradona, Zico, I saw them all. From close in too. And yes, they were all impressive. But there was, and only ever will be, one Jonnie Wales.

Hilton 0 Lumley 4

Newcastle United vs. Nottingham Forest
58 Dean Street, Gateshead
Autumn 1971

Cats And Dogs

Let me take a brief step back in time, to August 7, 1964
– my fifth birthday. In the early afternoon, Mam, who had
been looking bloated and out of sorts, went upstairs for
a lie down. Then Auntie June came and took me round
to her house, out of harm's way. Something was up. Was
Mam all right?

It wasn't until the next morning that I was allowed
upstairs to see just what the problem had been. There
I found Mam lying in bed with what appeared to be a
nasty hangover. On the bedside table were a whole load
of birthday cards, only they had pictures of babies on
them instead of the usual railway engines. Hey, silly, I was
supposed to open them!

Then someone said look what a lovely birthday
present you have, and there in the corner, just visible
under a blanket, were what at first glance appeared to
be the contents of a tin of dog food, but which closer
scrutiny revealed to be the battle-scarred head of a dozing,
newborn baby. I grimaced and was confused. Birthday
present? As I debated whether to call it Thunderbirds or
Stingray, Mam beat me to it: "Robert, aren't you going to
say hello to John?"

John Charlton Rowell was to be Mam's fifth and final
accident. According to my sisters he was my spitting

image, only in an exaggerated form. He had more pounds, more freckles, and more ginger hair than me, and they reckoned that, if at all possible, he was even uglier. Here at last was my twin sparring partner, five years late to the day. We were in for one hell of a fight.

With those prime meaty chunks and distorted features – not to mention Big Brother's fists itching for the bell to signal the start of the first round – it would have been more appropriate had John's introduction into the world been of the sort normally reserved for boxers before prize title fights: Lay Dees aaaaaand Gentlemen. Iiiiiin the red corner. Weighing in at eleven and a quarter pounds. Aaaaaall the way from Gateshead, Tyne and Wear. The Heaviest. The Fattest. The Biggest Baby in the World. Jonnyyyyyy ROW-WELLLLLL!

Mam was certainly going to have her work cut out refereeing the next ten years: "Guys, I want a good clean fight, heads up, no holding and no low punches". She didn't get one. Well, they had told me that John was my birthday present, an innocent but miscalculated act of generosity he was going to live to regret. For when you are five years old and somebody says here, this is yours, you take it literally. You take it to bits, plug it into the electricity to see if it works, and throw it off the wall when it doesn't. John became my personal punchbag, off which I bounced ideas, pillows, footballs and the occasional loose uppercut.

Characterwise we were similar and yet different. I was a pacifist, another way of saying that when it boiled down to it, I'd do anything to avoid a punch-up. John, on the other hand, had clearly taken the courage I never had to add to his own, plus a bit more. So whereas heights, fights, speed and the opposite sex were all out of bounds for me, John was quite the contrary – a right little rascal. He climbed trees and gave eye for eye out on the street. He raced down the steep back lanes on his three-wheeler bike using only his trailing feet for brakes. And he dropped his pants to show little young girls what a little old man looked like. We chewed our nails every time he left the house, yet somehow, miraculously, he always came back alive. Caked from head to foot in dirt, perhaps, but alive nonetheless.

John was my whipping boy. When he was still too young to form sentences, I would speak up on his behalf. "Yes, Mam, I must confess that it was indeed our John who ate the cake, despite your express warning that if anyone touched it before tea-time, he or she would be in for a darn good hiding." His unintelligible gagga-googas of protest fell upon deaf ears, and I must say I felt sorry for him as I listened to the alternate slaps and yelps from the safety of the upstairs bedroom – while quietly stuffing the last slice into my mouth. That's the great thing about little brothers: you can have your cake and eat it.

Even when John later learned to speak proper Geordie and defend his case, somehow I always made sure that he was the one who got into trouble. I would wind him up while he was watching telly by singing *John the scone with butter on*, then see how far I could poke my index finger into the side of his neck before touching on his soft spot. At which all hell was let loose, and we finished up on the floor in a rolling cloud of arms and legs. This was always guaranteed to push Mam's patience over the edge, and within seconds she would come running in from the kitchen with the dreaded belt. Experience taught us not to hang around in the hope of negotiating a peaceful settlement, and we immediately made for the bathroom – the only room in the house that could be locked from the inside. John would set off like a whippet, only to be overtaken by Big Brother greyhound on the staircase, and by the time I had reached the upstairs landing Mam would be within striking distance of his ankles. Since I couldn't possibly afford to put both pairs of legs at risk, I reluctantly decided she would have to be content with just the one pair, and locked the door. Poor John. Half an hour later, by which time Mam had long since calmed down and returned to her mashed potatoes, I would nonchalantly wander downstairs, take my place on the sofa, push my face into John's and stick my tongue out for good measure. What a Big Brother B****** I was. It went on for years: we played, we fought, we fell out ("I'm never playing with you again, ever"), five minutes later we made up, and then it started all over again. We were inseparable.

Naturally, my love for football rubbed off on John. We mostly played in the back lane, using garage doors for a goal. Being too young to know any better, John always played between the posts, while I whipped in banana kicks from down the lane, aiming for the top corner and well beyond his tiny reach. Even though I say so myself, I was pretty hot stuff against my four-year-old brother, but he stuck to his task and developed quickly. He first raised my eyebrows by stretching a finger out to tip previously unreachable top-corner efforts over the bar. To which I responded with sharper shooting. To which he responded with sharper reflexes. The better he got, the closer in I came, to the point where I wouldn't shoot until I could see the fear in his eyes. He went to ridiculous lengths to keep my efforts out, bouncing off the posts and the tarmac like a pinball. Yet not once did he complain of having hurt himself. Is this how all the world's mad goalkeepers begin life – as younger brothers?

When we were older, circumstances forced us – or rather allowed us – to play much of our football indoors. Mam and Dad were either at work or down the Black Horse, Audrey was married, Ellen was at Matlock Teacher Training College, and Gloria was out with her mates. Which meant that John and I had to "look after" the house. We didn't mind this at all, in fact we almost shoved Mam and Dad out of the front door, since their absence gave us the freedom to delve into our full repertoire of football games – with maximum hubbub and minimum outside interference. We certainly had very understanding neighbours.

One of the many beauties of football is that all you need to play is a playing surface, a goal and a ball. Indoors, our pitches were the front room, the kitchen, the bedroom, in fact every room in the house except the dining room – and that's only because we didn't have one. The curtains, the sofa, even the gap under the work surface between the fridge and the washing machine, all doubled up as goals. And anything you could kick without breaking your foot was used as a ball, from a folded-up pair of Dad's old socks to the real thing. As often as not we rolled up a double page from the Daily Mirror, which we wrapped in sellotape so as to make it compact and roughly spherical. Game on!

We kicked off and 58 Dean Street braced itself for the battering it was about to receive. The worst sufferers were the ornaments. The problem was that Mam and Dad had a whole bunch of friends and relatives who seemed to be forever returning home from cheap holidays with cheap souvenirs for gifts. Our house trembled like a china shop under the weight of all those Eiffel Towers, Hexham Abbey thimbles and Vatican ashtrays. John and I were mindful of the negative impact any careless footwork might have on our pocket money, so the first half of the evening was gentle, tactical and consequently uneventful. But as soon as the first dubious tackle came in, the desire not to lose increased, as did the number of shots off target. And it wasn't long before the Royal Society for the Prevention of Cruelty to Ornaments was banging on the front door.

The final whistle was the sound of voices coming up the front street, at which we hastily hid the ball, re-arranged the furniture, and sellotaped the broken ornaments back together. By the time Mam and Dad had stumbled through the front door, John and I would be happily sitting on the sofa watching News At Ten. It wasn't until the next day that Mam noticed things weren't exactly where she had left them some twenty-four hours earlier: "Who knocked the head off the little old man sitting on the park bench next to his dog that your Auntie Yvonne brought us back from Devon?"

"No one, Mam, it just fell off while we were watching the telly." We got away with murder.

When we had to baby-sit for our Audrey's first-born, John and I would take it in turns to play ball, while the other looked after the baby. One indoor "solitaire" ideal for such occasions involved nothing more than throwing the ball off the wall and diving to save the rebound. First it was Newcastle's turn, then the other team's, then Newcastle's turn again, and so on. Having lost a fight with a pot of tea when I was two, I had a very sensitive left elbow, and only ever played the game upstairs, where I used Mam and Dad's double bed as a six-yard box to cushion my falls. But John the circus acrobat would have dived on a bed of nails, so the front room carpet on which he normally threw himself about was marshmallows compared to the back lane.

One day, I was too busy giving baby its bottle in the kitchen to take any notice of the live running commentary coming from next door. So when, game over, John came running in to announce that Nottingham Forest had just beaten Newcastle United, I nearly dropped the baby's bottle. After all, being a Magpie like myself and, more importantly, just as big a cheat as Dad, John letting Newcastle lose was unthinkable.

I could see from the twinkle in John's eye, though, that the Moonies had been at him, and this was immediately confirmed by his next statement: "Nottingham Forest won so I'm supporting Nottingham Forest from now on". Even the baby yelled out at the news. In those days you had to be a complete lunatic to support a drab outfit like Nottingham Forest, so I spent the next hour or so reasoning with John the way you might reason with a suicidal maniac, pleading with him not to jump. But despite my promises of a couple of penny chews if he changed his mind, and a good thumping if he didn't, there was no budging him. His mind was made up.

What of course I didn't realise at the time was that John's switch in allegiances had nothing to do with Nottingham Forest being preferable to Newcastle United. He was simply getting his own back after all those years of Big Brother persecution. Me being black and white all the way down to my pinkies, he knew that to betray the Magpies was to betray me, a subtle, almighty kick right where it hurt. In short, it was his way of saying "I hate your guts". Oof! John stood by his decision too, thus starting a family link to Nottingham Forest Football Club that would become much deeper than any of us could ever have imagined. One that would last for all of twenty-seven and a half years; that would bring tears of joy and of sorrow; and which – strangest of all – would mostly centre around the fat-legged, three-months-old baby now screaming for its bottle back.

Newcastle United 5   Nottingham Forest 6

Football vs. Rugby
Greenwell Junior High School, Gateshead
September 1971

Rugged

> *This little piggy went to market,*
> *This little piggy stayed at home;*
> *This little piggy had roast beef,*
> *This little piggy had none;*
> *And this big fat piggy went grunt-grunt-grunt-grunt-grunt,*
> *picked the ball up and ran with it.*

My football career took a sharp downhill turn after the Jonnie Wales experience. I went to the first series of school trials, did "all right", qualified for the final stages, then mixed up the dates and that was that. Had my parents been the sort you see on the touchline at school matches, insulting the referee and barking at their sons to ignore teacher's instructions and "get up front, man", maybe they would have encouraged me to have another go. After all, just because Jonnie Wales was better than me didn't mean that I couldn't still hope to play for a second-rate team like Sunderland. But with my academic side showing few signs of progress, my parents were more concerned about my schoolwork than my footwork.

My years at Greenwell turned out to be about the lousiest three years of my life. The combination of growing up in Gateshead and a comprehensive school education doesn't exactly fill your boots with the self-assurance you need to kick ass in the real world later on, but when on top of that you are rejected by your best mates, you start wondering what the hell's going on. The problem was that they, unlike me, were beginning to take their first steps into adolescence. They chased girls, I didn't care. They smoked cigarettes, I didn't dare. They listened to Slade, which I couldn't bear. Suddenly I wasn't one of the lads any more, and Mam was my only friend.

Probably to overcome my relationship difficulties and chronic shyness, I sought to win over my class-mates by becoming court jester. I messed around so much that the teachers were forever moving me and my desk to the other side of the class out of the way of my eggers-on. The back of my head was on first-name terms with the teachers' right hands, and it was a miracle that I managed to avoid the headmaster's cane.

Partly to impress all those around me, partly because I simply enjoyed the taste, I sucked sweets in class. Wine gums, pineapple cubes, sherbet lemons, they all passed between my lips during lessons. One stand-in French teacher, highly unimpressed at the way our Geordie tongues were struggling with all the hee-hawing that goes on over the Channel, became especially irate when she realised that my own speech impediment wasn't so much down to the shape of my mouth as what I had in it.

"You boy! Come here!"

I stood next to the teacher facing the class, with a big smile across my face to show everybody I was in total control of the situation.

"Don't you not think that eating in class isn't something that you shouldn't be doing?"

Hallo? I was good at maths but not even my quick brain could deal with that many double-negatives. I debated whether to tell her to concentrate on her English rather than try to teach others French, thought better of it, and hazarded a reply: "Er, no miss?".

Et vlammm! "Well maybe that will teach you not to eat sweets in class in future!" That slap didn't half hurt, but it did wonders for my popularity ratings.

Besides French, at Greenwell we learned the rudiments of two other languages: German, which was optional; and Bad, which was compulsory. At Kells Lane, a whole variety of "nasty" adjectives had been used for emphasis, but at Greenwell, "flipping", "flaming" and "flimming" were all given up for just one, new, highly expressive f-word:

Consonant, please. K. Vowel please. U. Consonant please. F. Another consonant please. C.

You have thirty seconds. Tick-tock tick-tock…

Not that I ever used it myself, of course.

With school being a time of suffering, breaking up for the summer holidays was the happiest event of the year, more important even than Christmas Day and the F.A. Cup Final. Six whole weeks without homework was a lifetime ahead of us. September was so far away it might never come, and even if it did, surely by then the world would have been put to rights and you wouldn't have to pay for ice-pops any more. The prospects were lip-smacking: hot days, warm evenings, pleasant dreams, all-day games of football.

The excitement lasted all of two weeks. After days spent playing one-against-one dribblies against Bri Dixon, my new chum from up Beacon Lough way, he soon fathomed out that when I dropped my shoulder to the left it meant I was going to knock the ball to the right, and when I dropped my shoulder to the right I was just off balance. Either way, he won the ball, at which it was his turn to have a go, and the same thing happened. Clouds came and went, the sun rose and dipped, and still there we were, two puppets on a string, dancing and dropping shoulders under the moonlight in an unsuccessful attempt to fool each other.

If I had rushed out of the school gates on the last day of term as if the place were on fire, I was now ready to kiss and make up. Bored out of my mind, I spent the rest of the holidays shrivelled up on the sofa like a dying insect, an absent-minded finger working its way up one of my nostrils for comfort, begging for school to rescue me before my head caved in or someone came and sat on me.

The big day finally arrived and I no longer cared that ice-pops were as expensive as they'd always been. From the moment I walked in through the school gates my mind focused on the first games afternoon of the new term, and with it the chance to have another go at tackling Jonnie Wales, as well as express my footballing skills against boys other than Bri Dixon – boys who would fall for my shoulder-dropping every time.

The changing rooms were pandemonium as we exchanged our grey nylon shirts for football strips, waiting impatiently for Mr. Brabham to come along and split us into teams. But then above the din there was a shout of: "All right, all right, shut up you lot". Heads turned and in walked a thick, unfamiliar moustache wearing an equally thick, unfamiliar tracksuit. A bit of a thickhead by the look and sound of things, but no big deal – we'll soon be out there kicking that ball around!

And then he started. "Right, you lot, I'm in charge round here from now on so if you've got something to say, you say it to me… if anybody's got a problem with that, then that's his problem and I don't want to hear about it… at the end of the day, it's the result that counts… any sissies will be straight under the showers and won't be coming out until I've seen them… you can't tell a sausage by its skin… a stitch in time saves nine… I've got a donkey in my sports bag so you won't know what's hit you…"

And so on for a good half hour, at the end of which there were more questions on our faces than in an entire Mastermind series. Who is this guy? What does he want? Why is he wasting valuable football-playing time in this way? Then, as if by magic, he pulled out this egg-shaped, leather object and our organs nearly dropped. There, in his hands, was a very strong case for his pleading insanity and getting away with it. "Right, everybody outside! Today we are going to sort the men out from the boys. Today we are going to play *rugby*." Rugby? Who in his right mind wants to play a dangerous game like rugby? But rugby it was, and a few minutes later we were all out there avoiding this oval object like the plague.

Or almost everyone. A few hog-shaped individuals – those who normally dreaded games lessons because they were crap at football – excelled at this new "sport", quickly establishing themselves as teacher's piglets. Here were lads we'd been taking the mickey out of for years, both on and off the football field, and now it was their turn to squeeze a smile through those pork chops.

Take Jelly-Pants. Up to that fateful September afternoon, Jelly-Pants had probably resigned himself to being Jelly-Pants for the rest of his days. But rugby gave his life new meaning. One minute he was at the centre of the bacon sandwich technically known as the scrum, making virile grunting noises and nibbling at ears; the next he was diving in at feet and earning house-points for flattening little pillocks like me. The nickname "Jelly-Pants" went straight out of the window, and now, to his (suddenly very large) group of mates, he was known quite simply as "Bezz". Goodness, you could even envisage chatting up sows with a nickname like that!

One rosy-cheeked individual stood out in particular for possessing all the physical attributes of the ideal rugby player. He had a Billy Bunter head, cauliflower ears, and if there was a neck under all that blubber it certainly never saw the light of day. Most importantly – that which made rugby and him the perfect marriage – he had a brain the size of a peanut. His Parma hams made rude noises as they rubbed past each other, preventing him from working up anything more than a trotter. He clutched the ball, set off at one mile an hour, and we all took it in turns to cling to his curly tail and other parts of his body without sliding off. Alas, to no avail. He continued, undeterred, right up to our line, where the teacher politely informed him to place the ball gently on the ground without dropping it. Try. Three house points.

To my amazement, several of the good footballers appeared to take a liking to these mass wrestling matches. Ronnie Ward was one. He might not have been in the same league as Jonnie Wales (no one was in the same league as Jonnie Wales) but he was nevertheless one of the best footballers in the school. Yet even he made the frightful mistake of giving up the beautiful game for egg-chasing. I still see him in the Gateshead Fell Rugby Club when I go home. Behind that mass of shoulder muscle, neck muscle, ear muscle and eyebrow muscle, I can just about make him out. What a waste of footballing talent.

Legend has it that rugby takes its name from the school of that name, since it was there, in 1823, that a sixteen-year-old "Jelly-Pants" by the name of William Webb Ellis caught the ball during a game of football and ran with it. Stupid, stupid boy. I hope that he was expelled for his appalling behaviour, because quite frankly, I just don't see the point. I mean, it is surely only in rugby that a player can run his studs down an opponent's back without the referee even blowing up for a foul. And it is surely only in rugby that players are applauded for kicking the ball into the crowd – in fact if you didn't know the rules, you'd think that was the whole objective. In football, other than perhaps at places like Hartlepool, a player would be substituted if he did that too often, since the game is designed to be played on the green bits in the middle, not in the surrounding stands.

It would be fine in rugby if, once off the pitch, the ball didn't come back – everyone could go home then – but no, the players then spend half an hour forming two lines for what appears to be the opening formation of a Morris dancing routine, the egg is duly thrown in, and "play" resumes amid much huffing, puffing, ranting and panting. And all this aggro for what? A game which is invariably won by the team that scores the most penalties. There are loads of penalties in rugby, given for the stupidest of reasons, like holding on to the ball for too long and standing in the wrong place. And while the kicker builds a little hill of sand to stop his ball from toppling over, all of the opposing players stand behind the posts, not one of them volunteering to go in goal. So all the kicker has to do is chip the ball over the bar. It seems ridiculously easy to me – I kick the ball over the bar all the time in football without even trying. And nobody ever claps me or awards me points.

Am I missing something, or wouldn't it be preferable to cut out all the ranting and raving and just award both teams five penalties each, the one who scores the most being the winner? That way the game could be played during half-time breaks at football matches, thus providing us footie fans with entertainment while we eat our pies. Now there's an idea.

Yes, I know you rugby fans out there will be offended by my words. As one "connoisseur" once said to me: "Football is a game for gentlemen played by ruffians, rugby is a game for ruffians played by gentlemen". Which just shows what he understood about life. No, sorry. To me, and, let's be honest, to most of the civilised world, football is a game for the masses, played by normal human beings; while rugby is a game for the massive, played by murderous, jockstrap-sniffing, sheep-tickling Afrikaner farmers.

A few of whom went to Greenwell. I could never have imagined having my head kicked in in such apparently legal circumstances, not to mention under the approving eye of the teachers. Yet despite my attempts to keep well away from the action during that first rugby lesson, somehow my name was put down for the school trials – they must have confused me with someone else. I didn't turn up, though – as far as I was concerned, un œuf was definitely un œuf.

Football 0   Rugby 1

Crystal Palace vs. West Germany
Earlswood Park, Low Fell, Gateshead
Late 1971

Cool And Crisp and Uneven

Subbuteo was, and probably still is, the greatest table football game ever invented. Explaining how it is played to the unfamiliar is like explaining cricket to the Italians – in Italian – so let me simply sum it up by saying it is a game where you flick miniature plastic footballers after a ball and whoever scores the most goals is the winner. Put like that, no wonder Dad described it as the "stupidest bloody game I've ever seen". But we kids loved it. The tense, action-packed matches made Subbuteo the fantasy football of our childhood and was the closest we ever came to playing in the first division.

The skill in Subbuteo is in the flicking. An experienced player will exploit the player's hemispheric base by doing fancy things like swerving around an opponent, collecting the ball and setting off upfield again, and all this thanks to just one, very deft tweak of the index finger. When it works, it's Kevin Keegan in his prime. When it doesn't, it's Eric Cantona in his – our boys were throwing themselves feet-first into the crowd long before the temperamental Frenchman was saying silly things about trawlers and sardines.

It was a while before we had our very own Subbuteo set. Santa Claus misunderstood the letter Mam and Dad had written on our behalf, and we ended up with a completely different football game. By the end of Christmas Day it was already back in its box and John and I were chanting,

We want Subbuteo!

We want Subbuteo!

Despite knowing that in our family, gifts other than at Christmas and birthdays were as frequent as Newcastle away wins, we pestered Dad on a daily basis. After all, wasn't it his fault that we'd ended up with the wrong game in the first place? And what with his two jobs and Mam's one, it's not as if they couldn't afford it: the basic set cost no more than a couple of pints – all he had to do was come home from the Black Horse ten minutes earlier than usual and the money was there!

We want Subbuteo!

We want Subbuteo!

Finally, to our surprise and joy, Dad gave in. What he bought us wasn't the World Cup Edition of our dreams, perhaps, but this was no time to look a gift box of bits of plastic in the mouth. In fact the only thing missing from the cheap set was Subbuteo's official, green baize pitch – a bit like having a set of snooker balls but no table to play on. Since we couldn't possibly join the Dean Street League without our own home ground, we took one of Mam's old cotton sheets, folded it in two to give it league standard thickness, penned in the lines with a magic marker, and hey presto we were in business.

The result was quite unfit for football: ripples formed during matches, making the snowy white surface about as playable as the "player" in January. But John and I soon mastered the unusual conditions, indeed the pitch turned out to be our secret weapon. It didn't matter how good you were, coming to play at 58 Dean Street was like travelling to Southampton – we might be crap but you'd have a hard job coming away with the points.

An even greater hazard in coming to our place was house-proud Mam. When five minutes before kick-off a knock on the front door announced the arrival of the away team, she would carry out one of her late but legendary ground inspections and quickly conclude that nobody was "coming into this midden" (which is how Mam described the interior of 58 Dean Street when five minutes had passed without her getting out the duster). We would then spend the next hour standing on chairs as she hoovered around us, tra-la-laing abominable old Scottish songs as she worked, while my disappointed mates grouped outside, chanting *You only sing when you're cleaning*. Like a bad Scottish winter, Mam was personally responsible for delaying the end of the Dean Street season by several months.

Even when the game did finally get underway, there was no guarantee that Mam wouldn't leave her imprint on it – literally – with one of her sudden pitch invasions. As we played away on the bedroom carpet upstairs, Mam would barge in, jump over the one-inch high fence surround, march straight across the pitch to fetch something from the wardrobe, and tread on three or four players in the process. My protests of "Mam, watch out!" fell on deaf feet, and in the days before superglue and supersubs, we invariably finished the game with nine men each. The headline in the following day's Subbuteo Times summed it all up: "Serial cleaner turns serial killer – four murdered at cup tie".

Fortunately Mam didn't travel to away matches, so when I set off with my West Germany team for my most important game to date – the semi-final of the Dean Street Cup – it was just me and the boys. On paper we had nothing to worry about. With the likes of Maier, Schnellinger, Beckenbauer and Müller we should wallop Bradders' Crystal Palace side every day of the week. But as I reminded my players during the team talk on the way down Albert Drive, the Cup is eleven bits of plastic against eleven bits of plastic. What's more, Bradders had never, ever been beaten, so with Crystal Palace currently cruising at the top of the first division there was no room for complacency. My aim was to sneak a draw and take Palace back to Dean Street for the replay, where I knew the uneven, snow-bound pitch and Mam's hooliganism would be worth at least a goal start.

I played out of my skin. With just seconds remaining the score was still locked at nil-nil, a replay was in sight and the supporters in my mind were singing *Wembley, Wembley, here we come*. Then Palace made one, last-ditch assault. Bradders manoeuvred his centre-forward into a dangerous shooting position and I scrambled around the pitch to prepare my 'keeper for the coming shot.

In Subbuteo the goalkeeper manned his penalty area thanks to a rod fed from under the goal (bear in mind this was long before Peter Schmeichel started going up for corners), and right now my hand was trembling so much that it looked as if poor old Sepp Maier was having a fit. It didn't matter that Bradders completely fluffed his flick. For what would normally have been a straightforward stop for a world-class goalie like Maier, the ball trickled as if in slow motion past his shaking limbs before nestling quietly into the bottom corner of the net.

"In the nick of time!" cried Bradders, as we both instinctively looked up at the clock. It clearly showed we had been playing a good fifteen seconds over time, so I stared appealingly at the referee in the hope that the goal might be disallowed. But since the referee was always the biggest boy in the room – in this case Bradders himself – my pleas were waved away, the goal stood, West Germany were out of the Cup.

If Mam had seen it there would have been a riot, but she hadn't and I sulked all the way home. I never did get my own back on Bradders. Soon after there was a mass exodus of boys from the area, and the Dean Street Subbuteo League folded as a result. John and I, on, the other hand, continued to extract enjoyment from the game for years to come. One Christmas, when I was, erm, thirty, we bought ourselves a brand new set – the World Cup Edition this time – and played throughout Christmas Day. All the old butterflies were there, as were the disputes over whether his player had fouled mine, and whether my flicking technique was legal. Above all, we were reminded just how fantastic Subbuteo was, how wrong Dad had been in calling it "the stupidest bloody game he'd ever seen". Certainly, the day I have a son of my own, in his first letter to Santa Claus – whether he likes it or not – Subbuteo will be right up there with the Hornby train set. And this time I'll make sure I write the damn thing myself to avoid any confusion.

Crystal Palace 1   West Germany 0

Hereford United vs. Newcastle United
BBC Grandstand
Every first Saturday in January since 1972

Mud, The Great Leveller

I hate Januarys. It's freezing cold and all your Christmas presents are either broken or eaten. Worst of all, though, the F.A. Cup is once again upon us, gleefully introduced by BBC Grandstand...

Frank Bough: ... And now here's Bob Wilson with "Football Focus".

Bob Wilson: Thank you Frank and a Happy New Year to all of you. Well, today's the day when the meek will be taking on the mighty in the third round of the F.A. Cup, and we'll be focusing our attention on those teams of butchers, bakers and candlestick makers all dreaming of becoming giant-killing legends...

[Here we go again, cue the old clip of the long sideboards – haven't they got any other goals in the Match Of The Day archives?]

... And it's Radford for Hereford...now Tudor's gone down for Newcastle...Radford again...ohhhhhhh, what a goal! Radford the scorer! Ronnie Radford!

I can't bear to look as Radford runs off arms aloft, more amazed than anyone in the whole ground that his shot from all of three thousand miles out has gone flying into the top corner, with Newcastle keeper Iam McFaul rooted to the mud. Tiny kids invade the pitch to celebrate what will later win "Goal Of The Season", and Hereford United of the

South-West Plonkers League are on their way to knocking the great Newcastle United out of the F.A. Cup.

I was in the back yard kicking a ball about when Dad came through to break the news. I say that because the test of every Newcastle fan worth his weight in hops is remembering precisely what he was doing when he learned of Hereford's historic victory. Put into perspective, that defeat was as humiliating as Italy losing to Andorra or Muhammad Ali losing to Richard Dunn – the only difference being that Newcastle losing to Hereford did actually happen.

For years after I prayed that we might come across Hereford again, just to set the record straight, send them back south with a toe-cap in their ears, and above all put those BBC demons to rest. But the opportunity never arose. In the end, I decided I just couldn't take F.A. Cup third round day with Bob Wilson any more, and fled the country.

> We hate Bob Wilson and the BBC,
> We hate the Cup in Januar-y,
> We hate that man Radford Ronnie
> We are the Geordie – boot-boys.
> Na, na-na-na, na na na
> Na, na-na-na, na na na
> Na, na-na-na, na na na
> We are the Geordie – boot-boys.

Hereford United 2   Newcastle United 1
(after extra time)

Me and the skins vs. The skins
Blankenberg, Belgium
August 1973

Brass Monkeys

If music be the love of beer,
Play on!

We were a very musical family. My granddad had worked
as a pianist for the silent movies, Uncle George was one of
the best trumpeters in the north, and his sons Ray and Ken
followed in his footsteps; Ken even appeared on Hughie
Green's Opportunity Knocks for his sins. Dad himself played
piano and trombone, but of his own children I was the only
one to show any real potential. He taught me to play the
piano when I was five, and I loved it all the way through to
the age of twelve. That was when, asked to exhibit my finger-
tapping skills in front of the schoolclass, I discovered to my
consternation that the three, strategically-placed, chipped
ivories that had helped me find my bearings on the piano
at home weren't a standard feature on keyboards elsewhere.
What therefore started out as a rendition of my personal
favourite, Beethoven's Für Elise, quickly developed into Für
Gott's Sake Get Off Das Bloody Piano. Dad spent weeks
trying to entice me back, constantly "harping" on about the
"pleasure there is in music". But since my hormones had
already begun telling me to grow my hair long if Dad said cut
it short, our own musical branch of the Rowell family came
to an abrupt halt, with no heir to the stool.

Then there was the brass band. It was Uncle George,
then conductor of the Washington Colliery Brass Band, who
originally convinced Dad to go along and play trombone. And

from as early as I can remember, every Sunday morning John and I would go along with him to "listen in". Those Sunday morning practice sessions were a nightmare. Let's face it, not many people would admit to actually enjoying brass band music, even when those performing seem to know what they are doing. But I was there when they were still practising. Other than toothache and watching Sunderland, I can't think of anything worse than spending an hour in the company of thirty or so puffy-cheeked, pop-eyed "musicians", all farting random notes across the room at each other in an attempt to make themselves heard above the din.

Of course the brass band, like Sunday football, was really just a way of escaping from the missus to have a few beers with the lads. When the practice session was (thankfully) over, the instruments were put back into their boxes rather more quickly than they had been brought out an hour earlier, and the band lads raced off to be first served in the working men's bar at the other end of the corridor. Certainly, there were far more encores at the end of the drinking session than at the end of the practice session, and it wasn't difficult to see, judging from the ruddy cheeks and frequent outbursts of laughter, that this is what Dad had meant by the "pleasure there is in music".

While all this merriment was going on, John and I would slide up and down the wooden corridor in our socks, battling to kick an empty cigarette packet into the other's doorway. If we were lucky, at the end our patience would be rewarded with a "bagatuda" – a packet of Tudor's salt and vinegar crisps. But with Dad being "well-popped" by the time he came out, as often as not he would simply forget.

I'm not sure if we improved our footballing skills at the Washington Welfare Hall, but crisps or no crisps, it was all infinitely preferable to the only other alternative on offer for Sunday morning entertainment – church with Mam. There the only let-up from the indescribable boredom came from a loud and squeaky one our John would let fly during Behold The Great Creator Makes. The aroma and our hysterics filled the church, and it wasn't until three hymns later that we managed to calm down. After that, our eyes only had to meet ever so briefly and we'd be giggling our heads off again.

With all that breaking of wind our John would have made a fine brass brand player, but in fairness to Uncle George and the Washington Colliery Brass Band, they did actually get their act together when letting off in public. They figured well at the annual Durham Miners Meeting, and travelled to Blackpool and London to compete in many a national drinking contest. Perhaps the most cherished memory, though, at least as far as our family is concerned, was when former peanut-farmer and recently-elected American President Jimmy Carter came to Geordieside to trace the steps of George Washington. Naturally, the Washington Brass Band played for him that day – I think it was *Jimmy, Jimmy, show us your nuts* – and they were just about to start their second number when Mr. Carter, visibly suffering from the combination of jet-lag and hoompa-poompa, went across to interrupt. Proud Dad still has the photo on his piano of the meeting between George and the Georgian, the two great leaders. It's a lovely picture: Uncle George is visibly touched by the President's warm comments, something along the lines of "hey that fanfare stuff was just great and by the way I think your toupée is off of centre."

Put booze and music together, or better still booze and more booze, and you have all the ingredients of a holiday. So when the band was invited by the Mayor of Blankenberg to spend a week performing in Belgium, the prospects of a one hundred and sixty-eight hour drinking marathon were too good to miss. For the first time in the history of Washington Colliery Brass Band, the cornets, euphoniums, double basses, trombones, baritones and horns all came together in perfect harmony to respond with *Oh Yes Please We'd Love To*. The only downside was that they were going to have to take their wives and families along.

I could see the sort of week we were in for as soon as we boarded the boat at Dover. England's first ever travelling hooligans decided that some serious rehearsing was in order and piled into the lounge bar downstairs. The problem was that most of them had never been past the boats on Saltwell Park lake, so it wasn't long before the joint effects of the English Channel swishing and swooshing outside, and the beer swishing and swooshing inside, had their guts gurgling for fresh air. The first to crack was Geordie Pickering, who came racing up from the lounge as if the ship were about to sink, just in time to send his innards overboard – then back down for more. Then, from our wind-in-the-face ringside seats up on deck, we watched on as one by one the other lads popped up like trumpet valves to carry on where Geordie Pickering had left off – and this before we'd even left the harbour! By the time the four-hour crossing was over, there was more of the Washington Colliery Brass Band in the English Channel than on mainland Belgium.

John and I spent the next seven days trying (in vain) to dissuade the grown-ups from entering the next bar. The nearest we came to tourism was a bus-trip to a café in Bruges, and another to a bar just over the border into Holland. Other than that, with what seemed like twenty-four hour opening times, there was no let-up. The only fun we boys had was the occasional game of snooker, at which we struggled like hell to make breaks, what with there being no pockets on Belgian tables.

John and I did have our own supply of drinks, though. For weeks before the "holiday", Mam had been building up a stock of cans of cheap pop, so that by the time we boarded the coach at Washington there were enough crates of the stuff to see us through a nuclear holocaust, never mind a week in Blankenberg. Our can-opening generally took place in our hotel room during the afternoon, while the grown-ups caught flies after their liquid lunch. Now John and I were big fans of fizzy drinks, but there's only so much pop you can take. Bored out of our lives, and with our bellies ebbing and flowing, we were constantly banging on our parents' door:

"Mam, I'm bored".

"Well have a lemonade".

"I've had one."

"Well have an orangeade."

"I've had one of them as well."

"Well bloody well have another one!"

And the renewed sounds of snoring told us that this was her final word on the matter. It went on day after day: they drank their pop, we drank our pop. We might just as well have been on holiday in Gateshead, for other than the colour of the beer nobody would have noticed the difference. Ah, "the pleasure there *ish* in *mews-hic*."

As luck would have it, on the very last day something as rare in Belgium as it is in Gateshead occurred: the clouds gave way to sunshine. The band lads and their partners suddenly remembered that Blankenberg was a coastal resort, and that within fifty yards of the hotel was a huge, sparsely populated beach. For once, instead of going straight from their lunchtime session to their rooms, they rushed off to the sands to catch sunstroke.

As they all lay there cooking and squirming like lobsters, John and I started kicking a ball around. Now the sight of a ball to a Geordie who's just had a bellyful is like a red rag to a bull. In a matter of minutes two teams had been organised and twenty Johann Cruyffs were racing around like a bunch of schoolkids. It didn't seem to matter that both teams were wearing the same colours – pink going on red – since nobody had the intention of passing the ball anyway. With wives and girlfriends watching, every player was keen to show off his silky skills.

Not so silky as it turned out. In their desire to impress, they had all overlooked the fact that even when they'd been at their peaks – some twenty or so years earlier – they hadn't been particularly good footballers. And it certainly wasn't the combination of beer-gut and blistering sun that was going to help them set the world alight. As a result, the game didn't last very long: some slid in for tackles and never got up, some sneaked off for a quick fag and never came back, others ran off to puke in the moats of nearby sand castles.

But the game did last long enough for this fit little fourteen-year-old – all dressed up in his Hilton house colours – to show the world how good he was. Overflowing with sugary water and pent-up frustration, I was on carbohydrate overdrive that afternoon, and ran rings round the lot of them. The alcoholic cloud that had cast a shadow over the whole holiday suddenly broke out into a heavy downpour of compliments, and on the coach trip home the eyes in the back of my head could sense the band lads pointing discret but admiring fingers in my direction as they told their wives how brilliant I was. Not even some clever so-and-so getting out his cornet to play *Edelweiss* at three o'clock in the morning was enough to wipe the smile from my face. Some day, assured drummer Bill Davis – whose claim to fame was once keeping goal for Scarborough – I would make it as a professional footballer.

How many times did I hear that in my life? That some day I would "make it"? Hundreds of times, and always from people who had never seen or even heard of Jonnie Wales, and who at best had played in goal for Scarborough. Never one to question the true value of praise lavished upon me, though, I believed all of them for a while. It was only many years later, when opponents started coming up to me after matches and saying, "you must have been good in your day", that I realised it was all starting to get a bit late.

Me and the skins 15   The skins 2

Newcastle United vs. Our John
St. James' Park (first leg) and 58 Dean Street (second leg)
March - May 1974

Chilling

Not a lot of people know this, but Newcastle United once had a rich F.A. Cup tradition, at least among those old enough to be able to recall the last time they had won it. Indeed for a while the obsession with going to London to visit the Queen was considered a fair excuse for not "wanting" to win the League. After all, playing in the Cup Final meant a day out at Wembley and a new tin of dubbin to clean your boots with. Not only that, the match was shown live on television. It was the big occasion, bigger than all forty-two league games put together.

By the early seventies, though, after years of looking as if we weren't the slightest bit interested in any of the competitions, the Cup tradition excuse wasn't so much wearing thin as going completely shiny. Then in 1974 the Magpies put together their first decent cup run in ages, and immediately there was talk on Geordieside of this being a freak year – our year. From the moment the quarter-final draw gifted us a home tie against none other than our John's second division Nottingham Forest, we sensed that the gods were with us. All of a sudden, people I'd never seen show much interest in football – such as our Audrey's husband Brian – loved football. They hunted around their lofts for their black-and-white scarves and consulted their Newcastle street maps to find out where Saint James' Park was.

After six hours queuing in the cold to be sure of a ticket the day they went on sale, and four more queuing and waiting for the game to start on matchday itself, I was ready for my bed by the time the players showed up. *Ten hours* to see two second-rate teams kick a ball around for a sixth of that time. We must have been mad. Nowadays at most I'd give them ten minutes, and even then only on the condition that my match ticket, pie and Bovril were served on a plate when I walked up to the ground at five to three.

The buzz inside the stadium and the great roar that went up when the game did finally get under way were a clear message to our boys that hey, we've waited a long time for this so don't go and mess it up or there'll be hell on. Yet I knew, just knew, that this was not going to be one of those cup-ties where the first division outfit wins by a couple of "logical" first-half goals and everybody goes home happy. For a start, this was Newcastle United, and if ever a team was capable of screwing up the unscrewupable, it was us. But much more important was the fact that, if we thought we had the gods on our side, Forest surely had the devil on theirs, in the image of the nine-year-old poltergeist standing in big brother's shadow at the front of the West Paddock. I say poltergeist because from a very early age our John had developed an uncanny ability to send household objects flying across the room at great speed, usually in my direction and with alarming accuracy. I was absolutely convinced that on this, his very first visit to St. James' Park, his evil little mind would play havoc with the most important object of them all, the white, round, bouncy thing the twenty-two players had just started battling over.

True enough, in the time it took you to read the last paragraph, that most agonising of sights – a wave of ripples in the netting behind Iam McFaul – proved that my fears hadn't been unfounded. And the thousands of Forest supporters noisily renting the Gallowgate End that day exploded in the realisation that they might not just be there for the beer.

John himself was surrounded by Newcastle fans but

this didn't stop him from celebrating. Fortunately, he was wearing one of those Parka coats that had been bought about ten sizes too big (this to allow for a few years' growth and the hosting of the occasional birthday party), so he was able to jump up and down under its roof without anyone noticing. His little head spun round and round inside his hood like the possessed little girl's in The Exorcist, and I knew that somewhere the other side of those bursting seams was the widest, cheesiest grin in the history of Cheshire.

0-1, 1-1, 1-2, and eleven minutes into the second half John pulled off what turned out to be his final act of sorcery for the day, sending his hero Duncan McKenzie flying across the goalmouth. Penalty! Pat Howard was sent off for disputing the referee's decision, the spot-kick was tucked away, and by now the outer extremities of John's mouth were up behind his ears.

The real "fun", though, was just about to begin. The referee's doubly controversial decision had upset all of us, and no one more so than the big fat man now scrapping with the police just behind the Leazes End goal. This in turn sparked a riot, as three hundred boys came spilling out onto the pitch, and Newcastle versus Forest gave way to cops and robbers. The only way out for the young invaders now was back into the crowd, but where? They couldn't run back to the Leazes End since that's where all the policemen were coming from. And the Gallowgate End was no solution, either, because the Forest fans would have happily kicked their little heads in. So they came piling into the paddocks instead, which is exactly where we were standing – the very first line of infantry.

The sight of all those feet desperately throwing themselves into the crowd around him frightened the life out of our John, and this gave me a brilliant idea: if I removed him from the ground now, not only would his head still be in one piece, his departure might also bring a return to calm and – you never know – a Newcastle comeback. This would of course mean the personal sacrifice of leaving a Newcastle game before the end (for the first and last time in my life, I hasten to add), but to me it was a case of the lesser of two evils. I whispered something to the back of John's Parka hood, detected the faintest of nods, and ten minutes later we were sitting in the relative quiet of the number twenty-seven bus.

As the next thirty minutes' events would bear out, it was a far, far, better thing I did then than I have ever done. John was smiling on the other side of his Parka hood when our Audrey opened the front door and said "you'll never believe what happened". At the sound of the words "Newcastle four", John's mouth took on the size and shape of an empty garage, forewarning us of great claps of thunder brewing beyond those quivering tonsils, and we all dived for cover. I must say I felt deeply saddened for my little brother in his moment of grief. I didn't even have it in me to punch the air. In any case, I hadn't even been there to see it, and at school on the Monday nobody, but nobody would believe that Newcastle's 4-3 turnaround was exclusively thanks to me.

Nor did the Football Association. They put the Forest players' sudden loss of form down to the pitch invasion, and promptly ordered the match to be replayed on neutral territory. In all, it took Newcastle three attempts to beat Forest, but beat them we did, and eight weeks later the team was on its way to Wembley to face Liverpool. Never was there such a "this is our year" air as before that final, and the whole of Geordieside was draped in black and white in celebration of the coming victory. Malcolm Macdonald felt so sure the pot was ours he issued public threats across the Pennines that he was going to tear the Liverpool defence to ribbons. It seemed that all that was left for us to do now was have a quick word with royalty and collect the cup.

Mine seemed to be the only guts in the whole area that were saying hey, wait a minute, we do still actually have to play this game, Liverpool have a pretty good team, that kind of stuff. OK, so Newcastle had never lost at Wembley, but the current team had never played at Wembley! I'd never lost on the Centre Court at Wimbledon either, but it didn't automatically mean I was ready to thrash Jimmy Connors, did it? But nobody wanted to listen, and in the end even I put my behaviour down to undue pessimism – after all, one million Geordies couldn't all be wrong, could they?

Couldn't they? Well, they hadn't bargained for our John. As three o'clock approached, there was little Beelzebub, sitting perched on Dad's protective knee, his cropped hair, wooden smile and droopy eyelids giving him the look of a mischief-minded ventriloquist's dummy. And was he there to egg on big brother's Newcastle? Was he bugger. As I dared steal a glance in his direction, the when-I-get-you-I'm-gonna-eat-you glare he threw me sent shivers down my spine. Bloody Nora.

The only black-and-white stripes to get near the Liverpool goal that day were those of Geordie athlete Brendan Foster, who won a pre-match race around Wembley's cinder track. Thereafter it was a day to forget. The Newcastle players came off the pitch wondering just what had hit them. Whether it really was John who had turned them to stone, as I believed at the time, is a matter for debate. Dad blamed Newcastle's humiliation on rather more terrestrial factors: an ineffective midfield, a non-existent attack, and that other little devil, two-goal Kevin Keegan. Well, I suppose he did have a point!

Either way, Wembley had long since emptied and the Liverpool players were well on their way home with the cup by the time Beelzebub's head had finally stopped spinning. And when it did, with no Parka hood to conceal it this time, there for all to see was the very last, cheesy grin of the 1973-74 season. Freaky.

Newcastle United 0   Our John 3

Saltwell vs. Dryden
White House Sports Fields, Gateshead
Autumn 1974

Cold Feet

The years between the ages of eleven and fourteen are supposed to mark the change from boyhood to manhood. And so they did – for everyone else but me. I must have been off sick the day the doctors came to jab us full of puberty. The other boys woke up the next morning with bodies several feet taller and voices several keys lower, desperately impatient for games afternoon to arrive, during which they could show off their brand new, takes-both-hands willies in the changing rooms. As for me, I remained as squirty and as squealy as ever, and continued to keep my cocktail sausage under wraps in the showers. Never did I feel so ill-equipped to face the world.

It is during those same, maturing years that the budding young footballer learns the fundamentals of the eleven-a-side, team game. This basically involves knowing more or less where to stand, and passing the ball occasionally. Only I missed out on all of that too, since my own footballing development had been pretty much restricted to dribble-dribble-shoot down at the "player".

Playing for the school tennis team was little consolation. Tennis was considered a "puffs'" game in our school, which is perhaps why it was so easy to get into the team. With Bri Dixon at number one puff and myself at number two, we set a school record of losing every doubles match over a four-year period. Bri at least came away with one major trophy, though. In our final year, the upper sixth, we were entered in the mixed doubles at the County Durham tennis tournament, partnered by two girls from the year below. As usual I showed up in my faded blue house colours, teamed up with a girl called Jill, lost every game and caught the bus home. Nice and straightforward, no messing around. Bri on the other hand turned up in his sparkling whites, partnered a girl called Angela and had trouble concentrating when she bent down at the net. It was love at first service and they married ten years later.

Then, out of the blue, came a call-up for the school football team, for the first time in four years. It has to be said that this was less a result of my brilliant performances during games lessons as a reduction in the competition for places, on three counts. First, when we changed schools at the end of the third year, about half of the pupils went to Heathfield while the rest of us moved on to Dryden. Looking back, there must have been some sort of agreement that Heathfield would have first choice of footballers. For example, Jonnie Wales went there, as did, much later, the even more famous Paul "Gazza" Gascoigne (how our Gloria got in I'll never know, since she was a really crap footballer). Dryden, on the other hand, was mostly left with cloggers.

Second, the girls were becoming a major distraction. My mates were chasing after them like there was no tomorrow, but I might just as well have spent a couple of years in outer space for all I saw in that department. It was a good job I wasn't all that bothered, mind, for my features oozed a lot of things, but never sex appeal, and my eau de sports bag fragrance acted as a deterrent to all but fleas. In any case, I was much too shy to pop what at that age was the world's most daring question, "diyye wanna ganoot with us?" to even the most duck-billed of the species.

The third factor, less important early on but which over time had them toppling like Ravanellis, was G.O.D. Every Geordie turns to G.O.D. at some stage in his life – it's a question of "when" not "whether" – and once converted, there's no looking back. For G.O.D. is everywhere, G.O.D. is all-conquering, G.O.D. is good. G.O.D. is Gannin Oot Drinkin, and thousands of talented Geordies fall by the footballing wayside as a result of turning too much water into urine. Once smitten, twice smashed, and in no time at all G.O.D. becomes the centre of all social activity: "wor lass", the kids, even playing football, all take second priority.

So there you have it; Heathfield, the lasses and G.O.D, three boats others caught and I missed, and which together explained why my name was up there on the noticeboard to face Saltwell School.

The call-up went right to my head. During the days building up to the match I could be seen strutting around the school, ignoring everything and everyone, totally in love with myself. I even overheard Malcolm Trout, the disrespectful little prat, say, "Just look at Rowelly, he thinks he's Pele". Señor Edson Arentes do Nascimento to you, mate.

The night before the game I tucked up in bed – football held lovingly in my arms as usual – but the excitement was too much and I couldn't sleep. Instead I lay there in the dark, carefully planning the next morning's scintillating dribbles and sensational overhead kicks. Ten hours later, on one of the coldest and most miserable Saturday mornings of my life, I hit the mud with a thud. Unable to manage a touch of the ball even during the pre-match knockabout, I sensed that somehow this was not going to be my day. The huge, sticky pitch and hard leather ball – which my spindly legs had trouble kicking more than a few yards – were unfamiliar territory to me.

Then, as we lined up for the kick-off, I looked across the halfway line to survey the opposition, and nearly jumped out of my Littlewoods boys' underpants. It was like a scene from Planet of the Apes: eleven, fully-grown homo erectus standing there with their sleeves rolled up, their hairy faces sporting the confident looks of lads who had not just kissed girls but stuck their tongues in as well. They stamped and clapped and grunted encouragement to each other, just like the New Zealand rugby team: "Come on, let's get stuck into these humans!"

In pathetic contrast, there stood I, my sleeves pulled down over my hands to keep out the cold, and my twiglets for legs looking as though only the Indian rope trick could save them from buckling under. Whatever the opposite for "up for it" was, that's exactly how I felt.

After just a few minutes the ball deflected my way outside their penalty-box and shouts of "cross it!" rained around my ears. I panicked, got my knickers in a twist in the mud, and in no time at all hundreds of four-inch long aluminium studs came crashing into my ankles. The same thing happened a minute later, and again a minute after that, so from then on I did everything I could to be where the ball wasn't, thus surviving to the end without breaking any limbs.

I've played badly on a number of occasions over the years, but those ninety minutes were undoubtedly the worst I have ever spent on a football pitch. I had a stinker – the morning-after-ten-pints-and-a-curry kind of stinker. What's more, I did the stupidest, craziest thing I could ever have done that Saturday morning – I asked Dad for a lift up to the game. Now Dad has many qualities, but diplomacy is not amongst them. I'd hardly put the latch on the Skoda door when he started laying into me, criticising every single aspect of my game. He was disappointed, embarrassed and shocked at just how badly I had performed in the company of my peers. I couldn't get a word in edgeways, which was perhaps just as well, since I had nothing to say: there was simply no case for the defence.

It took two cups of tea to calm Dad down when we arrived home, and when it had all gone quiet he looked across to check whether I was sufficiently devastated. Seeing a tear roll down my fifteen-year-old cheek, he realised that maybe he'd gone too far, tried to back-track with a "you did very canny, son", but that only sent another tear rolling down the other cheek. The situation was in any case irrecoverable. He knew very well I'd been rubbish. I knew very well I'd been rubbish. I couldn't even muster up the energy to give our John a confidence-boosting seventeen-nil thrashing in the back yard.

As bad as I had been, the dearth of willing legs at Dryden gave Mr. Smith no option but to keep selecting me match after match. It's true that my confidence did improve ever so slightly as the season progressed – I even scored a tap-in in one game – but on the whole I was way out of my depth. As indeed was the rest of the team, and we lost most games by a baker's dozen. At the end of term I decided to retire to the relative rug-by-the-fireside comfort of the "player", and leave the serious stuff to the men. School career over.

Saltwell 7   Dryden 2

Bolton Wanderers vs. Newcastle United
Burnden Park, Bolton, Lancashire
14 February, 1976

Mac-nificent Day

Supermac, Superstar,
How many goals have you scored so far?

I earned two pounds twenty a week delivering newspapers for Donald Marshall's. The wages there were the best in Low Fell, and needed to be. My round, which I had taken over from an exhausted Bri Dixon, was the most gruelling in the shop, starting out at the bottom of Orchard Gardens off Church Road, and finishing up somewhere near Luton. This I did twice a day, six days a week, plus Sunday mornings.

You had to be a bit of a weightlifter to get through the Sunday round. My customers were the sort who liked big words as well as big boobs, and insisted on ordering the big fat Sunday Times and Sunday Telegraph to go with the Sunday Slush. It's not even as if I was rewarded for planting all those trees in their letter-boxes, either – the very same people would draw their curtains and switch off the fairy lights when they saw me coming up their road at Christmas-tipping time.

It must be said that I was not what you would call the model paper-boy, and was lucky to have such a forgiving man as Mr. Marshall as my boss. I often turned up late, sometimes not at all; I missed doors out and sold the resulting spares; whole newspapers were reduced to shreds as I played tug-'o'-war with the Evening Chronicle-eating bitch at the top of Popplewell Gardens (no wonder her dog looked so terrified!). But one Sunday morning I pushed Mr. Marshall's patience too far.

I had been delivering long enough to feel up to the challenge of going round without the help of the little book telling me which house received which newspaper. As usual, I started out with the odd numbers up the left-hand side of Orchard Gardens, then came down the other side to do the even ones. Then off to Cherry Tree Gardens cul-de-sac and the same again. It was just when I was turning the corner into Hope Avenue that the dressing-gown from 7 Cherry Tree came running after me, complaining that for some reason he'd received his neighbour's Sunday People instead of the Sunday Mirror. I thought better of telling him that there was no difference, that he'd find the same vicar-with-his-trousers-down stories in both, but at eight in the morning on his day off he didn't look in the mood, so I gave him what he wanted.

But hold on a second, if he's received his neighbour's paper, what has his neighbour received? And his neighbour's neighbour? And then it dawned on me: I'd forgotten all about our new customer at 5 Orchard – the very first house in the entire round. And so I spent the next couple of hours retracing my steps, knocking twenty or so bemused, wrinkled bodies out of their beds to correct my mix-up. And by the way, was there any chance of a tip this Christmas? Slam!

All things considered, it was going relatively well until I knocked on the door of the miserable bloke at 20 Orchard. It was clear from the look on his face that my asking whether he wouldn't mind handing back the big thick juicy Sunday Times in return for his regular News Of The World, was about the same as asking whether he didn't fancy a kick in his dangling gonads, and my peace-keeping mission thus came to an abrupt end. Half of Orchard Gardens was queuing up outside Marshall's on the Monday morning, and it wasn't to leave tips. So I handed in the sack before the sack was handed to me.

With the commitment of Saturday-afternoon deliveries out of the way, there was now no excuse for not going along to watch Newcastle's home games. For reasons already explained, I hated watching the Magpies, and no doubt would have stayed away altogether had it not been for Malcolm "Supermac" Macdonald, our bandy-legged, cocky Cockney of a centre-forward. Supermac was the most exciting player I ever saw. At least once in every game, he would pick the ball up from somewhere in his own half, charge past ten players and smash it past the 'keeper. And sometimes it came off, too.

It's such a shame that so few of Supermac's wonder-goals were televised. That was the price he paid for being a big fish in a small puddle, the sort of puddle that the BBC and ITV had little interest in. But when we travelled to second division Bolton for the fifth round of the F.A. Cup, the Match Of The Day cameras came with us, and the whole nation was about to be treated to the kind of fireworks we got to see every week.

With its match-stick men, grey skies and decrepit old football ground, Bolton was surely where Lowry came to paint his *Going to the Match*. Emerging from the Burnden Park turnstiles into the away end was like taking a step back into a previous life. The clocks must have stopped ticking the day Nat Lofthouse netted his last goal for the club, but the cancerous spread of rust clearly hadn't. Two hours before kick-off, those empty, neglected old stands were crying out for someone to sit there and listen to their tales of former glories over a pint and a few Woodbines.

By kick-off time, though, Burnden Park was like one of those forgotten old churches that only fills up when Stars On Sunday comes to town. Every matchstick in Bolton seemed to be there, and at moments of intense excitement the home crowd would drum up its one and only chant – Bol-ton, Bol-ton, Bol-ton – and although not particularly original, it echoed eerily around the stands to produce one hell of a racket. As they chanted, you had the uncanny feeling that all those Bolton supporters were staring at you and you personally, like forty thousand Mona Lisas following your every move through the zombie eyes of Bolton's past. This feeling of being watched, the stamping of feet on moaning floorboards, and the rattling of corrugated iron in the wind were enough to put the shits up anybody. None of us would have been the least surprised if an air raid siren had gone off to tell us there was still a war on.

Bolton went one-up (Bol-ton, Bol-ton, Bol-ton); Supermac equalised (Bol-ton, Bol-ton, Bol-ton); then came one of the most thrilling goals I've ever seen. From a Tommy Craig throw-in out on the left, Supermac turned and walloped it with his right peg from all of forty yards. (Bol-ton, Bol-ton, Bol... WHAT THE F...)

There was a banner held up by some of our supporters which said, "Jesus saves but Macdonald scores the rebound". Well with all due respect, not even He would have got near this one. The first thing Bolton 'keeper Barry Siddall knew about it was the shaking of the goal behind him, and he scrambled to safety for fear it might collapse. Goodness knows what would have happened had Supermac hit it with his good foot. What a goal, I mean what a goal.

My heart was still pounding from a season of Supermac excitement when just a few months later, Gordon "there'll be no more stars in this team" Lee suddenly sold him to Arsenal. The transaction cost the Londoners exactly a third of a million pounds, a huge amount in those days, but that was nothing to what it cost us. For Supermac's departure was the end of thrilling football as we knew it, and we all went back to delivering newspapers.

Bolton Wanderers 3   Newcastle United 3

Me vs. John
31 Beaconsfield Avenue, Gateshead
Christmas 1977

Bad Light Stops Play

Supermac's replacement, the appropriately named Paul Cannell (as in "who the Paul Cannell is he on a Saturday afternoon?") was manager Gordon Lee at his peak. OK, I still went to the odd match and I still bought The Pink, but when Monday came I no longer day-dreamed in class the way I used to when Supermac was around.

With it looking increasingly unlikely that the club would be coming round for me to save the situation, I started concentrating on my schoolwork, and twelve months later – dodgy old suitcase in one hand and equally dodgy 'A'-levels in the other – I closed the garden gate behind me and took my first, bold step into the unknown. Destination: the world. First stop: a Foundation Course in Accountancy at Sheffield Polytechnic. I climbed onto the number twenty-seven bus for the last time and reflected upon my parents' final, tearful words of advice: "Eat plenty toast, it'll make your hair curl."

Well, I practically lived on the stuff during my first three months. Until one morning I looked in the mirror to check how student life was treating me and realised that if my goldilocks were doing any curling, they were doing it the wrong side of the plug-hole, somewhere out there in the North Sea. It wouldn't be very long before "blow-dry" and "Robert Rowell" were never again to be used in the same sentence, and that, as far as I was concerned, was the last time I'd ever listen to anything *they* had to say.

Not that I had any intention of listening anyway. By the time I had stepped down from the train at Newcastle Central Station at the beginning of the Christmas break, I'd seen it all: I'd kissed the girls and made them cry, started using words like "dogmatic" and "fascism" (the meanings of which still escape me to this day), and had become an authority on everything from the Holy Bible to Stella Artois. In short, Sheffield had transformed me from greasy-haired, zit-faced little boy to greasy-haired, zit-faced pain in the backside.

None of this bothered my parents, of course. I might be their globe-trotting success story, but I was still their greasy-haired, zit-faced little boy, and they were just glad to have me back alive, to fill me with Quaker Oats before returning me to the wild. They were practically on their hands and knees when I walked through the front door, and amid much pomp and ceremony I was escorted to Dad's favourite armchair next to the gas fire, where I was duly crowned King of the Castle.

It was from one's new throne that His Rowell Highness spent the next days and weeks holding court as one's subjects ran around making cups of tea, flattering one's ego, and listening carefully when one proffered words of wisdom. It was also from there that one was able to observe daily life in the Rowell household with the detached curiosity of an outsider. Both Mam and Dad were still working, this in order to keep their number one son in beer and themselves in candles. Dad was winding down towards retirement at the Team Valley post office, and in general leading a life of "Rowelly". Whether he was at work, watching television or at the dinner-table, a cushion never seemed to be very far away. As for lifting a finger around the house, his idea of do-it-yourself was do-it-your-bloody-self.

Dynamic Mam had meanwhile taken over Uncle George's fish-and-chip shop, the last of a hundred jobs she held over the decades to help keep the family afloat. This was a highly lucrative but thankless way of making a living, especially due to its prime location opposite a pub. When the Black Horse closed its doors at night, all its merry men staggered out and made a not-so-straight line for Rowell's. Financially-speaking, this was the chippie's best time of the day. Decibel-wise, it was also its loudest. For drink transforms even the most bashful of Geordies, and there's no place like the nearest chippie to show the world just how funny ten pints can make you. "Don't give him that last pie, missus, he supports Sunderland." W-A-R-F. "Aye, all Sunderland supporters to the back of the queue, please." W-A-R-F W-A-R-F. "Hey, pet! If you're a Sunderland supporter you have to go to the back of the queue with the rest of them – unless you fancy a snog like!" W-A-A-A-A-R-F.

The other problem with running a fish shop, at least in Mam's case, was Dad. Dad was the self-appointed managing director, marketing manager, purchasing officer and accountant. In balance sheet terms, a liability. When he had his way, he bought the cheapest potatoes (never mind the quality, feel the weight), and told Mam off when she gave out too many chips. His revolutionary formula for attracting customers was to leave the door wide open even in the thick of winter (between late August and mid-June), so that the smell of boiling fat would remind the inhabitants of Low Fell that Mam's chips were the best – which of course they were.

When it came to running the production line, though, it was Mam who controlled the temperatures. For as soon as the fat-friers came on Dad was off like a smoke alarm to the Black Horse. There he made full use of his book-keeping skills by occasionally looking out through the pub window to Rowell's across the road, and trying to guess the evening's takings from the length of the queue. Then he would be off to the bar to invest the last half-hour of McGregor's best profits into the next half-hour of McEwan's Best Scotch, "The One You Cannot Come Home From".

Ah, the dreaded drink. In our home it was the cause of no end of Greek dancing and cheap plate smashing. Not because Dad came home drunk every night (he didn't), but because he didn't always take Mam with him on her nights off! Like most other Geordie households, the woman's place was in the home, and the man's was in the wrong. So if Dad was at best second division when I was away, he was strictly Federation Breweries Northern League when I came home, and on my first day back Mam was up at five in the morning pulling out the ingredients for Number One's breakfast. When my spots eventually sucked the rest of me downstairs I was given the full treatment. "What would you like, son?" Mam sang it, she was so happy. "There's orange juice, grapefruit, corn flakes, French toast, Weetabix, sausage, bacon, eggs and black pudding, toast and Marmite; I'm sorry I've no kippers but if you want I can get your Dad out of bed to go and get some."

The savoury smell of Scotland wafted its way along the passage and up the stairs, and it wasn't long before Scrooge could be seen making his way down, his dentureless mouth slavering at the prospects of his first full breakfast in ages (when the King wasn't there, the cupboard was bare). Dad's raw gums edged gingerly into the kitchen, testing the terrain with a rather cagey "panna have a puppa pea pet?" (well, you try saying it without your teeth in).

Mam's singing stopped in an instant, a sure sign that Dad might just as well have stayed in bed for his troubles. From my luxurious vantage point at the dining-room table, and with the Big Breakfast Show laid out before me, I sat and watched as Scrooge came scampering out from the kitchen, cowering to protect himself as old Ma Rowelly played conkers on his bald head with her rolled-up tea-towel. It was a scene I wouldn't have blinked at in the past, but I now lived in another world and could only watch on in hilarious amazement at this lightning display of perfectly-timed swipes and insults that had Low Fell's housewives queuing up outside the front door for private lessons. "I'll cup of tea you -swipe- you old waster you -swipe- you've been nothing -swipe- but a bloody menace -swipe- since the day I married you -swipe swipe- get yourself out the house you old goat -swipe- and don't ever come back!" Leaving Dad in no doubt whatsoever that on this particular morning at least, he could forget his "puppa pea".

Looking back, it is surprising that Mam even let Dad sit at the same table as me during meals, but it wasn't long before I left the table anyway – and not because of Dad. One of the tough lessons I'd learned during communal life at Poly was that whilst there were no bodily odours more sweet-smelling than my own, opinions did vary on the subject, thus the desirability of washing occasionally. But our John was only thirteen and still had not grasped the utility of everyday items such as soap. His shaggy hair and woolly appearance wouldn't have been out of place at a sheepdog trials, and his unease at simply being *him* was evidenced by a whole repertoire of annoying mannerisms, from cracking his fingers to flicking his head to one side, earning him the nickname – given by a stunned new brother-in-law Stewart – of "King of the Habits".

John came into his own at mealtimes, where he demonstrated how table manners must have been twenty thousand years B.C. – Before Cutlery. Knives, forks, even teeth were but idle bystanders as the largest spoon in the house shovelled huge quantities of meat and potatoes into the cement-mixer (itself left wide open for the occasion), where they were briefly tossed around before mercifully disappearing into the great beyond. One was suitably disgusted, of course, and tut-tutted disapproval all the way to the next room where one finished one's meal in peace. Lardy-da.

Poor John. I gave him hell, correcting his English, poking fun at his habits. I genuinely thought I was doing him a favour, yet little did I know he was actually developing a serious hatred of his big brother's guts. King of the Castle? King of the Hassle more like, and his daily brotherly-love curve hit rock bottom at around one o'clock in the morning, every morning, when after a night out on the beer and a visit to Rowell's, I would wake up in a spin and spew my pie, fish and chips all over the bedroom, splashing John's sleeping, shaggy mop in the process (no wonder he later broke with generations of Rowell tradition by choosing not to become an alcoholic).

The trouble with little brothers is, one, they eventually

grow to be just as big, if not bigger, than you; and two, they have elephantine memories: every insult, every beating, every humiliating moment is notched in their brains, to be used against you in evidence when get-you-back day comes – in my case the day before I was due to return to Sheffield. I'd just given John yet another thrashing at darts in the back bedroom when we started shadow-boxing, throwing fake punches at each other: playful, non-contact stuff, just like in the good old days. It all happened very, very quickly. One instant he was standing over there and I was standing over here, the next he was nowhere to be seen and I was contemplating the Milky Way. My floodlights failed, my legs did a jelly-pants and I nearly dropped through the floor. There was no need for a count – in the time it took me to recover my senses they could have removed every tooth from my mouth and I wouldn't have felt a thing.

That punch had me in more of a spin than ten pints down the pub ever did. It split atoms, warped time. It moved mountains, emptied oceans, eclipsed suns. It was the Big Bang. It hit me so hard it must have started out in the front garden, yet I had been much too full of my own greatness ever to see it coming. Boy did that punch knock the ass out of the King of the Castle.

Whether John had meant to hit me that hard, or even hit me at all, was beside the point. The Big Bang marked the end of time as I knew it. When my vision finally recovered, it was a very different version of John that was standing there. This was John the human being, with eyes, a nose, a brain, emotions, and a meteoric right fist to boot – there was certainly no question of asking for a rematch. The Big Bang seemed to trigger an expansion in John's confidence in everything we ever competed at. He started scoring one hundred and eighties at darts and forty-odd breaks in snooker; his Queen led my King a merry dance around the chessboard; he did the Rubik's cube in well under a minute, then sat back and laughed as I fumbled away. Worst of all, at football, and it breaks my heart to say it… so I won't.

It turned out that John's nerves weren't the only ones tested by my presence that Christmas. Towards the end of the holidays, Dad began asking what time my train was leaving on a worryingly frequent basis. And even Mam was beginning to tire of the lakes of vomit and waterlogged beds that had become a regular feature of the morning after the night before. The enthusiastic goodbyes told it all: everyone was happy to see the back of Robert Rowell, that worldly sage. And nobody more so than our John. With me out of the way, the throne was now vacant. The King is dead! Long live the King!

Me 0   John 1
(first round knock-out)

Newcastle United vs. Wrexham
St. James' Park, Newcastle
28 January, 1978

Soggy-oggy-oggy

Taxpayers wouldn't have been best pleased with the way we students went about spending their money. For if we crammed in a lot of things during those first, intense months at Sheffield Polytechnic, studying wasn't one of them. The Ballard Student Hall of Residence was more like a holiday camp than a place to live. The basic message to all the young girls and boys thrown into its melting pot seemed to be to go forth, enjoy yourselves and do a bit of multiplying. As for the Poly, it was three miles away in downtown Sheffield and consequently much too far to provide a rational alternative to beer and butties at our only point of contact with the outside world: the Ranmoor Inn just a hundred yards down the road.

Even football took a back seat, and a good job too. On the playing side, I wouldn't have been able to run more than fifty yards without tripping over my beer-gut, and as for my beloved Newcastle, they were rock bottom of the first division (thanks mainly to ten consecutive defeats early in the season), and I did everything I could to hide my Geordie accent.

Then, one day in January, from a distant radio came the draw for the fourth round of the F.A. Cup:

"Number twenty-three – Newcastle United – will play number thirty-one – Wrexham."

I must confess that before leaving Gateshead I didn't even know where Wrexham was, but Ballard Hall was full of lads from the valleys, all of whom supported *Wrrreggsham* (as they pronounced it in that up-hill-down-dale accent of theirs) in their former lives – indeed by emigrating to England they had practically halved the team's home gates. The Welsh boyos were easily identifiable, thanks to their eighteenth-century haircuts and huge chips on both shoulders. They suffered terribly from sheep-sickness, and didn't seem to care much for England or the English. Not to mention our language: whereas the Brummies, Geordies, Cockneys and Liverpudlians could just about communicate with each other without an interpreter, the Welsh insisted on gurgling away in that silly Celtic language which for the rest of us had disappeared when the Romans invaded. Their idea of fun was teaching us how to say Llanfair-piggledywiggledy-oggledygoggledy-heydiddlediddly-oghoghogh (or whatever it was), all this while they sniggered and ogged between them, a sure sign that they were having a bloody good bleat at our expense.

In the Wrexham tie, then, I saw at last an opportunity to get my own back. With goodness knows how many divisions separating the two clubs, I felt confident enough to turn my Geordie accent back on for the occasion, for we were surely going to fry *Wrrreggsham* for breakfast.

In Trefor and Paul, I had befriended two of the least abnormal of the Wrexham faithful (well, somebody had to), and I invited them to take a break from their "studies" and head north to witness the sort of racket we Geordies could make when we were winning six-nil and it wasn't even half-time. At least that was the idea. Only seconds of the match remained when a Newcastle player booted the ball into the crowd and I finally let go a sigh of relief: the tennis score fantasy had turned out to be just that, and we could count ourselves lucky to have edged it by the odd goal.

Then, in the time it took the referee to gather enough wind in his lungs to blow that last peep-peep-peeeeeep that would send everyone home, the ball went ping-pong-pang and land of my bloody fathers, Wrexham were level.

Trefor and Paul nearly jumped out of their fleeces. Had I known then what I would know ten days later – that we'd get slaughtered four-one in the replay – I would have held a pointing finger over their heads, shouted "Wrexham supporters!", and left them to the lions. But I didn't, and instead had to suffer their bleating all evening. Call it sour grapes, but the only kick I got out of the two days was in not letting them sleep together in the double bed back at Mam and Dad's – the noise would have kept the whole household awake all night. Behhhhh!

To round off a wonderful weekend, on the Monday morning I received a nice letter from the course-master congratulating me on all the heavy boozing I'd been putting in and all the hard work that I hadn't. He recommended I reconsider whether being an accountant was really something I wanted to be. What a stupid question. Of course I didn't want to be a bloody accountant, it's just I wasn't good enough to be a professional footballer so what else was I supposed to do? I wisely invested what was left of my bank overdraft in photocopying the notes the more conscientious of my fellow students had taken during lectures, took my head from out of the boobs and into the books, and got to work. Several months later, with Newcastle United long since relegated, I surprised all but my mother by scraping promotion.

Newcastle United? Sorry, old bean, never heard of them. Football? I say, goodness no. Accountancy, that's my game!

Newcastle United 2   Wrexham 2

IF...

If you can keep your head when all around you
Are playing crap and blaming it on you;
If you can trust yourself when team-mates doubt you,
To take the next corner, and fluff that one too;
If you can drink 'til closing the night before,
Yet still be up at half-past eight;
If you can open the dressing room door
To hear "Get changed quick, you're effing late!"
If you can squeeze into socks too small for dwarves' feet,
Don fifties shorts and unwashed shirt;
If you can wear borrowed boots of solid concrete,
Caked in last week's hardened dirt;
If you can climb hills that bask in no sun's rays,
To play in snow and pea-soup fog;
If you can skate and slide on winter days,
To crowds of one man and his dog;
If you can thump and smack and slog a ball
High into the clouds, yet never where intended;
If by the time you've heard your team-mate's call,
You've been tackled, robbed, cheaply up-ended;
If you can shout "What? Penalty? You must be jokin'!"
After leaving studs in your opponent's knee;
Or watch while someone's nose is broken
Under the approving eye of the referee;
If you can force heavy legs and heart and lungs to
Soldier on when long since gone,
And so chase back when there's nothing in you,
Except the will to scream "Come on lads, come on!";
If you can fill the unforgiving ninety minutes
With an hour and a half of kick and run,
Yours is the Earth and everything that's in it,
And – which is more – you'll be a Sunday footballer, my son!

Charterac vs. Brown Cow
Graves Park, Sheffield
1 February, 1981

Bloody Hot

I wouldn't forget in a hurry my introduction to that alien being, the Sheffielder. It was the day I stepped onto a Sheffield bus for the first time

- *Close Encounter of the First Kind* -
"How much is the fare to Ranmoor, please?"
"Seven pence please, love."
I jumped back. Love? Was he chatting me up or what? Maybe I hadn't heard correctly. I tried again.
"Seven pence? Is that all?" And the old man next to me butted in with:
- *Close Encounter of the Second Kind* -
"Aye, love. Labour council, love."
Pukka Pies! Another one! I felt sure the driver's hand stroked mine as he gave me my ticket, and it was backs to the fire-exit after that.

That same evening I went down to the Ranmoor Inn with my new student friends, and was happily emptying my bladder in the men's toilets when a smallish, middle-aged man walked in. He stood right next to me, casually opened his flies, glanced across and asked me whether I was:
- *Close Encounter of the Third Kind* -
"O'reet love?"

And I came running out of there with the stuff still dribbling down my leg. Firkin Ale! I thought I'd left Gateshead to discover the opposite sex, and I'd ended up in a town full of puffs!

I would later (thankfully) discover that "love" was simply a word Sheffield folk, especially the men, stuck bizarrely but harmlessly on the end of everything they said, whether they were speaking to their great granddad or next door's wheelbarrow. I must say I wasn't totally convinced at first, but it wasn't long before I was going around using it myself (which incidentally got me into no end of scrapes when I let it slip in the pubs back home). Just as I pretty much adapted to all the other Sheffield expressions and customs, like saying "ah" and "nee-ow" instead of "yes" and "no", and joining in the cries of "good arrows!" when someone scored more than twenty-six at darts. I even reached the stage where I was able to sup Ward's beer without pulling a face, for it, like Sheffield, was an acquired taste, and over time I grew to appreciate everything about the place, love.

There were a couple of aspects of Sheffield language and life, however, which I never completely came to terms with. The first, much harsher on the eardrums than the "love" thing, was the habit Sheffield men had of calling each other "cunks". I was told that what this really meant in Sheffieldspeak was "very good mate"; that calling someone a cunk was simply a way of expressing deep friendship without having to be soppy about it. So I shouldn't take offence, then, when depending on the circumstances I might be referred to as a reet cunk, fat cunk, daft cunk or soft cunk. On the contrary, as long as I was some sort of a cunk, I should be mighty pleased with myself. Well, as I say, that's what I was told.

The other thing I never totally came to terms with, despite one or two memorable moments during five arduous seasons of the stuff, was the Sunday morning football.

Sheffield claims to be the birthplace of the beautiful

game, for it was there, in 1857, that the world's oldest football team, Sheffield Football Club, was formed. But that was a long time ago, and if a whole dictionary of adjectives could be applied to the way the game was played there in the early eighties, "beautiful" certainly isn't the first one that springs to mind.

The main problem was where the game was played. Sheffield is built, so they say, on seven hills, and other than down by the Don river, there isn't much level ground. Since the industrial revolution hit the place long before the ball had been invented, it was the factories – like the ones I was now going around auditing as a trainee accountant – that got their grubby paws on all the low-lying flat bits. Which meant that football had to be played up on the surrounding moors, with pitches on one-in-three climbs and where, no matter what time of year it was, it always snowed on Sunday mornings – and horizontally at that.

No wonder the city turns out so few decent players. Go on, apart from the occasional clogger, how many top professionals can you name that originate from Sheffield? (Let me save you from wasting half an hour flicking through the Rothmans: the answer's none.)

To play in the Sheffield Imperial Sunday Football League, then, you either had to be mad or a prison case. Many were both. Your average Sunday footballer was an explosive mixture of long studs and short IQ, the first to help him up muddy inclines and down opponents' shins, the second to numb the nervous system – no brain, no pain.

George Bests they were not, but when it came to kicking the ball high up into the air, screaming encouragement at team-mates and putting the shits up opponents, they were unrivalled. Expressions like, "Tha's a reet mardy chuff, thee" (If you don't stop your moaning, I'll kick your head in), "Tha knows it when tha plays against me, love" (Stay clear of me or I'll kick your legs off), and the rather puzzling, "Thee, Tha, There, Thum!" (I smell the blood of a Geordie bum) were all designed to put you off your game. In my case at least, it worked, and I spent many a Sunday morning jumping out of the way of fifty-fifty tackles, or standing out by the touchline disguised as an icicle.

One particular nutcase I came across committed the worst foul I have ever seen, stamping his studs down into the private parts of an opponent as he came sliding in to rob him. It was enough to have you singing Bee Gees songs for the rest of your days (I should know – I was the one writhing on the ground in agony). He had the cheek to plead to the referee that he was going for the ball (oh yeah, which one: left or right?), and all he got was a booking. For in Sheffield, you had to break someone's leg to stand any chance of being sent off, and even then your victim's screams of agony would probably be drowned out by the collective cheers of, "Best pukkin' tackle o't match that, love!"

My twinkle-toes might just as well have spent the season in hibernation for what use they were on those frosty hilltops. Or at least that's my excuse for being crap in a crap team. Charterac loosely represented the Sheffield Chartered Accountants Society, whose team I joined when I went into articles. We might have had the strongest balance sheet in the league, but out there on the pitch all our bean-counting skills were good for was totting up the cricket scores posted to the debit side of our profit and loss account. Annual income: twenty-six goals. Annual expenditure: one hundred and seven goals. Result: relegation, love.

The following year we did at least win promotion, though this was not so much down to our scintillating form as other teams dropping out through financial problems (it's true that one pound a week subs is asking a lot of a Yorkshireman). But promoted we were, and I calculated that if we managed to gain promotion every year from then on, my dream of one day playing against my beloved Newcastle United would be realised when I was exactly forty-five years old.

Which seemed a bit long to wait, so I decided to cut out all the middlemen by writing to Sheffield United Football Club to ask for a trial (I could be excused for thinking I might stand a chance: the last time they had won anything was when pieces of string were still used for crossbars). But despite citing, among other things, a personal best at keeping the ball up with my head of 402 (that I had set in my tiny bedsit), they politely suggested that I get lost. And I resigned myself to being a Sunday footballer for the rest of my days.

Life as an amateur footballer did have its advantages over the professional game, however, the most important of which was the rule on alcohol consumption. Whereas professionals aren't allowed a drink for up to seventy-two hours before a match, our going out to get smashed on the Saturday night was absolutely mandatory. Indeed waking up on the morning of the game with anything other than a violent hangover was considered unsporting behaviour.

The pattern was pretty much the same every Saturday. We would do the rounds of the city centre pubs, then move on to a club to keep the flow going. Most Sheffield nightclubs were like cattle-markets: the men would drink heavily and watch from the sides as this great wave of Harmony hairspray rose and dipped below the strobes. We usually chose The Limit, a casual, punky club, and the only one in Sheffield where you could get in without being threatened by the bouncers for wearing the wrong clothes or the wrong face. I would then spend the next two hours chatting up (mentally, at least) the girl I had singled out as the one I was going to marry, have children and maybe even sex with some day. All this while lubricating the larynx with double-priced *Courage*. The beer was never very good at The Limit, and I was glad when I'd had enough, but two hours' worth contained just about sufficient alcohol to make me feel like the world's most desirable man. So, armed with a whole string of highly original, do-you-come-here-often chat-up lines, Mr. Gift of the Gab would finally wade across to the lady in waiting, slur a brief dance request in her face, take "nee-ow" for an answer, and, secretly relieved, return to the bar. Had big ears anyway.

Now excess booze has always had the effect of dragging

my eyelids down over my cheeks, and on the eve of the game against the Brown Cow they were so low they were sweeping the floors. There was only one safe place for such a situation: the porcelain palace. In the delicious comfort of cubicle number three, I sat down and closed my weary eyes. I wasn't asking for much, just a few minutes break from all those girls trying to rip my shirt off. Then I'd be right as rain, out there pogoing to Terry Tapeworm And The Intestines with the best of them. Just a few minutes, that's all, just a few minutezzzzzzz...

If it hadn't been for my Charterac team-mate Simon, I might still be sitting there now. As The Limit said goodnight to the last of its customers, he it was who climbed up onto the loo door and poured half a pint of lager over my head to wake me up. What? Closing already? But the night is still young! Simon chose the sensible option of going home – after all, we had a match the next day – but not me. I was starving. It was time for a *Chubby's*.

Chubby's was invented for people like me, people who, pregnant with all that beer swilling about inside, suddenly get a craving for bad food. They made the greasiest doner kebab this side of the Aegean, but at two in the morning I was so hungry I would have eaten turdburger with ketchup – easy on the ketchup, mind love.

When I finally stumbled out of Chubby's looking and smelling like a dripping sandwich, my shouts of "Taxshi" had Sheffield's cab-drivers disappearing into the night faster than the dark, leaving me with a three-mile slog home to Ranmoor. What the hell, it would sober me up in preparation for the Sunday morning. I jogged all the way up to where our firm's offices were at the top of Glossop Road, then set off on the final stretch, a mile walk home I did every evening after work, and so familiar I could have done it with my eyes closed... now there was a thought.

With my eyes open, it looked pretty straightforward: Fulwood Road stretched out, quietly and uninterruptedly into the distance, and there was a high wall all the way along the side to help me feel my way. To make life even easier, I decided to grant myself up to ten peeps during the journey, in the highly unlikely event of a loss of bearings. Ten peeps? Pooph! That would take me as far as the Derbyshire countryside, never mind Ranmoor! And off I set.

(Let me pause briefly to issue a warning to any children watching: walking with your eyes closed along a major road can be very dangerous. The feats you are about to read about were performed by a trained idiot, and should never be attempted under any circumstances.)

The first three paces were brisk and assured. Then my knees started arguing over which one should go first, then the road went all soft, then I was grappling with a hedge (what? Derbyshire already?), and peep number one found me in someone's garden. What's more, another step and I was goldfish food. This in itself should have had the red lights flashing inside my head, but when you've drunk as much as I had that night, all lights are on green.

I woke up the next morning with the usual symptoms of splitting headache, churning stomach and burning backside. I lay there looking at the ceiling of my bedsit, and painstakingly pieced together the events of the previous evening. Had I drunk too much? Probably. Had I spent too much? Probably. Had I upset anyone? Probably. How had I got home?

Oh yes, I'd walked it. Or rather run it. No, I'd walked the last bit. *With my eyes closed*. Idiot! (smile). There was the chatting to the hedgerows... the goldfish pond... the...

Instinctively my head turned on the pillow, and there it was: a lake of dried blood as big as a frisbee.

The trafficlight!

Wanker! *Wanker!* That was it, I'd never touch another drop of alcohol in my entire life. And then the realisation: oh God it's Sunday, and I'm late – late and still drunk. With no time to nurse my third eye, I threw on some clothes, left my neighbours with a bomb disposal job in the shared toilet along the corridor, and dashed off to catch the bus.

The lads were changed and about to leave the dressing room when I arrived. The clinking of studs on concrete gave way to the peeping of referees whistles, and I was left alone to hunt around for the remains of the playing kit: a pair of Stanley Matthews shorts, two odd socks with holes in the big toes, and a number thirteen shirt.

It took me the best part of the first half to find our pitch. I'd run a half-marathon by the time the referee signalled me to stagger on, and spent the next ten minutes trying to catch my breath while the ball bobbled about elsewhere. When the little round thing did finally catch up with me, the inability of my eyes to focus on one ball rather than ten left me kicking thin air and falling on my backside. And chuckling to myself. For if normally such an embarrassing air-shot would have had me writing letters of apology to each of my team-mates, today I was too much "under the influence" to be worried about what anybody might think. In fact with my headache now gone, my stomach settled, and the sun shining brightly, I was feeling surprisingly good about life. The alcohol that was still flowing freely through my system had totally relaxed me, and I began floating across the pitch in a way that I had never floated before. How this was going to affect my performance I wasn't totally sure, but I had a really hard time letting it bother me. For today I was going to enjoy myself, love, and stuff everybody else.

My usual game was to run around like crazy for ninety minutes, head down, never stopping to think, dribble-dribble-get rid. But not today. For once in my life I possessed that single, prized attribute which makes the class footballers stand out from the rest: today I had *time on the ball*.

I was Billy's Boots. I hardly seemed to move from a spot in the centre circle no bigger than a ten pence piece, from where I orchestrated the game almost at walking pace. I could have played with my eyes closed that day. Er, well, on reflection maybe not.

As if to prove how extra-terrestrial I was feeling, I did

something twice in the second half most footballers dream of doing just once in an entire lifetime: I scored two goals direct from corner-kicks, one with my left foot, the other with my right. Who cares if the slope had more to do with the bend on the ball than the inside of my boot? When there's a quarter of an hour to go and you're on your first ever hat-trick, there's little to be gained from analysing the action replays.

I had to wait until the last seconds of the match for my golden moment. Thirty yards out, I looked up to see the goalkeeper off his line, and sent a delicate lob up and over his head. As I half-turned in celebration, the ball somehow managed to clip the underside of the crossbar and bounced into the keeper's arms. My closest opponent said "bad luck, love", the referee blew for time, and I thought not to worry, I'd get that hat-trick sooner or later.

Hat-trick or not, my performance was the talk of the pub afterwards, principally because nobody had ever seen me play like that. Whatever had become of Robert Rowell the blue-arsed fly they had all come to know and love? Was it something to do with the stigmata in the middle of my forehead? A miracle? But I merely sat there all smug, as if I'd just worked out how to do Rubik's cube and wasn't letting on. In any case they would never have believed me.

In an effort to repeat the bizarre experience, I went over the top during quite a few Saturday evening sessions after that – except of course the bit about playing Blind Man's Bump with stray trafficlights. It didn't work, though: on the Sunday morning I invariably played like a cunk – in the true sense of the word.

Charterac 4   Brown Cow 2

Rotherham United vs. Sheffield United
Millmoor Ground, Rotherham
21 February, 1981

Lovely Day For It

And here's to you, Mrs. Robinson,
Jonnie loves you more than you will know,
Wo, wo, wo.

A rather conservative gentleman once said that "quintessential Englishness" was all about cricket and village greens. Well, unless quintessential means boring old fart, I'm a Scotsman. Because in that remote part of England I come from, not only do you have to travel twenty miles before coming to your first village, you have to travel another twenty to find one whose green is being used for cricket instead of burning witches, and twenty again to find one where rain hasn't stopped play (or burning, as the case may be).

No, to me, Englishness, or at least the male Englishness I long for now that I no longer live there, is a day out with the lads. A day in which there are no difficult decisions (another pint? sure!), a day in which we are relieved of all earthly responsibility. One which allows us to escape from the missus if we have one, or forget about the loneliness of our plight if we don't.

The grandest celebration of male Englishness, without doubt, is the four-courser with the boys that starts around midday on a Saturday afternoon: English beer in an English pub for lunch, an English pie and Bovril at an English football match for afternoon tea, more English beer for dinner, all finished off with a late supper, and that great, traditional English challenge: an impossibly hot Indian.

What makes this kind of Englishness so special is not the football itself – of the thousands of teams that turn out every Saturday afternoon, perhaps five play football that is actually worth watching. No, those ninety minutes are just a way of justifying the hours and hours of booze, banter and general bloody good time that go on around, and sometimes during, the match itself. After all, "Do you mind if I go to the match, love?" sounds so much more excusable than "Do you mind if I go out for a good drink with my mates and go to the match while I'm at it, love? Love?" Which in the end is what it amounts to. It's surely not for the footie that grown men travel such silly distances to take in such silly games as Altrincham vs. Blyth Spartans, Stoke City vs. Ipswich Town, Watford vs. Portsmouth, or Darlington vs. Chesterfield. I should know, I went to all of them. Each one was a truly memorable day out too, just don't ask me what the final scores were!

This is an unquestionably sad reflection on the habits of the "ordinary" Englishman, but I am yet to find a more satisfactory way of spending my Saturday afternoon without the wife wanting to come along and spoil it. Certainly, looking around my circle of friends and judging by the number of people who attend football matches every week – around a million in total, most of whom are male pub-lovers – it would seem that I am not alone. So much for cricket and village greens.

This pursuit of Englishness has taken me to over thirty English league grounds (which is nothing compared to some). I've been to Old Trafford, Anfield, Highbury, Hillsborough and Elland Road, to name but a few. But my favourite has to be… Millmoor.

Millmoor? Ay, Millmoor, love. Home of "The Millers", Rotherham United. Why? Because a day out at Millmoor had just about everything an Englishman could ever ask of his Saturday: the beer was good; the company was good; there was no anxiety (no matter how much I tried, I just couldn't get worked up over Rotherham United); and the only risk of violence was a Rotherham supporter banging his own head off a wall. If only we didn't have to go to the matches themselves it would have been perfect.

Admittedly, Rotherham the town doesn't appear in too many holiday brochures. In fact you wouldn't go there at all unless you took the wrong turn off the M1 or your mother's life depended on it. Rotherham is to Sheffield what Sunderland is to Newcastle, an outback of dour people who, when you tell them a joke, at best they get it and are not amused, at worst they don't, think you are "tekkint piss" and punch you in the gob. If you really want to have them cackling in Rotherham, fall off scaffolding and break your neck.

I could quite happily have lived several lives over without going near the place had it not been for a lad at our firm who supported Rotherham United. As a chartered accountant, indeed as a human being, John "Robbo" Robinson was a bit of a one-off. For a start, not many people who come from Rotherham can claim to be chartered accountants, and most of those who do are just lying about their exam results. Second, whereas most accountants spend a good deal of their leisure time switching on and off their calculators, Robbo was a sort of exception that proved the rule, a real punk rocker. He wore pinstripes by day, pink hair by night, and his unconventional ways (chuckling when a client went bust, spitting in the corridors) didn't at all go down well with the partners. The only thing that saved him from the sack was that he happened to be damned clever. In short, he was the perfect partner in crime and together we made a right couple of likely lads. There was just one problem: Maria, Robbo's fiancée, was forever trying to prevent "that Robert" from leading dear Jonnie astray.

I'm not sure who was leading who astray when it came to match days. We always kicked off in traditional English style, at a drinking spot within walking distance from the ground. We usually chose the Catholic Club, where we met up with Robbo's brother Steve, and his old mates, Shep and Whitey. Like most worshipping men's clubs, it was grubby, smoke-filled and full of middle-aged Sun readers wearing honest-to-God-I'm-not-really-baldy hairstyles (you know the one, where the parting starts just above the neck). Also scattered here and there were cloth cap-clad pensioners, who never seemed to move from their seats, yet whose pint glasses were always three-quarters full. Occasionally one would lean over and grumble something to your knees, like "mind that bitch Thatcher did naat for us old'ns," but other than that they were harmless. Finally there was the picture of the Pope on the wall, whose saintly expression was taken to be a clear blessing for all the boozing, page three gazing and dart-throwing going on below. In the name of the lager, the Sun, and the double finish. Amen.

The reason we liked the Catholic Club was because there, at least, we knew we could have a seat and a good pint, with none of the pushing and shoving to get to the bar that characterises most pubs near football grounds on match days. We were never in any particular hurry to be at the match ahead of kick-off, and drink-up time often lasted well into the first half. Then, once at the ground, I would insist on further delaying the proceedings by stopping off for my Saturday lunch: the world-famous, patent-pending, Rotherham United several times reheated sausage roll (I say "world-famous" because it was a Rotherham United several times reheated sausage roll that played the part of the little monster that came spurting out of that unfortunate man's stomach in *Alien*).

Rotherham's ground itself was invariably half-empty, so we had no trouble at all reaching our usual spot behind the goal at the exotically-named Tivoli End, along with all the other Alcoholics Anonymous. A quick glance at the surrounding expressions was enough to tell us how the team was doing: bleak looks meant Rotherham were winning handsomely, frowns meant it was goalless, and lots of lower jaws sticking out was a sign to the handful of opposing fans down the other end that *Tha's gonna get tha puckin' heads kicked in.*

Watching Rotherham United was a very sobering experience. Robust men with robust, Sunday morning names (Breckin, Stancliffe) played robust Sunday morning football on a Saturday afternoon, and we paid for the privilege of being there. As if that wasn't enough punishment, at half-time the Treeton and Catcliffe Brass Band, or whatever they were called, would come on to play what always sounded like funeral music (a clever marketing ploy that had us all running off to buy Rotherham United several times reheated sausage rolls), and their departure ten minutes later was aptly met with deathly silence.

To fight off the depression that usually accompanied the second half sobering-up process, we would think up alternative forms of entertainment. We teased the girls who sold confectionery along the side of the pitch, asking for things we knew they didn't have, like pints of lager and Pizza Calzone; we competed to see who could throw a Toffo highest in the air and catch it in his mouth on the way down (there was plenty of space at Millmoor for silly games like that); we heckled the players at corners (centre-forward Ronnie Moore once mouthed at me to eff off – fame at last!); we even compared shoe sizes. Then at last the final whistle was blown, at which Robbo and I gratefully made our way back to Sheffield, to carry on where we'd left off a couple of hours earlier.

This laid-back routine went on every fortnight for a couple of seasons, but things became very serious the day Sheffield United came to town. First, Rotherham were challenging for promotion, so expressions around the town were sterner than ever. Second, Sheffield United was the big (and envied, and hated) club from just down the road – you could have fitted Millmoor itself into the shadow of their main stand. It was a bit like Wales entertaining England: to the travelling Sheffield fans a case of "what are we doing here?", to the Rotherham United supporters nothing less than the derby of the century.

We'd never seen a Rotherham match from beginning to end, but this time we were determined to be there for every one of the ninety minutes. So in the interests of ground proximity we decided to give the Catholic Club a miss in favour of the spit-and-sawdust *Millmoor*, which was so close to the stadium you bumped your head on a turnstile when you stumbled out of its front door.

An advert on the back of the Rotherham United programme announced: *If you've not called in the Millmoor Hotel this week, you're not a full supporter*, with below a translation for those reading in Neanderthal: *Ay up! Asta bin int' Millmoor?* This was no place to take your girlfriend. Nor was it a place for away supporters. Half an hour before the Sheffield United game, with the pub now bursting with the beach-ball beer-guts of "full" supporters, a lone away fan walked in, innocent as you like, and in no time at all a huge circle had formed around him. A hundred fingers pointed at the tip of his ashen nose, and with a vehemence I had never quite witnessed before (nor have since), they chanted:

Puck off Sheff U!
Puck off Sheff U!

And puck off he did. Even Robbo was startled by the display of uncalled-for hatred. Full supporter or not, never was I so happy to leave a pub.

Alas, there would be no time for the Rotherham United several times reheated sausage roll today, and when we entered the ground it was so packed we had to forsake our usual position behind the goal for a spot along the touchline not far from the corner-flag. Worse still, we were standing just in front of Sheffield United's own version of the "full supporter", a big, bouncy-looking fellow totally unflustered at being all alone in the wrong end of the ground. You could have hung curtains on all the ring-pulls that dangled from his watermelon to indicate where his nose and ears were, and as for the location of his mouth, this became clear immediately after kick-off – one inch away from my right ear. His vocabulary was limited to screaming "Good decision!" when the referee awarded a free-kick to Sheffield United, "Bad decision!" when it went the other way, but nobody had the guts to clock him one, and by five past three the inside of my head was stone cold numb. I wasn't at all used to this kind of Saturday: no papal visit, no sausage rolls, no fooling around behind the goal, and good decision bad decision rattling my eardrums every thirty seconds.

With twenty minutes left of what was a thoroughly grim encounter, Sheffield United were one-nil up ("Good decision!"), and DEPRESSED was etched in big grey letters across all the surrounding foreheads.

Just then, Rotherham's tiny right-winger, Tony "Tiger" Towner, picked up the ball and set off on a dribble along the touchline just below us. One man, two men, three men and their dogs went to mow a meadow as he turned the Sheffield defenders this way and that, before cutting inside and slotting the ball past the goalkeeper. Mayhem. For once "Bad decision!" was drowned out, as Towner came running across to celebrate right in front of us.

I looked around for Robbo in order to kick and punch him in the customary fashion, but he was nowhere to be seen. Had the rowdy Sheffield United fan eaten him? Then I looked up and couldn't believe my eyes: he had somehow managed to climb over the line of kids sitting on the front wall and was now standing face to face with the great Tony Towner himself. All eleven thousand, nine hundred and four of us watched on as the two grown men held out their arms like long-lost lovers, before running forward to embrace in classic Hollywood style.

Then, in an instant, Towner was off – after all, he had a game of football to get on with. As for Robbo, he wouldn't be seeing any of it: the only bobby in the ground now had a firm grip on the back of his jacket, and was marching him along the very touchline his hero had just run ragged. One minute later he was busy undergoing intensive questioning in the relative quiet of the South Yorkshire Constabulary police hut.

"Right then, sunbeam. Name?"

"John Robinson."

"Address?"

"63 Tapton Crescent Road, Broomhill, Sheffield."

"Occupation?"

"Chartered Accountant."

"Oh, we don't get many o' those in 'ere." And while the founder of the Institute of Chartered Accountants turned in his grave, Robbo was let go.

In the meantime I too had left the ground, in the hope of catching Robbo's last words before they sent him down. In the deserted back street outside, it was a visibly shaken (if free) John Robinson, Chartered Accountant, that I met up with. We had no intention of going back in now – so much for our resolution to see the whole ninety minutes – and we were well on the way to Sheffield when Robbo's car radio announced that Ronnie Moore had sneaked an eighty-ninth minute winner.

The picture of the Tiger Robbo embrace was in all the local papers on the Monday, and even made one or two of the nationals. But Robbo himself was nowhere to be seen. Like a disgraced M.P., he drew the curtains on the outside world, this in the hope of preventing Maria from finding out about his public love affair, and thus from drawing, in turn, the curtains on their relationship. He succeeded too, and it was several years before she came across the newspaper cuttings. But by then Robbo had said goodbye to pink hair (indeed "hair") and Saturdays with "that Robert". He'd even said goodbye to Rotherham United in favour of the more fashionable Sheffield Wednesday, and – sin of all sins – started taking Maria along to matches. In short he'd become a right quintessential, and the whole episode was instantly forgiven. So here's to you, Mrs. Robinson!

Rotherham United 2 Sheffield United 1

Robert Rowell vs. Marco Tardelli
Sheffield and Madrid
1981 - 82 season

Scorcher

The "perfect goal" satisfies six conditions:

1.   It is an absolute corker, one that Jonnie Wales would have been proud of.

2.   It comes at an important moment in an important game.

3.   There are goal-nets (I'll come back to this in a later chapter).

4.   There is an element of surprise ("Oh my God, it's gone in!").

5.   It is celebrated in style.

6.   The scorer's sweetheart is at home, waiting to congratulate her man and put his dinner on the table.

It also helps, of course, if I happen to score it. Every dog has its day, every Sunday footballer too, and my greatest ever goal was a Matt le Tissier-style dribble-dribble-postage stamp (i.e. top right-hand corner) effort on the first day of the 81-82 season. My team-mates enthused afterwards that it was the best goal they'd ever seen, and I wasn't going to argue with them. However, if I am honest I have to admit that even that goal fell one short of perfection, seeing as it didn't satisfy condition number 6 (alas no girlfriend, in fact not even a table to put the dinner on).

Which brings me to the question: if there were one goal in footballing history – just one – that I could go back in time and score myself, which one would it be? My immediate answer gives me goose pimples just thinking about it. This goal had everything. And no it wasn't Geoff Hurst's third in 1966. In fact my favourite goal was scored by a foreign player for a foreign team in a foreign country. Disagree if you like, but what I consider to be "the greatest goal of all time" was the one that effectively closed the curtains on the 1981-82 season. Only, it was scored on the world's highest stage and in front of 90,000 spectators, not forgetting the countless millions of us watching at home…

And the winner is…

Marco Tardelli for Italy against West Germany, 1982.

The occasion is none other than the final of one of the most memorable World Cups ever. It is halfway through the second half and Italy are leading one-nil.

Ee-tal-ya! Ee-tal-ya! Ee-tal-ya!…

It is nearly fifty years since the Azzurri last won the planet's most prestigious trophy, and this in itself is a national crisis for a people that would happily lose a World War if it meant winning a World Cup (come to think of it, they would happily lose a World War, period). But this year, after eliminating both Argentina and a magnificent Brazilian team, luck might just be on their side. They have a very solid team: Dino Zoff, the forty-year-old goalkeeper and captain, Claudio not-so-Gentile, the defender who kicked and tugged Diego Maradona to bits, the "Brazilian" Bruno Conti on the right, goal-poacher Paolo Rossi, and veteran Gaetano Scirea at the back. Not forgetting their legendary coach, the pipe-smoking Enzo Bearzot.

Ee-tal-ya! Ee-tal-ya! Ee-tal-ya!…

The Italians are controlling their lead as only the Italians know how. Another German attack comes to nothing and Italy break away. Conti…to Rossi…to Scirea out on the right. Scirea takes his time, there is no hurry… to Bergomi…back again to Scirea. Can they hold on?

Ee-tal-ya! Ee-tal-ya! Ee-tal-ya!…

Midfielder Marco Tardelli makes his way towards the

inside-right position. He raises his hand, indicating to Scirea that he is free. Scirea obliges.

Ee-tal-ya! Ee-tal-ya! Ee-tal-ya!…

Tardelli's control is imperfect, the ball bobbles away slightly, and two German defenders come in to close him down.

Ee-tal-ya! Ee-tal-ya! Ee-tal-ya!…

The German team is not pretty (as usual), but they are mean (as usual). They shouldn't be in the final at all. Their semi-final against Michel Platini's artistic French team will always be remembered for the way Schumacher, the German madman-cum-goalkeeper, came running out of his box, fists and feet flying, to knock Battiston for six with a disgraceful challenge when the Frenchman was clean through. The injustice of it all means that today the rest of the world wants the Italians – admittedly no softies themselves – to win the final. Plus the fact that we always want the Germans to lose anyway.

Ee-tal-ya! Ee-tal-ya! Ee-tal-ya!…

Right now the Battiston incident is the last thing on Schumacher's mind, as he steadies himself on the edge of his six-yard box – you never know, Tardelli might fancy his chances…

Ee-tal-ya! Ee-tal-ya! Ee-tal-ya!…

[Camera shot from behind the goal – my favourite] Tardelli, slightly off balance, realises that the only thing left for him to do now is swing his left boot and hope for the best. Schumacher, seeing this, does what all goalkeepers do when an opponent shapes up to shoot: a little jig on the spot to flex the toes.

Ee-tal-ya! Ee-tal-ya! Ee-tal-ya!…

He needn't have bothered. Tardelli's left foot connects better than a Jack Nicklaus drive, and by the time Schumacher's eyes have sent a message to the brain saying, "ball moving quickly, to your left, at waist-height, dive now …"

…HOOOMPH

... the ball is already bouncing out from the netting just inside his left-hand post. Schumacher kicks out at the ball in disgust, since he knows, instinctively, that this means it's all over – no team, not even his own, pulls back two goals against the famous catenaccio defence. Tardelli, on the other hand, is asking himself whether it really is he who has been chosen among five billion earthly citizens to score the greatest goal in footballing history, the thunder in his ears assures him that it is, he picks himself up off the ground, and...

Goooooool! Goooooooooool! Goooooooooooooooool!

Never have I seen such a beautiful, explosive mix of amazement and joy. You can see the souls of sixty million Italians on Tardelli's face as he gallops off, arms pumping, zig-zagging his way past the rugby tackles of his team-mates on his way to the touchline. There President Pertini, arms raised to the heavens, is waiting to salute the man who has just clinched the World Cup for his people. The world is won, the world is one, the world is Italian.

And then they all pile on.

Years later I was shocked to hear Tardelli complain that that goal had ruined his life. That people in the street pestered him about it all the time, as if it were the only good thing he had ever done. It made him feel, he said, like a three-headed freak. Well, if you're watching, Marco, all I can say is come off it. I for one would have given a million goals for just the one goal you smashed past Schumacher. Partly – no doubt about it – because yes, it was a corker. Yes, it did come at an important time in an important game, and yes, there were goal-nets, etc. etc. But mainly because, when you returned home to Italy, you must have had the freedom of Totti!

Robert Rowell 5   Marco Tardelli 6

Rotherham United vs. Newcastle United
Milan, Italy
2 October, 1982

Warm Front

They all said I would fail. The head of the accountancy course was so sure of it he even promised to pay for every pint of beer drunk in celebration if ever I should pass. But to the surprise of everyone, in September 1982 I qualified as a Chartered Accountant. The course master was true to his word, and coughed up all fifteen pints' worth. Were it not for my bank overdraft problems, I might have framed the cheque. Instead I cashed it in and went out for more.

With my apprentice contract up, I was at last free to move under accountancy's equivalent of the Bosman ruling. Ever since the Hereford United humiliation, I had always intended to flee the country at the first opportunity, but where to? Most newly-qualifieds who sought jobs abroad went for lucrative packages in remote places like the Cayman Islands and the Bahamas, where there were no taxes and no football. Not me. Because of my ancestral links, France was my natural first choice, but they told me that an "E" grade in 'A'-level Donkey Noises fell well short of the level of language mastery required. So I plumped instead for Italy, purely for its hotbed of soccer status. The Italians had just won the World Cup, and the country's rich clubs were attracting the very best, offering the highest wages and the most competitive stage in the world to the likes of Michel Platini, Paolo Roberto Falcao and Liam Brady.

As luck would have it, the Italian accountancy profession was in a rather primitive state. Its firms were hastily importing the well-reputed Anglo-Saxons to help shake off the image of shady old men sitting in dark rooms doing triple-entry book-keeping (debit, credit and hide-it) – it seemed that all you needed was a 15-digit calculator to cope with all those millions of lire and you were in.

I had been looking for a way out of agonising through the upcoming Rotherham-Newcastle fixture, and found it in the form of Alitalia flight AZ 614 to Milan. As the plane climbed out of Heathrow airport that Friday November evening, I had good reason to be nervous: a big interview on foreign soil and my first ever flying experience. My anxiety wasn't eased by the presence of this gum-chewing, designer-stubbled terrorist type who kept wandering up and down the aisle as if he was waiting to pick the best moment to hijack the plane. It was only when he slapped down a sandwich on the table in front of me with a reluctant *prego* that I realised that he was one of the cabin crew, and with a sigh of relief I returned my attention to the book I'd bought for the occasion, entitled The Italians. It was full of interesting information about their traits and customs, my own favourite being:

Q. Why don't Italians have freckles?

A. Because they'd just slide off.

I don't know what it is about touching down at Milan's Linate airport, but there is no other place in the world where I feel so happy on arrival. Maybe it is the relief of Alitalia getting us down safely, in what is more often than not ridiculously thick fog (the Italian passengers always applaud this, as if they knew something about the state of the aircraft the rest of us didn't); maybe it's the fact that as soon as I emerge from the plane, I find myself there, in Italy, possibly the greatest country in the world. Even on that very first visit I felt an immediate sense of belonging to the place, that this was *my* country. In fact, had there been as many free drinks on my flight as the Pope obviously used to knock back during his, I might well have had the urge to bend down and kiss the ground.

I sighed when I saw the huge queue at passport control, but hadn't bargained for the speed of Italian formalities. Judging by the jaded expression of the passport controller, we'd obviously dragged him out of the wrong side of bed just to be there. The only sign that he was still alive came from a barely perceptible twitch of the left hand that drooped lazily over the ledge in front of him, this to indicate that he was anything but interested in our passports and would we do him a favour and *va fan culo*? By the time it was my turn, we were being flicked through at twenty to the dozen, so I could be excused for not bothering to produce my own papers for inspection. After all, he wasn't going to look at them, was he?

"Stop! Passaporto!"

Who, me? I handed over the passport originally issued when I was a long-haired, world-despising seventeen-year-old, and watched as his face – and indeed his whole day – lit up at the challenge of finding something, anything, its photograph had in common with the egg-headed twenty-three-going-on-fifty-four-year-old now standing in front of him. He turned the passport this way and that, finally gave up, and with a wry smile said *È cambiato un po, lei* – it is thanks to him and his fellow passport controllers all over the world that I now know how to say "you've changed a bit" in fifteen different languages.

As I waited for my suitcase, I observed the work ethic of Italian customs officers. There must have been ten of them, linking arms and chatting amongst themselves as even the most suspicious of individuals wandered past. To this day I have never, ever seen anyone stopped at an Italian customs – except, that is, for young girls carrying big chests. That's when every customs officer in Italy suddenly takes an interest in his job. They all pile around to embarrass the poor girl by examining her underwear, checking her bra size, that kind of thing – and that's before they've even opened her case! Ah well, at least the Italian customs officers are open about it, unlike their British counterparts, who examine ladies' lingerie in a way only the British can – very matter-of-fact, seen-it-all-before, no-this-doesn't-turn-me-on-one-iota – before rushing off to the toilets to play with themselves.

The sliding doors opened, I fought my way through the great mass of mammas all noisily waiting to welcome their thirty-something, still-living-at-home sons back to Pastaland, and jumped into a yellow cab. I'd hardly had time to show the driver the piece of paper with the address of my hotel, before a grunt of acknowledgement sent the car screeching off at head-jerking speed into a traffic jam all of ten yards further on.

There we were, hundreds of yellow cabs all leaving the airport at the same time, jostling like grains of sand in an egg-timer to be first through the bottleneck when the lights changed. Motors were duly vroomed up to Formula One levels, red turned to green (no sign of amber), ten lanes of traffic squeezed into two, and miraculously nobody was killed in the process.

My weaver-beaver driver was clearly unhappy with his slow start off the grid, and spent the rest of the journey turning this way and that in an effort to win a place on the podium. At one point, with no way through on our side of the centre-line, he happily pulled out onto the tram lines in the middle of the road. With one of Mussolini's solid steel, orange passenger tanks hurtling straight towards us, its driver tinkling his bell to inform us that he was big and we were small, my chauffeur simply accelerated towards him. I thought to myself, hang on a minute, I hope he's not playing who's going to jump out the way first, and closed my eyes for just long enough to visualise my lifeless body being cut free from the wreckage. When I re-opened them, the tram was nowhere to be seen. Pizza Calzone! It *had* jumped out of the way!

Then an amber-gambling nun in a *Cinquecento* overtook us at a red light (no doubt she was banking on divine protection) and I thought that if this is how the nuns drive, just what do you have to do to pass your driving test in this country? For those interested, here's the answer :

EIGHT STEPS TO SUCCESSFUL DRIVING IN ITALY

1. Take no lessons.

2. Wear sunglasses at all times, especially in heavy fog and driving rain.

3. Hang your left arm lazily out of the window and put your right arm around your girlfriend (or the back of the passenger seat head-rest if you haven't got one).

4. Steer occasionally, using your knees.

5. Roll down all the windows and play Italian junk music as loudly as your radio will allow – the ba-jung ba-jung ba-jung is guaranteed to make other motorists move aside to let you through, if only to see what kind of an idiot had attached his ice-cream van to their rear bumpers.

6. Blast your horn and scream at a fellow-motorist every thirty seconds (they especially appreciate it if you shout things like *And your sister!*). And don't worry about locking your doors first – the likelihood of an Italian actually gathering up the courage to come and bop you one is extremely remote indeed.

7. The inside lane is for undertakers only.

8. Be prudent and stop at green lights – you never know what might be coming the other way.

By some sort of a miracle, we reached my hotel in Via Hoepli, opposite la Scala opera house in the centre of town, and I unravelled myself from the get-ready-to-crash position in order to pay. The driver wrote down four hundred billion trillion lire on a piece of paper – presumably so that I could better understand the extent to which he was ripping me off – at which I pointed out that this happened to be three hundred billion trillion lire more than indicated on the meter. At this he pulled out a tatty tariff card covered in drawings of aeroplanes, dogs and half-moons, but I really couldn't see what this had to do with anything – after all, I wasn't *carrying* any aeroplanes, dogs or half-moons! He explained further: "Eh! Heez hair-o-porto supplemento, heez bagaglio supplemento, heez heev-neeng supplemento, heez hevery-goddam-supplemento-hyou-can-teenk-of-supplemento. Eh! Eh!" Ah well, at least I didn't leave him a tip.

On the Saturday morning – probably about the time back home when the Newcastle United team bus was passing through Scotch Corner – two girls from the firm, one American, the other Italian, came to collect me to show me around Milan. Now I'd always been led to believe that the Americans were a straight-teethed, obese, loud-mouthed, loud-dressed people, but this girl's teeth weren't straight at all. As for the Italian, other than her bulging eyes, bulging hips and bulging complexion, she was a bit of all right, so when she kissed me on both cheeks without so much as a how's your padre? I went beetroot from head to toe. Goodness me, I wasn't used to being kissed just the once, never mind twice – if a girl did that to you in Sheffield it was a case of, "now then big boy, thy place or mine?". Then she introduced herself as Titsy Anna and I thought hey, I'm in here. Who knows? Maybe skinny, big-nosed, white-faced egg-heads went down in Italy the way bronzed, big-muscled, well-endowed Italians went down in Britain. I'm definitely coming out here to live!

We visited the Duomo cathedral, la Rinascente (Milan's equivalent of Harrods), and the Galeria Umberto Primo, a beautiful old arcade where we ended the afternoon with a drink in a swanky café. That was where I discovered my staple diet cost three quid for half a beer, and I was just beginning to have second thoughts about coming to Milan when Titsy Anna's parting double-kiss left me in no doubts that she and Italy were for me. The American tried to kiss me too. No way, honey, I'm taken.

The big interview with the firm's senior partner was supposed to take place that same evening over dinner, but when I arrived at the hotel there was a note in reception saying that a certain Dottore Salvio was going to pay me a visit at eight. Presumably this was the firm's doctor just wanting to check that I was fighting fit, so I put on a clean pair of underpants for the occasion. I needn't have bothered, though. It turned out that Dottore Salvio didn't know his kidneys from his liver, and around his neck, instead of a stethoscope, was a tie with a knot the size of a swollen ankle (I would later learn that the illustrious title of Dottore was practically given to anyone capable of making such knots). In fact Dottore Salvio was the firm's senior partner, and off we went to the restaurant next door.

We sat down, il Dottore ordered antipasto della casa, and immediately started spouting off in Italian. I was just about to interrupt him to say that I would rather conduct the interview in English when I twigged that he *was* speaking English, or rather *Heengleesh*. This is a twisted form of English spoken only by Italians, in which the letter "h" keeps popping up where it shouldn't, where the original English words are distorted beyond recognition (for example, "as well" usually ends up sounding like "ass hole"), and where the enthusiastic swinging of arms has you ducking and diving like a featherweight boxer.

"High ham very, very appy to welcome Hugh heen Heetalee. Hugh know, Heetalee heez be-owty-fool country. High laaaaaaav Heetalee. Eh! Heez normal – high ham Heetalee man. Bat I teenk Hugh wheel like Heetalee *ass hole*. So, tell me, Hawaii Hugh choose Heetalee."

The first secret of good interview technique is to let the other guy do all the talking. This I was happy to do, what with me not having a clue what he was going on about, and the richest assortment of starters I'd ever seen having just landed in front of me. It was just as I was putting the fork to my mouth that I realised il Dottore was staring me straight in the face, as if expecting an answer.

"Er, yes?"

"High said, Hawaii Hugh choose Heetalee?"

"Oh, I see, right." And thus began the most important interview of my whole life. I was on my best, boring behaviour – after all, my relationship with Titsy Anna depended on it – and I gave the answer I was sure he wanted

164

to hear. "Well, I see Heetalee, erm, Italy, as an excellent opportunity to broaden my horizons in an international environment." One out of one. Good start.

"Hand hawhat Hugh teenk breeng person-hally heen term hoff hespery-hentsa."

"Well, if by that you mean what do I think I bring personally in terms of experience, I believe it is above all the professional approach of the British Chartered Accountant to what is, if I may say so, a relatively immature environment from a financial standards point of view." Two out of two. So far so good, but oh dear, was that a yawn?

"Hand let me hask, ass hole, hawhat heez hyour long-time ham-beetion?"

I'd been waiting for this one. "Doctor Saliva, let me be quite clear. Some day I intend to have your job." Foccaccia! If that doesn't clinch it, nothing will.

Another yawn, I was sure of it this time. We'd been talking barely five minutes, yet il Dottore was already bored, like he'd heard it all before. There then followed a lengthy silence, during which every time I swallowed my food the whole restaurant looked round to see who was making the huge thumping noises. Things weren't going well, but I didn't intend giving up on my dream of Italian football and Titsy Anna without a fight. I needed this job, so I tried a different tack.

"You see, Doctor Saliva, I believe that what the Italian accountancy profession is crying out for today is…"

"…Hugh know, Hugh look like Bob-hee Charl-ton."

"Ye what? Er, pardon? Scusi?"

"High said Hugh look like Bob-hee Charl-ton. Ha! Now zer was a wounder-fool Heengland team."

And it was plain sailing after that. The career crap left the table with the empty antipasto dishes, and we got down to the serious business of pasta alla football. At the end of the meal the waiter left the bottle of San Buca on the table, and one by one we toasted Bobby Charlton, Gianni Rivera, Bobby Moore, Paolo Rossi. By the end of the night we'd run out of players, and even il Dottore's having to carry me out of the restaurant wasn't enough to jeopardise the offer of a three-year contract.

I woke up the next morning a happy man. But this was nothing to how I felt when we landed at Heathrow. For there I learned that while Titsy Anna had been giving me two on each cheek, Kevin Keegan had been giving Rotherham two in each half. What a perfect way to round off the weekend! Just wait until I see Robbo! But the silly chuff was missing from our usual rendezvous at the Bull's Head that Sunday evening, just as he was on the Monday, the Tuesday and the Wednesday – in fact I didn't come across him again for months. No doubt my loss was Maria's gain, but I wasn't particularly bothered. Hafter hall, high was hoff to Heetalee, and what a way to go!

Rotherham United 1   Newcastle United 5

Milan A.C. vs. The Rest
San Siro, Milan
Every Sunday of the 1983/84 season

Not A Cloud In The Sky

When the formal job offer came through, I immediately went out and bought a Learn Italian In Six Weeks cassette course. Six weeks? Easy-peasy. It would be a whole six months before I jumped on that plane – I could probably fit in German, Spanish and Chinese while I was at it. What they forgot to point out, though, was that you could only do it in six weeks if you had an IQ in excess of 180 and didn't go to the pub every night. After the initial enthusiasm of ripping open the package and rushing through lesson one, it wasn't long before the books had lost themselves under a pile of dirty washing, and that was the end of that. So when I finally left England, the only thing I'd learned was the Italian for "My name is Paolo Tosi. I am a lawyer living in Holland. I am returning to Italy for the holidays." Now how was I supposed to order a beer with that?

The most difficult part about my departure wasn't so much the wrench of saying arrivederci to family and friends – I'd done that before and would do it again – no, much more of an emotional challenge was going to be getting past the little old woman. There were two little old women living along from my bedsit on the dank corridor I christened Death Row. One minded her own business, the other minded mine. It all started when I came home from work one evening and found her outside my door. The polite young man in me had a quick chat, five minutes maybe, she went away happy and I thought nothing more of it.

Until the next evening, when she stood there blocking my door like a goalkeeper. I don't know if you have ever tried it, but getting past a little old lady barring the entrance to your home is no easy task – you can't just knee her one. So I got the full life story this time – a good half hour's worth – and just before toddling back to her prison cell she kindly offered me a Twix. I didn't have the heart to tell her I hated chocolate, and courteously accepted. This was a big mistake, since she was an ever-present at my door after that, and before I knew it there was an EEC chocolate mountain in the corner of my bedsit.

This daily invasion of my time and privacy very quickly got on my nerves. I soon realised that the Twixes simply acted as vouchers with which she bought my time – one Twix earned her fifteen minutes, two Twixes half an hour, three and I could forget any plans I'd made for the evening. Particularly off-putting was her habit of talking about her home town of Hessell, with liquid emphasis on the "ss", so that every time she mentioned the place – approximately every ten words – the gap in her crooked teeth let fly a jet of spittle in my face. I tried all sorts to fend her off: varying my times of arrival, pretending I was drunk, being drunk, but she was equal to all of them. The Twix that broke the camel's back, though, was when I wandered into the Bull's Head one evening and my mates started chirping,

On the twelfth day of Christmas my true love sent to me:
Twelve chocolate Twixes,
Eleven chocolate Twixes,
Ten chocolate Twixes…

and I thought, that's it, I'm going to put an end to this bloody lark once and for all. The very next day I informed her that on account of a rare illness my doctor had diagnosed, I had to cut out all the chocolate bars from my diet, replacing them with cans of lager instead. She took this news very badly, as hoped, and I thought great, at worst this time tomorrow I'll be knocking back the Carlsberg, at best she'll stop Hesselling me altogether.

I was wrong. When I came home the next day, dear old "Jaws" looked as if she'd been keeping goal all afternoon. Her hands were empty but her look was mean, and the only thing she said was, "Aren't you friends with me any more?" "Of course I am", I lied, a howler of an own goal as it turned out, since she all but took this to be a licence to move in with me.

Things took a further turn for the worse when she got wind of my departure for Italy. She started wearing lipstick, dressed up for our evening rendezvous, and twice even tried to tempt me back to her cell "for dinner". I dreaded "goodbye" day like the plague, for fear she would stick those bright red plungers on my cheeks and burst into tears. You never know, she might even insist on coming with me!

My breakaway plan was simple, if heartless. Deciding that it was far better to have her on my conscience than in my suitcase, I woke up very, very early that July morning, packed my worldly goods into my Adidas bag, opened the door ever so quietly, breathed in and did a runner. Maybe it was just paranoia on my part, but I felt sure I heard the snick of a door as I turned to run down the stairs, and as I waited at the busstop on Fulwood Road, my heart pounded at the thought of Jaws advancing along the corridor TUM-TUM TUM-TUM, down the staircase TUM-TUM TUM-TUM TUM-TUM, along the drive to the main road TUM-TUM TUM-TUM TUM-TUM TUM-TUM and…

… here to the rescue came the number 60 bus. I jumped on, said "seven please, love" for the last time, and breathed a sigh of relief. I'd made it. I was FREE. And on the off-chance anyone at Sheffield Midland Station, or Heathrow Airport, or anywhere in between, asked whether I'd come across a man called Robert Rowell, that a dear little old lady from Hessell was looking for him, I knew what my answer was going to be straight away: "Ha, sorry, no speak Heengleesh. Mi chiamo Paolo Tosi. Sono un avocato e lavoro in Olanda. Torno in Italia per passare le mie vacanze."

If this was the only Italian I knew, it didn't much bother my new employers when I turned up at the office on my first day, since they didn't have any work to give me anyway. This was because Milan closed down for the month of August, as its inhabitants took their fights over square metres from the city's roads to the Mediterranean beaches. Instead I was sent for a one-to-one, eight-hours-a-day, crash course in Italian. This was so effective I was already dreaming in the language after the first day (the book is red, the book is red, the book is red), and after four weeks of cooking like a pizza in one hundred degree temperatures, I came out speaking more Italian than I could ever have learned in ten years at school.

My confidence, though, was limited to the classroom, where the teachers spoke slowly and deliberately. Outside, the only place I dared go was the supermarket, and that was only because when the cashier announced my melon and Parma ham came to the princely sum of *quindici mila cinquantacinque lire, per favore*, it didn't matter that I didn't have a clue what she was saying, all I had to do was hand over the biggest note in my wallet and let her do the rest. Curiously, the change nearly always included a few sweets, this to replace the tiny amounts of lire for which coins hadn't existed since Dante's time. I liked this quaint practice, since it gave me something to suck on the way home, but then one evening I discovered – too late – that it wasn't always sweets they gave you. On a crowded street, I gleefully removed the wrapper and handed over the little brown cube to my waiting saliva juices. Within seconds I was surrounded by a crowd of people all wondering whether I was about to die, as I coughed up Italy's answer to a cold cup of Bovril. Had they never been to an English football match before?

At the office, colleagues just had to look in my direction to set my armpits dripping, and the slightest movement of lips had my ears closing up like oysters, thus blotting out altogether any remote chance I had of understanding what they were about to say. I admired Stewart, a Glaswegian lad who started at about the same time and became a good friend, for the carefree way in which he threw himself straight into the thick of it. Inevitably, he screwed up on occasions, particularly with his habit of translating literally into Italian, phrases that were no doubt commonplace back in deepest Greenock, but of little use in sophisticated Milan. For example, if someone riled him by referring to the Scots as English (few Italians make the distinction), he would offer them a *quadrato andare Giacomo* (square go, Jimmy), or invite them to *scegliere una finestra culo intelligente, tu esci subito* (pick a window smart arse, you're leaving). The Italians looked at him as if he were from a different planet, and they weren't far wrong.

Thankfully, Italian is an easy language as languages go, and it wasn't long before I was fluent. Having taken all that trouble to learn it, then, I was understandably peeved when in a bar or restaurant the waiter would insist on replying to my pretty good Italian in pretty lousy English. I found a quick way of dealing with such show-offs, though, that never failed. This consisted of saying something in broad Geordie like, "hoo hinny, warraboot gannin to gerruz summit t'eat?" That didn't half shut them up. "Ha, sorry, no speak Japanese."

But what about Titsy Anna? I hear you ask. Actually, I was hoping you wouldn't. The first time I came across her was in the corridor at the office. She was more made up than a stolen car, and if she saw me she chose not to show it, brushing past and nearly knocking me over with the whirlwind of a fur coat she was wearing. I couldn't believe that all that romantic snogging in Piazza della Scala had been for nothing. Then I found out the harsh truth: one, Titsy Anna wasn't Titsy Anna, she was Tiziana; two, Italian girls give the two-cheeked kiss to any spotty-faced Tomaso, Ricardo or Eraldo; three, she was engaged to be married to some I-can-keep-her-going-all-night hunk of an Italian.

With Titsy Anna safely out of the way, I was now able to concentrate on the main purpose of my move to Italy. My poor employers: I must have cost them a fortune, what with the moving costs, language lessons and as much pizza as I could eat. Well, if they were expecting a return on their investment at some stage, they were going to be very disappointed. I wasn't in Italy for the work, I was there to savour the football Italia experience. Their part of the deal was simply to keep my fridge full of beer.

I made my priorities clear the very first day. I hadn't even unpacked my bags when I rushed off in a taxi to the Stadio Giuseppe Meazza, or San Siro as it is better known around the world. Even back then, before the 1990 World Cup transformed it, in my opinion, into the most beautifully sculptured slab of reinforced concrete in the world, it was awesome, a gigantic, two-tier arena, wrapped all the way round in gently climbing ramps that took spectators from the very bottom to the very top. There was no game that day – this was July – I just wanted to admire it from the outside, get a feel for the place, and check which tram I was going to suffocate to death in on match days.

I chose (A.C.) Milan (pronounced Mee-lan) as my team. This was because, of the maximum two *stranieri* (foreign players) Italian clubs were allowed in those days, Luther Blissett was one, having signed from Watford in the close season. And it seemed quite natural as a proud Englishman that I egg on our lad abroad.

On paper, Blissett was a bargain. Those were the days when English clubs were held in high esteem (on account of their considerable success in international competition) so it was assumed that if Blissett could score a thousand goals for Watford in one season, he could double that in Italy. Instead, he turned out to be (yet another) case of Italian club directors getting it all wrong. The problem was, in Italy the game was, and still is, played very differently. Back home, Blissett was used to running into the acres of free space left by ball-watching defenders before smacking the ball home, but in Italy, it wasn't quite that easy. The emphasis was on defence, and strikers were usually forced to play all alone, backs to goal, with about six defenders breathing all over their anatomy. Close control was the order of the day:

receive, lay it off, receive, lay it off. On Blissett's debut, we saw what we were in for the very first time the ball chanced his way. His first touch sent it spinning away, and as he tried to trap it under his studs, it bounced up into the air and into the path of a pleasantly surprised defender. It was the same story every time, a gangling spectacle of head, knees and elbows all bobbing about trying to get this bloody spherical thing under control, and each time an opponent came waltzing in to save him (and me) from further embarrassment. The Milanisti showed remarkable patience at first, as Italian fans always did with their stranieri, but by the end of the season they couldn't wait to see him go. After scoring just five goals, *Meess-eet Blee-sseet* was shoved on a plane and sent back to Watford.

Replacing Blissett the following season was il Rasoio, Ray "Razor Blade" Wilkins, and he at least gained renown for his ability to spray forty-yard passes direct to team-mates anywhere on the pitch. Anywhere, that is, except forwards – the Milanisti loved him for that and he lasted several seasons. No doubt one of the reasons Wilkins did well in Italy was that he had the desire and the ability to fit into his new surroundings. Of course any player moving to a new club has to go through some sort of acclimatisation period, but this is complicated all the more when there are the additional obstacles of culture and language. Players of South American origin, such as Falcao, Zico and Maradona, all settled into Italian football very quickly. For a start they happened to be world-class, which does help. Secondly, they had no trouble moving from one Latin country to another. In Rio de Janeiro, for example, people queue for train tickets in the same way as they do in Rome, which is by sneaking in from the sides. Such customs seem incredible to the please, you-go-first Brits, but as the saying goes, when in Rome…

Over the years I noticed a close correlation between a player's mastery of the Italian language and his match performances. And the average Briton's stubborn inability to progress beyond "the book is red" phase possibly explains why so many of them failed. Perhaps the most embarrassing of them all, both in and out of the classroom, was Ian Rush. Rush struggled from the start. In his own words, "I couldn't settle in Italy – it was like living in a foreign country!" Only learning about five words of Italian didn't exactly qualify him for dressing room jester, and T.V. interviews reduced the poor lad to a stuttering, mumbling wreck. Here is how he once replied, for example, when questioned about the poor early season form of la Juventus:

Tch…ohh…o-no-so…pekay…tch pfff…Juve eh…pfff…se…no se…se nuova giocare…ehm…pfffss…e difficile quest'anno pe Juve…eh pfffss…ah…o-non-so…

Don't worry if you didn't understand that, neither did we.

In Italy, teams from the same city often share the same stadium, so although Milan was my favourite team, every other Sunday I would also go along to San Siro to watch Inter (pronounced Een-ter). I just couldn't seem to get enough, and compared to going to a match back home, where supporters were (in those days at least) treated like horse dung, in Italy you were properly looked after. In Britain, the miserable grey weather, diabolical catering facilities, perhaps one, solitary shop selling souvenirs, and grown men peeing in the washbasins because the queues for the urinals were too long, were enough to put you off camping holidays for good. Certainly, you never had the impression that you were wanted, even when you went to watch your home team. In Milan, on the other hand, you felt good about going to matches from the minute you left home. Usually the sun was out (most Italian stadiums – San Siro included – didn't even have roofing), people were laughing, talking animatedly, and generally looking as if they were having a wonderful time. Before going inside the stadium you might pick up a delicious, freshly roast *porchetta* sandwich from one of the hundreds of food vans, or stop off at a stall to buy a pennant or scarf. San Siro was often *esaurito*, sold out, but I never had trouble finding a ticket, as long as I was willing to pay over the odds. Typical of the Italians' attitude to shady dealings, nobody seemed to mind that the *bagherini* (touts) had control of all the tickets, and not once did I see them being moved on or arrested – rumour had it that the clubs themselves were at the heart of everything that was going on.

Unless you had a ticket for one of the VIP areas, there was no numbered seating, just concrete *gradinate*, so you took a cushion along (in your team's colours) to park your bum on. No matter where you were you had an excellent view of the action, since San Siro, unlike many other Italian grounds, didn't have an athletics track, so you weren't half a mile from the action. It was a veritable two-tiered temple of soccer, and each week sixty or seventy thousand fanatical Italians transformed the concrete giant into a kaleidoscope of colour.

All clubs had a hard core of nutcases, who usually called themselves *ultras*. At San Siro they gathered on the upper tier behind one of the goals (the Milanisti had one end one week, Interisti the other the next). Their cheerleader sat on the front railings facing the crowd, announcing with the help of a megaphone what they were all going to chant next: perhaps *Ma-radona, figlio di putana* (Maradona, son of a bitch), *Roma! Roma! Va fan culo!* (literally, Roma! Roma! Go make bottom!), and my own personal favourite, *Pruzzo, Pruzzo, vieni a pescare con noi, ci manca verme* (Pruzzo, Pruzzo, come fishing with us, we're out of worms). Youngsters earned a few thousand lire by working their way around the gradinate, selling Grappa! Noccioline! Mars! Coca-cola! – and earned a few thousand lire more by cheating you on your change. Even the man on the tannoy sounded as if he was enjoying himself, sending booming echoes around the ground when announcing the team formations, or promoting the quality of Annabella's of Pavia, "the capital of the fur coat" – I don't recall them advertising luxury goods at Rotherham.

And then there was Mauro. As well as being a passionate Milanista, Mauro was pretty much everything you would expect of the stereotype Italian. He was dark, charming, immaculately groomed, elegant every day of the week, wore an overcoat even in the middle of summer (for fear of catching a cold) and sunglasses in winter. He didn't so much smoke cigarettes as make love to them. Admittedly, as a drinking buddy, he was a disaster. He would sit there with the same half-pint all evening, while the throats of both Stewart and I screamed out for him to adopt the British custom of getting a round in. He just couldn't understand what it was with us Brits that we could appear quite normal during the week, then go out on Friday nights with the sole objective of getting smashed. At pub-closing time he would run off home in disgust, while the two of us rolled around in the gutters giggling our heads off.

Like all Italians, Mauro's opinion of the English game was very condescending. How many times did I hear him say how much he enjoyed watching our matches on television, only to add (with no irony intended) that this was because our gaping defences, negligible technique and zero tactics always ensured end-to-end action and lots of goals! I couldn't believe that the league I'd followed since I was a boy, the Big League that Brian Moore and other British T.V. pundits had always assured us was the greatest in the world, could be regarded like some sort of slapstick circus.

Clowns like Blissett did nothing to improve that image, and over time I began to understand what Mauro was getting at. The Italian-in-the-street's awareness of football tactics was at least on a par with that of your average Premiership manager. In Britain, we tend to read the match programme while waiting for the game to start, but at San Siro the talk was all about whether such-and-such a team would play zone defence or man-to-man, whether they'd go for 4-4-2 or 4-5-1, that kind of thing. No wonder it is said that Italy is a nation of sixty million football coaches.

There was a carnival atmosphere leading up to the game, temperatures rising to boiling point when the two teams emerged like Roman gladiators from a long, covered tunnel, protecting them from wild coins and oranges. Flames and fire-crackers exploded everywhere, and tons of tiny pieces of paper were released from the sky, slowly fluttering earthwards and finally settling on the pitch or in the hair of those below.

Then at last the game started, and... yawn. Both Milan teams were middle-of-the-table sides in those days, and *Serie A* football was generally uneventful, cat-and-mouse stuff – most teams, whether they were playing home or away, adopted the *prima non prenderli* approach (first let's keep a clean sheet, then take it from there). Much more entertaining were the antics of Mauro. As soon as the referee blew that first whistle, Dottore Jekyll became Signor Hyde. He spent most of the game standing up, this to better insult Milan's opponents, Milan's own players (when a seventeen-year-old left-back by the name of Paolo Maldini made his home debut, Mauro immediately wrote him off as a *sega*, wanker), not to mention all those behind him whose view of the game he blocked, and who were forever screaming *seduti*! (siddown!). My mother thought Mauro was such a charming young man, but then she never saw him inside San Siro.

Mauro wasn't alone, of course. It didn't take much to have the whole stadium up in arms, literally speaking. A questionable decision from the referee would meet with universal yells of *arbitro cornuto*! (referring to the presumed red-card activities of his wife while he was busy officiating), accompanied by a splendid display of well-rehearsed arm movements that you had to see to believe. Imagine Luciano Pavarotti singing Ti Voglio Bene Assai while directing the traffic at Piazza della Reppublica, multiply the result by sixty thousand, and you get the idea. Certainly, were synchronised arm-waving an Olympic sport, the Italians would win hands down. Or rather up.

I remember almost nothing of all the games I saw, other than that I loved absolutely every minute of it. And the great thing was, when the game itself was over, football most certainly wasn't. I'd rush home from San Siro just in time to see Domenica Gol, the first of a whole host of television programmes dedicated to the day's action, and round off four consecutive hours of football-viewing later that evening with La Domenica Sportiva, the most serious programme of the lot. This was introduced by the deep-voiced Sandro Ciotti, for those who hadn't yet had enough football for one day, and a long-legged blonde called Maria Teresa Ruta, for those who had and just wanted to finish the weekend by drooling over a bit of skirt.

Winning was of course everything, but just as important for the individual players themselves, and which drove some of them to near-suicide, were the *pagelle*, or marks out of ten, given on Monday by the sports press. Anything below an acceptable six (*la sufficienza*) and your days were numbered. More than that and you could breathe for another week. The winning team's players invariably scored higher marks than the losers, no matter how their victory was earned. This was because in Italian football, there was no place for luck. Football was a science, not an art, a team won because they were better on the day. Programmes like Il Processo del Lunedì ("Trial on Monday") spent hours dissecting the games, analysing why the result was *logico*, not whether.

Surprises, too, were rare: a small-town provincial team playing away to the league leaders, for example, would invariably choose to play with just one *punta* (striker) in the hope of earning a nil-nil draw, but also – just as important – to limit the damage in the event of defeat. After the match you might see their coach smiling with satisfaction, as he described his team's 2-0 defeat by Juventus as one he would happily have settled for before the match. How much of the inevitability of some of these results was down to match-fixing we will never know (Milan had been relegated to Serie B for its involvement in a betting scandal as recently as 1980), but it was rare for the best team on paper to go away without at least a point.

The discussions and debates over penalty decisions, the ability of a manager to get his system working, the *rendimento* (form) of certain players, went on all week. You had to pity those (admittedly few) Italians who hated the game, for football was all around us. Bill Shankly once famously said, tongue-in-cheek, that football was more important than life and death. In Italy there would be nothing tongue-in-cheek about such a statement. How else can you explain the existence of several sports-only daily newspapers, ninety per cent of the contents of which were dedicated to football? And when I say sports newspapers, I am not talking about the Daily Sport with pictures of nude girls everywhere. This was all serious stuff: twenty pages of in-depth match reports, analyses of players' performances, interviews with everyone from il Presidente down to the *massaggiatore*, rumours, counter-rumours and every statistic imaginable, from the average boot size of the Serie A top strikers to the number of times Beppe Dossena had had sex since the beginning of the season. A page or two was usually dedicated to what was happening abroad, too, so you had more chance of reading about Hartlepool's pre-season friendly against Rochdale in the Gazzetta dello Sport than the Hartlepool Mail.

Media coverage aside, the thing that struck me most in those early days was the laid-back attitude to cheating – perhaps the one national sport with more participants even than football. In fact wrongful behaviour wasn't so much the cheating itself as being caught out. Look at all the rolling around on the floor that goes on in Italian football, yet to the spectators this was as acceptable an element of their game as heavy shoulder-charging is in ours. Thus, whenever a player was awarded a dubious penalty after diving in the box, the criticism wasn't so much levelled at him for having cheated his opponent, as the defender for being naïve enough to let him get away with it.

And of course the referee for not seeing it. Or maybe not wanting to see it, as the case may be. On this delicate subject, there are basically two schools of thought in Italy: on the one hand are those people, the Italian equivalent of Manchester United supporters, who choose to follow Juventus because they're always winning the league (including the 83/84 title – my first); and everyone else, who hate Juventus because – they say – every one of those titles was *bought*. Either way, it was the referees who bore the brunt of the passionate debates at our office on Monday mornings. Any non-Italian-speakers watching would have been alarmed to see all those accountants shouting and waving their arms at each other as if they were on the verge of a mass brawl – and that was just when they were discussing the weather!

What a great country, what a great people, and what a great job I'd landed. Forza Italia!

Milan A.C. 0   The Rest 0

Solese vs. Bollatese
Cascina del Sole, near Milan
September 1984

Stormer

During that first year in Italy, my own football-playing was limited to weekend coats-for-posts with Mauro and his mates. Other than accusing me of being a bit of a *Veneziano*, greedy beggar, which of course I was, Mauro was impressed by my skills, and quite surprised that anyone from Britain could possess such technique. I must be an exception, he said. Bollocks, I said, there were millions more where I came from, it's just that we didn't have time to dally on the ball in England the way they did in Italy. You should have seen Jonnie Wales, I said.

Later, I played in a couple of low key, big-bellied summer tournaments, my first taste of organised football. There I was able to see that, for all the Italians' apparent knowledge of the game, once the sunglasses came off and the shorts went on they played just as badly as the rest of us, eleven would-be Paolo Rossis running around like headless chickens.

Where Italian football did differ from the real thing, however, and this even at the lowest levels, was in the theatrics. In Sheffield, football was first and foremost a "man's game", two armies going into battle. The body language was aggressive, the English language was aggressive, and either you accepted the rule about any tackle below shoulder-height being legitimate or you were a "mardy puff".

In Italy, by contrast, each match was a meeting of two amateur dramatic societies, the Romeos versus the Juliets. Every missed chance was a *tragedia*, every tough tackle the work of an *assassino*, every one of the referee's "wrong" decisions an *ingiustizia*. And each time the victim of all this bad luck would look towards the heavens, hands held together in prayer, and ask *Dio Caro*, dear God, what exactly he had done to merit His wrath.

At the end of the game, it wasn't unknown for players to run off in the huff, or even for a whole team to run after the referee. They picked on him because, at odds of 11-to-1 on, he was easy meat, a dead cert, and for once the Italian thoroughbred Yellow Streak would come racing out of its stalls.

In England, five minutes after the final whistle and we were already into our second pint. Not in Italy. If the football was a comedy of errors, the lengthy, almost religious ritual that surrounded washing and dressing was straight from the first division. It lasted almost as long as the game itself, as each player extracted a huge toiletries bag Elizabeth Taylor would have been proud of, before donning bathrobe and flip-flops for the trip of all of two yards to the shower-room. One hour and two bottles of shower-gel later, ridiculous amounts of time were then spent on drying the wet bits between toes, grooming eyelashes and polishing willies. And so to the grand finale, a well-rehearsed reverse striptease that started with the knee-length socks, and culminated in the dark sunglasses, this to provide uninterrupted views down girls' blouses on the packed *metropolitana*.

There wouldn't have been much room in the take-no-prisoners British game for most of the Italians I played with. For if they didn't freeze to death first, they would have been laughed or kicked off the pitch within the first five minutes. On the other hand, I doubt whether many of those playing in the Sheffield Imperial Sunday League would have lasted long in Italy, either. All that British Bulldog gnashing of teeth, raising of boots and showing of studs didn't tend to go down too well with Italian referees, so the sort of challenge that was waved on in England would just as likely have received a yellow card in Italy.

It goes without saying that my tinky-winky, fair-weather style was better suited to the blizzard-free Italian game, where you were actively encouraged to express yourself on a football pitch in ways that didn't simply involve running your socks and mouth off for ninety minutes. It wasn't long before I was being courted by several (admittedly modest) teams, which – very important – all played in Saturday leagues, meaning I could continue going along to San Siro on Sundays. But then, on my return after the summer holidays, I received a surprise phone call from Daniele, a colleague I'd played alongside in a couple of office friendlies. "I was counting on you to join our team next season. We have a friendly this Sunday, so why don't you come along? I can't promise you a game, but at least you'll get to meet everybody."

A team that plays on Sundays? Might not get a game? Sounded like a bad blind date to me. But as the Serie A season hadn't yet begun, I saw no harm in going along just the once. And three days later I took a train out to the northern suburbs of Milan, where Daniele was waiting to drive me to the nearby community of Cascina del Sole.

"Robert, meet Federico, il Presidente."

President? President of what?

"Of Solese – you know, your new football club."

A little football club like this with a president? Now there was something to write home about. In the changing rooms I was briefly presented to the other players, as well as Piero, the formidable-looking *mister* (coach). He took one look at the supermarket bag in which I'd brought my boots and towel and immediately handed me the number 16 shirt – you couldn't get much further down the batting order than that.

Piero's team-talk went on for ages. This was, he said, *una partita importantissima*, a very important game, since today's opponents, none other than local arch rivals Bollatese from the division above, would provide just the test we needed before the season proper began. He then talked technical for fifteen minutes about the system we would be adopting. This was much more in-depth than the let's-play-it-simple kind of stuff I'd been used to back in England, as each player received detailed instructions on everything from how to kick a ball to where to stand at corners. I grasped none of it, of course, and gulped at the seriousness of it all.

I was glad to get out and warm up, and was comforted to see that the pitch was only marginally better than the ones I'd played on in Sheffield. Maybe this lot weren't that good after all. But after going back inside for the last formalities, and Piero's final words of encouragement (*Dai! Forza ragazzi! Andiamo!*), I followed the other lads to a different pitch, probably the greenest, best rolled, most beautiful football pitch I have ever had the privilege to walk across – Rotherham United's included!

A lot of people were milling about at this time, and I noticed that Federico, il Presidente, was collecting money. It was only when I took my seat in the dug-out that I realised what was going on. These people were actually paying to stand in the little *tribuna* (terrace) opposite. The last time I had performed in front of a crowd was in my final season in Sheffield, when I played in the heady heights of the Sunday league's premier division. But that had been just the once, for the big local derby, and even then there was no question of anybody actually paying to watch it. To me, people forking out three thousand lire (£1.25) to watch any team I was involved with – and in a pre-season friendly at that – was insanity itself, and a perfect illustration of the excessive importance given to football by Italians. I mean, didn't they have anything better to do with their Sunday afternoons? The answer, for a hundred or so of the male population of Cascina del Sole, was evidently no.

Solese kicked off and for the first ten minutes played the ball around without their opponents managing a single touch. The very simple reason for this was that no player from either team had yet left his own half. Just like in Serie A. There weren't going to be many goals at this rate, I thought, and I'd certainly chosen the wrong country in which to score my first ever hat-trick!

Bollatese eventually made their superiority count, scoring either side of half-time. The standard looked pretty good – too good for me – with plenty of passing along the deck and the emphasis on possession football. With twenty minutes to go, I had already decided what I would be saying to Daniele afterwards – that no grazie, I'd be keeping my Milan season ticket after all – when Piero, clearly deciding that the game was lost anyway, glanced along the bench.

"Robert, *preparati!*"

Gulp. I was coming on. Worse still, he wanted me to play on the left of midfield, which meant running up and down right in front of the paying public, still in vociferous mood despite the adverse scoreline. For once in my life bungy-jumping looked a doddle.

I was overawed. It didn't help that it was a scorching hot day, and that I hadn't played for two months. My opposite number sold me the same dummy three times in succession, and each time I happily bought it. I sensed what everyone must be thinking, that the Englishman with the testa rossa wasn't much good at all.

I waited an eternity for my first touch. When it came, I thought what the hell, the next fifteen minutes are the last this lot will ever see of me, put my head in the position it had occupied throughout the previous twenty-five years – face down – and left the rest to my legs. An opponent immediately came sliding in from the right, and I was pleasantly surprised to see that the trusty old right-foot-left-foot ball shift came off just as well in little villages in northern Italy as it had done all those years before in the back lanes of Low Fell. Hey, this wasn't as difficult as it looked!

I was never very receptive to team-mates' shouts of "pass the ball!" at the best of times, but today I had good reason: I was too taken in by the roars of delight coming from the stand a few yards away to my left. This really got the adrenalin pumping, and before I knew it I'd dribbled all the way to the penalty-area. That's when my body remembered just how long it was since I'd last kicked a ball, and just as I was about to collapse from exhaustion someone pushed me in the back. Pheep! Penalty! Two-one!

I have trouble believing those professional footballers who claim to be oblivious to crowd noise once the game gets underway, since the oohs and ahs that accompanied that opening effort all but knocked my head off. Love was definitely in the air, and from then on every time the ball was played down my side I could hear them cooing in anticipation. They had good right to be all worked up, too, for despite the hesitant start those next fifteen minutes of football turned out to be the finest, most exhilarating fifteen minutes I ever played. It was almost embarrassing the way every dribble, every pass, every audacious flick came off, and each time the crowd went mad.

In the very last minute, I set off on my umpteenth twist-and-turn, again was pushed over, this time just outside the box. Free-kick. The taker coolly slid the ball to the right of the wall, and there I was to turn and hit it first time under the 'keeper's body.

Did I say one hundred people? The racket the crowd made when that net rippled made it seem more like one hundred thousand, and their celebrations continued until well after the match was over. But the very moment I emerged from the changing rooms it all went very quiet. I felt like Mahatma Gandhi as the supporters stared in admiration before moving aside to let me through. Accompanying me was my very proud new coach, Piero, who insisted on driving his new star back to the station. It was just as we were climbing into his car that someone finally broke the silence: *Eh! Piero! Anche noi abbiamo lo straniero adesso*! Hey! Piero! Now we too have our very own *straniero*!

I confess that people don't often ask me what was the high point of my football career, but that must have been it, at the very moment on that late September afternoon when, for the community of Cascina del Sole, Robert Rowell became *lo straniero*. If only Jonnie Wales could have been there to see it.

Still revelling in the adulation, I squeezed my enlarged head onto the half-empty train knowing that there was no way I could keep the Milan season ticket now. The people of Cascina del Sole simply wouldn't let me. Anyway, they'd given me a bright green, brand new sports bag to replace my carrier, so I couldn't let them down now.

It took the hustle and bustle of Milan's Cadorna railway station to snap me out of my reverie. Cascina in Wonderland suddenly seemed like a million miles away, and I felt scared. Scared because I was convinced my dream quarter of an hour had been nothing more than a fluke. And although my outer layers were still beaming with pride and satisfaction, deep down inside I knew it could never last.

Solese 2   Bollatese 2

Solese vs. Longtaimago
Cascina del Sole, near Milan
October 1984

Early Fall

The official Italian league was a pyramid system run by the Federazione Italiana Giuoco Calcio, or F.I.G.C. At the top of the pile was Serie A, with Juventus, Milan and company, followed by Serie B, Serie C1 (north and south), Serie C2 (split into four regions), Inter-regionale (twelve), Promozione, Prima Categoria, Seconda Categoria, and finally Terza Categoria. The further down the pyramid, the more regionalised it became, so that Solese, which was in the Seconda Categoria, played all of its matches against teams in the northern suburbs of Milan.

The chances of some day bridging the six divisions between Solese and Juventus might have been pretty remote, but you wouldn't have thought so from the club's ultra-professional approach. We trained two evenings a week (and by "trained" I mean *trained*, not once around the block and off for a pint), and on match days we all had to be at the ground an hour before kick-off – there was no question of turning up last-minute the way we did in Sheffield. Whilst Italians are not normally associated with good time-keeping and organisation, when it came to football, everything was handled with uncharacteristic precision, and this from Serie A all the way down to the Terza Categoria. Other than Mussolini's trains, the only things that ever ran on time in Italy were football matches.

Solese not only had a president and a coach, we also had our very own physiotherapist, not to mention countless *dirigenti* (directors) who met in a little office down the end and whose roles I never really understood. The most important job of all, which ensured the club's continued survival, was that of sponsor, a position held by none other than good old Federico, president and turnstile attendant.

Whether Federico's considerable financial involvement was made possible by his day-job as village doctor was no concern of mine. I mention this because in Italy, the medical profession fell into that nod's-as-good-as-a-wink category of people who paid income taxes under the PHEW system – Pay Heef Ewe Weesh. This was simply because most small value sales and services, from eating pizza to obtaining a sick note, were paid for in cash or favours that the taxman never got wind of. One dentist acquaintance of mine, who not only extracted teeth from my mouth with no sign of a receipt (nor anaesthetic, come to think of it), wasn't even qualified to do so in the first place. And who could blame him for taking my thirty thousand lire under the table? In Italy, handing money over to the Government was like pouring water on sand – you never saw it again. And the election to parliament of former footballers and porn stars only emphasised the people's total *menefreghismo* (couldn't care less attitude) towards anything Rome tried to impose on them, from the wearing of seat-belts to owning up to your true earnings. As someone once put it, "in Italy, under the law, everything is permitted, especially that which is prohibited," and this universal lack of trust in the powers that be explains why Italy is such a nation of everyone-for-himself (and his family, and his friends) law-benders – admittedly the warmest, friendliest, most jovial law-benders in the world, but law-benders all the same.

Federico seemed to foot the bill for everything: club sports bag, tracksuit, even boots. We received travel expenses, and wages in the form of the occasional pizza and pint after training, or maybe some item of clothing that had fallen off the back of a *camion*. I even discovered that our centre-half had cost the club a million in transfer fees – lire that is – not to mention a couple of dreadful own goals early on in the season.

My popularity grew by the week. This wasn't down to my match-day performances, quite the contrary. I didn't play in any of the opening league games, since we were still waiting for the F.I.G.C. to obtain clearance from the football authorities back home over my disciplinary record. In that time Solese didn't pick up a single point, and my absence only served to make local hearts grow all the fonder. I'd played just fifteen (albeit fabulous) minutes in a pre-season friendly, and here I was being built up as some sort of messiah. Not only that, the whole of north Milan seemed to know who I was. When I went to buy new boots in a town five stops up the line, for example, the owner of the shop picked up on my English accent and immediately said, "Ah, you must be *lo straniero*. They say you are *buono*".

Never having so much as fouled anyone in my whole life – never mind been booked or sent off – just before training one Thursday night Piero pulled me aside to break the good news, that the club had at last received the go-ahead from the F.I.G.C. The Sunday following, he said, I was to make my league debut.

I might have stood half a chance had Piero left it at that, but then he went on for half an hour about how, after a string of defeats, he was counting on me to single-handedly change the team's fortunes. Goodness, I wasn't used to carrying the world on my shoulders. Worse still, in parting he casually dropped a huge bombshell: I shouldn't dribble so much, he said.

Non dribblare troppo! In the cold light of day, I was the first to admit that I should learn to pass the ball more often, but in the heat of the action you don't think about all that, you revert to back-lane basic instincts. Asking me to cut down on that part of my game was like telling our 'keeper not to use his hands. But I was in no position to argue with il mister, and I promised myself that when the day of reckoning came, I would carry out his instructions.

For the first Saturday evening in my entire adult life I didn't go out and get sloshed. Instead I stayed home, cleaned my boots (another first), watched television and what I ate, avoided sex (no problem there), and was in bed before midnight. After all, this was the big one, il Campionato. I'd even gone out and bought a bathrobe and flip-flops for the occasion.

We met up in the Bar Cesare for coffee before the game, and immediately I sensed all eyes and whispers upon me. Today, they all seemed to be saying, was the day of lo straniero. I was already a bundle of nerves as it was, but the poop factor hit maximum when I reached the ground. There, the shouts of encouragement from the supporters brought home just how much their local team meant to them, and how they were expecting me in particular to wipe out weeks' worth of sorrow in just one afternoon.

The pre-match routine was all very organised, almost military, no larking about. Piero gave us one of his marathon briefings, then we were all taken outside for a lengthy work-out, and when we were sufficiently knackered they called us back in for the referee's roll-call. The linesmen checked our studs to ensure that they were legal, and just as we were leaving Piero pulled me aside to remind me, just in case I'd forgotten, that dribbling was out of bounds today. We formed two lines with our opponents, the match officials trotted us out to the centre circle, and there we stood to attention in a long line facing the crowd, waiting for the referee to blow his whistle, toss his coin and get on with it. The team formations were even announced over the loudspeaker (the first time my name had been called out in public since I'd gone astray at the Town Moor fair as a kid), and about all that was missing were the national anthems. Then, finally, we kicked off.

I was pathetic. Or, as Piero put it afterwards, *in crisi*. Whether it was the pressure of being lo straniero, the restrictions imposed on my natural game, or simply me being crappy old me, every time I received the ball I thought back to what Piero had said, and passed it – straight to one of our opponents. Piero himself spent the full ninety minutes playing "Simon Says" from the dug-out ("Robert, move ten yards forward! Robert, move left a bit! Robert, do this! Robert do that!"). He, no doubt, knew what he was talking about, but I didn't have a clue. The tribuna was silent throughout, no doubt stunned by just how badly I was playing. In the end I felt like going over to say sorry guys, this is the real me you're seeing. The acting's over, *E finita la comedia*. But by then they'd long since given up on me and gone home.

Some of you are probably thinking, this Robert Rowell bloke must have achieved something in his football career to have written a book about it. You probably put the Longtaimago disaster down to debut jitters – as indeed did everyone else at the time – and can't wait to read about how I recovered to lead Solese to promotion to the Prima Categoria, before saying goodbye in order to join one of the big *Serie A* clubs.

If that's the case, go no further. I wasn't to know it at the time, but at twenty-five years old the high point of my career was already behind me. Longtaimago wasn't debut jitters, it was the start of a rich vein of bad form. In fact, about the only commendable performance I gave over the next weeks was when I was the only one of our players *not* to join in the lynching of an opposing stopper who'd punched our centre-half in the nose. I watched in horror as they set upon him like dogs, forcing him to leave the field with blood pouring from a head-wound. All this while some of our supporters – normally calm, middle-aged men with whom I'd drunk espresso before the game – bayed for more and tried to rip down the fencing so that they could get at him. Anyone who thought that football hooliganism was a uniquely British disease never attended a match at Cascina del Sole.

Piero was eventually *esonerato*, a nice way of saying that he was given the chop, and the new coach, Sergio, quickly moved me from left-half to left out. The only controversy surrounding his decision was why it had taken so long, but it looked like it wasn't going to matter much anyway; at about the same time I received an offer for a job that, if accepted, would take me away from Milan and Solese. It was the right thing to do, careerwise and moneywise, but I hesitated. For despite everything, despite no longer being an automatic first-team choice, despite being crap, I felt very much at home at Solese. My straniero status may have long since fizzled out, but the people continued to be extraordinarily friendly, and many a late Sunday afternoon was spent at our captain Paolo's house, feasting on his mother's delicious *brasato e polenta*. But then one evening at training a cheeky young brat put the ball through my legs, and that was enough to sway it. It was time to move on.

Solese 0 Longtaimago 1

Nottingham Forest vs. Newcastle United
City Ground, Nottingham
1 January, 1988

Balmy

If I told you I played in the side that won an Italian final in 1996, would you believe me?

Well, it's true, but football had nothing to do with it. A six-man team from our company fought off a hundred or so other challengers to win a national business management game. The prize was a flight to the destination of our choice. Half the lads sold their tickets and used the money to install double-glazing, the other half flew to Brazil.

I found Rio de Janeiro to be just like Geordieside: wide, open beaches, a party atmosphere and lovely, genuine people all looking to steal your watch at night.

And of course football matches going on everywhere. Don't get me wrong, the Statue of Christ and Sugar Loaf Mountain were both worthwhile visits, but the tourist attraction I looked forward to most was the display of forty-yard banana shots at the Estadio Maracanã, the world's biggest stadium. I couldn't wait.

I should have kept my saliva to myself. The Maracanã itself was in worse nick than Rome's Colosseum. What's more, for what was supposed to be an important cup game (Vasco da Gama versus International), there hardly seemed to be anyone there, the only evidence of local support coming from the steady pounding of a distant drum. Despite the whole ground being draped in Coca-

Cola advertisements, I couldn't for the life of me find anyone willing to sell me a bottle of the stuff. And in the huge, empty urinals I was able to take a fifty-yard walk while having a pee. This was all no doubt something to do with my having chosen to sit downstairs in the expensive seats (by expensive I mean no more than a couple of quid), which none of the people from the *favelas* could afford. The only other spectators in my section were a handful of ugly European men, all in the spectacular company of beautifully-tanned young ladies – the nice thing about Brazilian prostitutes was that they didn't just make you feel extraordinarily handsome, they were willing to do the most perverse things imaginable, like watching you get all excited over a football match.

As for the game, after an hour and a half of wondering when the players were going to stop warming up and get on with it, the referee blew his whistle and everyone started heading for the exits. In all that time the closest we'd been to a banana shot was a lame effort late on, that deflected into the net off someone's head, thus saving us from thirty minutes of extra yawning. The playing surface didn't help matters, mind you. Its bounce was straight from the Sheffield Sunday League, and the grass so long that the ball went missing for whole minutes at a time.

The next day I wandered over to the beach from our Copacabana hotel to see whether the standard of football was any better down there, and it wasn't long before I was getting stuck in with the natives. Although playing in bare feet on the soft sand was like trying to run in a bad dream, I was soon into my stride, and were it not for the milky-white skin and shouts of "haway, gerrit in the box man", I could well have been mistaken for a Brazilian myself. I still didn't come across anything approaching a banana shot, though, and in the end it was me who ended up impressing the locals, showing them how to head the ball like a proper Geordie (Robert de Niro chin-pull, Jimmy Connors grunt, and a generous serving of T-H-U-M-P).

I was left wondering what all the fuss was about. I mean, whatever had become of all those great Brazilian footballers? The answer was that they'd left for the rich and fertile continent of Europe. Most were playing in my own back yard in Italy, and one, Mirandinha, had only recently got on the wrong plane and ended up at Newcastle United! So when a month later I was back in Rio de Gateshead for the Christmas holidays, I travelled to the away game in Nottingham in search of that elusive banana shot.

Had it not been for the puzzled looks every time one of his team-mates yelled at him, you could have been forgiven for wondering who the boy from Brazil really was. Not that Mirandinha had a bad game or anything. It's just that he and all the reputed great players in the Forest side were totally eclipsed by a young rascal in the United midfield whose name I'd barely heard before: Paul Gascoigne.

Poor Neil Webb. The Forest and England star had no doubt expected to be the class midfield act on show that day – it's true he was a very, very good player – but it wasn't long before "Gazza" (as the world was to come to love and to hate him) was making him look as overweight as he and his contract later became. The just-who-the-bloody-hell-is-this expressions on the faces of Webb and the other Forest players reminded me of my favourite film of the time, Amadeus, in which the composer Salieri is suddenly confronted with his own depressing mediocrity after being upstaged by a hitherto unknown upstart called Mozart.

We were all Salieris that day, watching from the shadows as Gazza gave his solo, virtuoso performance beneath the floodlights. Gazza it was who curled one into the bottom corner in the first half (that banana shot at last!), and Gazza it was who put Mirandinha clear to seal our victory late on.

At San Siro, I thought I'd seen them all. I was wrong. Gazza was more awesome than anything I'd ever witnessed on the professional stage, the complete Jonnie Wales. The things he could do to a ball made the Kama Sutra look positively missionary, but what really made him a delight to watch was his sheer bloody cheek. He would take time to smile when others barely had time to breathe, and at one stage late in the game, right down below us, he stuck out his tongue and let out a great, Mozart-like belly-laugh after slipping the ball through a gasping opponent's legs. Even the referee looked as if he was enjoying it.

And that was the last I ever saw of him in the black-and-white stripes. Life in football is too short, and loyalty to a going-nowhere club like Newcastle is something only the silliest of fans still believe in. No reasonable-thinking person could really blame him, then, when the following summer he moved to Tottenham. Gazza's planetary movements have been well documented since his early days. His extraordinary gifts have at times taken him very high (Italia '90 World Cup, the Spurs Arsenal semi-final, the goal against Scotland at Euro '96), but his always wanting the ball so that he could show off has sometimes taken him very, very low (who can forget his appalling challenge on Forest's Gary Charles in the 1991 Cup Final?).

The then England manager Bobby Robson described Gazza as being "daft as a brush". Certainly his little numbers off the field were soon being talked about as much as his little numbers on it, and it was only a matter of time before his world-famous weaknesses for alcohol and chocolate would catch up with him. He'd be on the back pages one week as Wolfgang Amadeus Mozart, and front page headlines the next after Wolfing Down A Madness In Mars Bars. So much so that in later years he often looked more like one of his several-bellied mates than a professional footballer.

Doesn't matter. Such good and bad extremes are so often the price of genius. And to me, that's what Gazza was – a football genius. Which is why, in every game he ever figures, somehow he will always be the main attraction. Never was this more evident than on his return to Saint James' Park in what was just his second game for Tottenham, at the beginning of the 1988-89 season. The "betrayed" Newcastle fans marked the occasion by buying Geordieside out of Mars bars, hurling them at the lad when he showed up wearing the "wrong" colours.

Which is pretty much what the world has been doing ever since – hurling stuff at him. The Gazza-bashing wagon jumps for joy every time his self-destruct button goes off, and its passengers tut-tut in unison at his renowned inability to string two sentences together in "proper English". While not wishing to condone the more infamous of Gazza's antics, to them I say get lost the lot of you. For a start I know a good many people who couldn't string two passes together, so surely it's horses for courses. Second, the next time you sit back to enjoy a spot of classical music, just remember that the very Mozart now playing exquisite one-twos off your living room walls was no nine-til-fiver either. That when he wasn't writing music for our benefit, he too was belching in public or out on the town getting into all sorts of Gazza-like trouble. Certainly, had the Sun and Daily Mirror existed two hundred years ago, no doubt Mozart would have filled their pages. And who knows, maybe two hundred years from now football fans will still be enjoying video classics like Gazza – The Complete Nutmegs, while all the footballing Salieris of the twentieth century will have long since been reduced to one-liners in the A-Z of Football. In the meantime, let he who hath not sinned cast the first Mars bar.

Nottingham Forest 0   Newcastle United 2

Bar Sport vs. Rovinata
Lecco, northern Italy
9 April, 1988

Blue Moon

All the world's a football pitch,
And all of its people merely players…

In March 1972, the satellite Pioneer F was shot up into the heavens, its destination Jupiter, Pluto, and the back of beyond. On its side was a gold-covered aluminium plaque containing several inscribed messages about our planet, in the event an alien intelligence should some day cross its path. These included a map of how to get to Earth, a diagram of the composition of the hydrogen atom, and a naked man and woman waving "Hi".

…16 years later…

Earth-date: 9 April, 1988. Earth-time: two-thirty-ish. On a park football pitch in the town of Lecco on the south-eastern tip of Lake Como, a profusely sweating, baldy-headed Englishman was making a late dash into his opponents' penalty-box for a corner, twenty-five minutes into the first leg of the quarter-final of the CSI regional playoffs.

If you wanted to be rude, you could say that Bar Sport was the Italian equivalent of a pub team. We didn't have our own ground, we didn't have paying supporters (in fact we didn't have *any* supporters), we trained just once a week, and very strangely (I debated long and hard before admitting this one to you), the games lasted only sixty minutes. Otherwise we had the usual contingent of coach, president, directors, and of course a sponsor – not a doctor this time, but the Bar Sport, hence the name.

It was the first time in my life that I'd played for a "successful" team – by which I mean a team that won more games than it lost – and I was enjoying my football immensely. I had established myself as the *mediano*, a sort of defence-minded midfield general à la David Batty – in other words a midfielder who is hopeless anywhere near goal. The highs and lows that made up the unsteady heartbeat of my youth were pretty much behind me, and the wily, Liam Brady-type runs were but one a match. I passed the ball without having to be screamed at, and generally did what was asked. I wasn't brilliant, I wasn't terrible, just consistently "not bad".

Surprising then that the local rag, the Giornale di Lecco, should glowingly describe me as the team's "catalyst". Surprising too, as Mimmo stepped back in readiness to take the corner, that our coach Guido should shout across for me to go up for it. Who, me? Go up for a corner? But I hadn't scored a header in fifteen years!

At this stage, you are probably wondering what all of this has got to do with satellites being sent up into space. Actually, I'm not totally sure myself. But imagine for a moment that somewhere out in the Milky Way an alien spacecraft did at some point during the last thirty years come across Pioneer F. Now put yourself in the moon-boots of those aboard. After all those light years away from home – let's be honest – would you be interested in pictures of hydrogen atoms? Of course not. No, the first question on your mind is going to be whether these Earthlings have discovered football. Judging from the plaque at least, you would be forced to conclude that there was absolutely no sign that we had, and that this Earth place wasn't worth the detour.

What alien civilisations will perhaps never know is that our world is broadly made up of two types of people: those who eat, breathe and dream football…and the Americans. Bad news for UFO-spotters, it was this last lot who sent

Pioneer F up into space in the first place. Had it been the Russians or anyone else, the man on the plaque would have been kicking a ball, and the woman would have been, well, clapping as he did so. Surely this image alone would have had the little green men groping around for their telescopes. Even from far out in space they would have been able to see that planet Earth was literally covered in the identically-arranged patterns of circles and rectangles that are Man's messages to the gods. Not only that, closer inspection would have revealed that these ancient battle-grounds were still in use, that games were going on all over the place, that football was in fact the world game. And nowadays our skies would probably be full of Unidentified Football Observers – our team could certainly have done with a few supporters!

What makes football so popular all over the universe that, given accurate details of kick-off times, little green men in flying saucers would be all too willing to make a several million light year detour just to come and watch? What is it about this simple game that, as a child, made me and most other kids prefer dreaming of some day lifting the F.A. Cup to say, winning the gold medal in the Olympic rifle-shooting? And what is so special about the scoring of a point in football that is capable of sending normally sane earthlings into outer space in under a second?

According to Football and Art 1860-1960, what we have to understand is that "the nocturnal and sometimes transgressive images of football can be found in the Dadaist movement, German expressionism and pop art. The football player remains one of the emblematic figures of the twentieth century, enshrining a particular notion of modernity, theatrical performance and the redefinition of the self." Hmm. I must admit, that wasn't what I had in mind when I went up for that corner. No, football's much simpler than that. For a start, one of the game's great attractions is that unless you're a total donkey, anyone can have a go; you don't need the sort of growth disorder that produces basketball players and jockeys, nor the brain disorder that makes you want to have your face punched in for twelve rounds. Nor do you need a fat neck (rugby), fat belly (darts), fat wallet (polo), or fat just-about-everything (sumo wrestling). Nope, football is just you, your regulation-size mates, and a regulation-size ball.

But hold on, I hear you protest, you could say all those things about, say, handball, so what's the big deal? The answer to that question surely lies in football's unique use of the foot (or rather non-use of the hands), in order to move the ball around. For if kicking a ball takes just a few seconds to learn, it takes many a misspent youth to master, and in between it flies all over the place. This feature alone is what makes the business of moving the ball from defence to midfield, from midfield to attack, and from attack into goal such a tricky and yet intriguing process (unless you're watching Sunderland, of course). It accounts for all the ooh-ing and ah-ing that goes on at football matches, at every chance created, at every chance squandered, and explains why, in turn, we all go instantly and absolutely raving bonkers when the ball does, miraculously, end up in the back of that net.

Just imagine. Even the top strikers only get to score a "point", on average, about once every hundred minutes or so. No wonder then that so many of them feel no shame in rating the ejaculation that goes with scoring on a Saturday afternoon alongside the one that follows scoring on a Saturday night. As Italian striker Fabrizio Ravanelli put it, "Scoring is an extraordinary feeling. Only those who have got goals can understand what I'm talking about. You feel exhausted afterwards, just as you would after the other type of orgasm."

Others may mock, Fabrizio, but I know what you are talking about; on that day in Lecco when the little green men didn't turn up, I was the lucky one who somehow managed to get his head to Mimmo's corner, and at that gorgeous, heart-pounding sight of net bulging, for an instant I forgot I worked in the financial planning department of Black & Decker Italia, and spent the next ten seconds acting instead like I was the greatest footballer on Earth. It didn't much matter that when I ran over to the touchline, arms aloft and adrenalin pumping, I met with nothing but the confused look of a stray dog that happened to be passing by at the time. I couldn't have been happier had I been Alan Shearer scoring in the F.A. Cup Final.

If it is the rarity of goals in football that makes their scoring the cause for major celebration, I ought to briefly mention the difference goal-nets make to heightening the climax of the scoring moment. As anyone who has ever scored a goal will tell you, there is an immense thrill in seeing your top-corner effort thunder into that netting that you simply don't get when the ball just goes bouncing off, plop plop plop, down the hill. Not only that, everybody in the ground, from the scorer himself to the man sitting in row Z, sees the net swell at precisely the same instant, so we are all overcome, all at the same time, by this uncontrollable urge to jump up and down on the backs of complete strangers.

It is ironic that the very scarcity of points in football is what puts most Americans off the game altogether. Try telling them that there is such a thing as an exciting nil-nil draw and they will look at you as if you were a little green man from outer space. Whether it be points, cookies or plus-size garments, what they want is quantity, not quality. There again, they are not generally renowned as a highly-cultured nation – perhaps this is all the proof we need that football really is the greatest sport in the universe.

After the near-suffocation that comes with all your team-mates piling on top of you, my celebrations ended with a fifty-yard dash down the touchline for a series of give-me fives with the coach and substitutes, just stopping in time to avoid a give-me-a-kick-in-the-bollocks from those sitting on our opponents' bench. Having finally regained my place for the kick-off, still glowing at the shouts of "Bravo, Robert!" echoing in my red hot ears, I had difficulty containing a smile as I imagined the post-match pats on the back, the phone calls home to the folks, the gloating Sunday. Indeed so taken up was I in my own glorious exhaustion that an Unidentified Football Observer could have been hovering just ten feet above my head and I wouldn't have noticed a thing. But it wasn't, of course. And those little green men will never know what they were missing.

Bar Sport 1   Rovinata 0

Alfreton Town vs. Nottingham Forest
Alfreton, Derbyshire
August 1989

Cloud Breaks

In terms of the narrow age gap and a penchant for smashing up your Subbuteo players, our Steven was more like a younger brother than a nephew. He lived just opposite us at the top of Beaconsfield Avenue, and his flipping mother made sure he got to join in just about everything we ever did. On Saturday mornings, for example, Dad, John and I would often set off to the pitches down the Team Valley Trading Estate for a kick-about, and just as we'd be prizing open the Skoda door, our Audrey would pop her head out of number 30 and shout across: "Robert! John! Don't forget to take Steven with you!" What was worse, Steven's dad Brian would usually insist on coming as well – he was just as big a nuisance as Steven, since he couldn't kick a ball to save his life.

Our games always followed the same routine. Dad obliged by going in goal, John and I blasted shots at him until those sixty-year-old hands of his were dropping off, and Steven stood there, crying for a kick. Now and again we'd roll it his way, nice and soft so as not to knock him over. "No, not with your hands...bring your leg back... that's it! C-l-e-v-e-r b-o-y!" Then we'd get back to the more serious business of hand-blasting, and a few minutes later we'd have to give Brian a kick as well, just to stop *his* crying.

I left for Sheffield when Steven was just six, so it was John who suffered the brunt of his big-uncle-worshipping activities. But whenever I came home during the holidays, we always managed at least one kick-about, and each time I noticed that Steven's football skills were coming on rather more quickly than expected. "Don't pick it up" soon gave way to "don't kick it too hard", then it was "keep your elbows to yourself, you little git!", and it wasn't long before *we* were the ones begging for kicks.

When a scout from Nottingham Forest called Bill Emery came along to watch Steven play for the school team (the same school, incidentally, that both Jonnie Wales and Gazza had been to), and saw enough in the first half to not bother staying for the second, our delight was surpassed only by our surprise. OK, so Steven was a bit useful, and certainly he knew how to barge us off the ball, but surely he wasn't that good! I mean, this wasn't just any old Nottingham Forest, it was Brian Clough's Nottingham Forest, winners of two European Cup Finals!

When you're steeped in football the way we are, and your son, or nephew, or even third cousin, signs a YTS contract for Nottingham Forest, in an instant you have a new family hero. For sure, mine and John's passing exams and making decent livings from behind desks received lots of "we're-not-sure-what-you-do-exactly-but-well-done-anyway" type compliments, but Steven's just getting a trial with a professional football club paled all of our achievements into insignificance. We could have been Prime Minister and Chancellor of the Exchequer for all Dad cared; down the Key Club he wasn't boasting about us any more, it was all Steven.

The one person in the entire family who slightly resented Steven's new star status (though she was as proud as punch all the same) was his little sister Alison. And no wonder. Whenever we heard her familiar rat-a-tat-tat at the front door, John or I would shout out jokingly, "Sorry, you can't come in here unless you're a footballer!". With Steven about, we couldn't give two hoots about her getting her sums right or playing for the school netball team, what we wanted to know was what it was like to spend the whole day training with the Neil Webbs, Stuart Pearces and Franz Carrs of this world. Poor Alison. With confidence-boosting uncles like John and me around, her parents had a hard time preventing her from hanging herself from the light-fittings.

As well as preventing Steven's head from becoming too heavy for the rest of his body, John and I absolutely idolised him and his new environment. When we went to see the Forest-Newcastle match, for example, the day was memorable not only for the Great Gazza, but for the behind-the-scenes tour Steven gave us before the match. There, deep in the bowels of Nottingham Forest Football Club, John and I were like big kids in the lap of Santa Claus. John! Look! Steven's talking to Franz Carr! Hold on a sec! He's answering back! Franz Carr! Talking to our Steven! Bloody magic! And we nearly fainted from all the excitement.

To be honest, that day I was half hoping Brian Clough himself would come up to me and say something along the lines of, "Now then young man, I've heard you can play a bit, what do you say to coming along and giving it a go?" If only I'd given Steven a few more touches of the ball when he was a toddler, I could have boasted of having taught him everything he knew. But it was too late for all that now. Realistically, other than the one where you gather hockle in your gob and spit it out sideways – John and I were first division in that department – Steven had got none of his tricks off us. Not that it mattered, of course. Steven's success was our success, and when he had the cheek to waltz into the depressed Nottingham Forest dressing room after the Newcastle match, lifting his tracksuit top to reveal the true (black-and-white) colours of his youth, I thought, aye aye aye, if he's not working in a sausage factory by the end of next week, we could be onto something here.

Being away in Italy, I mostly learned of Steven's subsequent progress through his mother's tension-filled letters. I still have them, and they are a testimony of the ups and downs that a budding young footballer and his anxious parents go through on the rocky road to maybe-land:

"...Bill Emery tells us Steven is playing well for the youth team...

...we've heard nothing, so it's looking like they are going to release him...

...great news! Steven signed as an apprentice last week...

...I'm afraid the news is very bad, Robert – THE LEG'S BROKEN..."

Yet somehow Forest kept faith, Steven soldiered on, and my chance to finally see him play came just a week before his eighteenth birthday. Admittedly, the pre-season friendly between Forest's ninth team and Alfreton Town of the HFS Loans League wasn't the sort of match you'd normally even drive across Alfreton to watch, never mind travel the one hundred and fifty miles from Gateshead to Derbyshire, but you know me well enough by now to understand that I wouldn't have missed it for the world.

The game started well, and I must say I was quite impressed by Steven's technique and the way he controlled the midfield - he'd certainly come on a bit since the days when he used to shove us off the ball down the trader! Alfreton, though, had this lad who looked and played a bit like former Wimbeldon hard-man Vinnie Jones (the locals even nicknamed him "Vinnie"), and the way he was getting stuck in made me fear for a few budding careers. After about fifteen minutes there was this mass scramble for the ball just down below the tiny stand where we all sat, and when the ball finally emerged and the players untangled themselves, I looked round to see where Steven had got to.

I didn't have to look far. He was sitting all alone, just a few yards away, clutching his leg and grimacing at the pain. Vinnie had got him. My uncle-istic instincts made me want to go across and cuddle him the way we used to when he was a baby, and I struggled not to cry. Then, from somewhere behind me came a shout of, "Get up yer big pansy, you're not on telly now!" I felt sick. Steven heard it, we all heard it, but this was clearly one tackle he wouldn't be getting up from. I knew our Steven wouldn't fake injury, and in any case you always know when a player is really hurt, as it's the one time he doesn't roll back and forth across the deck as if he were on fire. If only I'd seen which idiot had shouted at him like that, I would have gone up and given him what for:

"Hey! You! That's my nephew you're screaming at!"

"Oh yeah? And what are you going to do about it then?"

"Oh, nothing, I just thought you might like to know his middle name is Brian."

Archie Gemmill, Forest Juniors' coach at the time, wandered across from the dug-out, sprayed Steven's leg and told him to get on with it – oh, the wonders of medical science in modern British football! Both he and the idiot behind me must have felt like right wellies when the ambulance pulled up. I was right, Steven hadn't been faking it, he'd broken his frigging leg.

I waved at a lonely-looking Steven as they carted him off in the back of the ambulance, then stood alone for a while in an empty Alfreton side street, wondering about his career. He'd had no luck, the poor lad. This was his second leg-break in two years, in exactly the same place as the first. To be fair to Vinnie, Steven said afterwards that it had been a fifty-fifty tackle, with no malice intended, but that wasn't going to mend his leg any quicker. So the next day, to raise Steven's spirits I went to pick him up at his digs and drove him and his crutches over to Sheffield, where I was planning to have a few beers with my old mate Robbo.

In the pub, everyone gathered around and listened with great interest, for this was their chance to talk to a real footballer. They weren't at all bothered about how Steven's leg was doing, though. No, what they wanted to know was what his legendary manager, Brian Clough, was like in real life (pretty much the belligerent, enigmatic, unpredictable bloke he was on television was Steven's answer, just for the record). Drinks were bought all round, and in no time at all Steven was back to his cheerful old self.

We arrived back at Robbo's three hours later in a slightly more joyful state than when we had left. To add to the merriment, Steven and I then discovered that we would be sharing the double bed in the guest bedroom. If this alone had us giggling, the trouble we then had getting Steven's tracksuit bottoms off over his plaster cast had us in stitches. As we chortled away, I tugged ever so gently at his tracksuit leg, but it wouldn't come, so I tugged a little harder, then harder still, finally jerking his leg up and down in one last desperate attempt to dislodge the bloody thing. It was all so comical that my raucous laughter completely drowned out our Steven's own shrieks.

Only Steven's shrieks hadn't been of the laughter variety at all. What probably saved his leg – and his career – was my collapsing in a stupor while still tugging away at his tracksuit bottoms. My last recollection before finally passing out was of the expression of speechless agony that had taken over his whole face, that told me maybe he hadn't been having the time of his life after all. Sure enough, when I woke up the next morning, Steven was looking me straight in the eye. "Uncle Robert, that's the worst pain I have ever felt."

"What? Vinnie breaking your leg?"

"No, you trying to get my tracksuit bottoms off!"

I just lay there, feeling guilty and hung over, and thought about how rocky a road it is for all those young lads who give up everything in order to have a go at becoming professional footballers. And I thought of all those jealous people, like the nutcase at Alfreton who shouted "get up yer big pansy, you're not on telly now", who resent the success and begrudge the salaries of top footballers, and who simply cannot begin to imagine what it takes to get there. All the sacrifice. All the pitfalls. The one-in-a-thousand chance of making it. The risk of suffering a major injury before you even come close to getting on the telly. Not to mention perhaps the biggest hazard of them all – career-threatening uncles like me.

Alfreton Town 0 Nottingham Forest 2
(just for the record)

England vs. West Germany
Abbadia Lariana, Lake Como, Italy
4 July, 1990

Italian Summer

Never was there more fitting a world cup tune than *Notti Magiche* ("Magical Nights"). From the moment all those gorgeous girls came on during the opening ceremony, Italia '90 was one glorious, captivating celebration of the beautiful game, a real *festa di calcio*: restaurant terraces full of smiling people tucking into their pizzas; deliciously warm Italian evenings; and of course acute tension, which built up to hands-over-the-eyes levels as the tournament reached its climax – even the earth stopped spinning for Italia '90.

Having been part of the Italian football scene for seven years, mentally I felt well-prepared for the whole occasion. But even *my* jaw dropped several feet the first time I emerged from a tower of steps to enter the new, three-tier colossus that was Milan's San Siro. What a stadium! Its rebuilding may have cost several times the original budget to complete (Italia '90 was a one-off opportunity for the few to screw the millions), but it was worth every last lira, it was that magnificent. It made even the most impressive of the English grounds – Old Trafford, Highbury, even Wembley – look like bus shelters in comparison.

Months before the first ball was kicked, I had bought a number of season tickets for the games to be played in Milan, thus enabling half my family to come across and watch. At first I was both proud and delighted to have my folks there for the world's foremost soccer tournament, but the Italians have a saying, "Guests are like fish, after three days they start to smell", and a couple of weeks with our lot was enough to drive me up the wall. It's not that I minded acting as interpreter all the time, even if it was a bit of a pain translating some of the rubbish they came out with ("Robert, tell the waiter he's a greasy dago, just for a bit carry-on"); and I could even handle the chaos that went with sharing my one-bedroom apartment with five other people, since I was at the office most of the time anyway. No, what really got on my nerves, and indeed all of our nerves, was that at the end of their two-week holiday England were still in the competition. Or, more precisely, still in the competition but playing crap. So by the time Cameroon were beating us two-one mid-way through the second half of the quarter-final (and running us off the park into the bargain), it had us all but grabbing at the nearest throat and squeezing it very hard.

That's when I cracked. With twenty minutes of the match remaining I stormed out and took myself off to the nearby lakeside. There the only disturbance to the dead quiet was a car jumping up and down on the spot with its windows steamed up – a young couple *in camporella*. Otherwise it was the ideal place to prepare myself psychologically for England's inevitable exit and the blood all over the floor when I got back. My heartbeat back to below a hundred, I returned home to face the music, saw through the patio doors that Dad was frantically rubbing his legs up and down, and knew immediately that Gary Lineker was in the process of pulling off one of his miracles. The next day, thankfully, my folks went home. And the England team stayed.

The Italians themselves were, as always, extremely pessimistic about their national team's chances. And, as always, they made it quite clear that anything other than winning the competition would result in a mass public lynching of coach and players. The team looked as though it could just about go all the way, too, with notably Roberto

Baggio turning on the class, and Toto Schillaci – the new Paolo Rossi – knocking in a goal a game.

Italy's games were however unwatchable. Not due to their style of play – quite the contrary – but because they were commented on by the most powerful, most annoying, most biased man in Italy: RAI Television's Bruno Pizzul. Never since Mussolini had a man been capable of brainwashing the nation the way Pizzul did. He shouted "Penalty!" every time an Italian player went down in the box, and when it wasn't given you were treated to twenty different replays of the "foul" in question – each clearly showing that the Italian player had cleverly jammed a leg between those of his opponent before taking a dive – and Pizzul, blinded by his love of the national team, would gravely give his verdict: an *errore clamoroso* (amazing blunder) by the referee. Five minutes later, Franco Baresi would all but rip off the shirt of the opposing centre-forward, and cool as you like Pizzul would comment on the purity of the tackle. It had me all but kicking the television over.

Just how powerful Pizzul was became clear the next morning, when try as I might, I found there was no point in reasoning with my colleagues. Every time I disputed Pizzul's wisdom they simply gave me the kind of look normally reserved for antichrists, and in the end the only way to avoid such impossibly stressful days at the office was to phone in saying I was sick. Sick to death of Bruno Pizzul.

If Pizzul was an expert at twisting national feeling this way and that, there was little he could do when, ten minutes from the end of the first semi-final, Argentina's Claudio Caniggia just managed to get his head to the ball before Walter Zenga, the advancing Italian goalkeeper, and all of a sudden it was nestling in the back of his country's empty net. The instant silence that immediately fell upon Pizzul and his sixty million fellow countrymen was such that, from where I was sitting at a friend's house in Como, you could have heard a noodle drop in deepest Sicily. One hour later, after extra time and penalties, the unthinkable had happened: Italy were out.

Possibly the most useful tip I ever picked up in Italy was that in order to avoid traffic jams, the best time to drive is when the Italians are eating, watching a football match or in mourning. So while I drove straight back to my apartment, the empty roads made me realise just how much it all meant to them, and I felt genuinely sad for all those close friends now sobbing in their bathrooms. But at the same time I was greatly relieved. All along I had dreaded the thought of England meeting Italy in the final, for win or lose my life thereafter would have been intolerable.

West Germany, England's semi-final opponents, had a really strong team, ploughing through their opponents like tanks through fields of daisies. Judging from the quantities of beer their travelling fans were knocking back on my local campsite, it was clear early on that they knew they were going to have something to celebrate.

I too was drinking heavily, but for different reasons: to help me overcome our inevitable exit. All I remember of our semi-final is the Germans smashing penalties about Peter Shilton's ears (was I really that drunk, or did Shilton fall over every time as if he'd been paid to let them in?), and Stuart Pearce and Chris Waddle missing theirs (for years later, Pearce's dressing room nickname would be "Germany"). Bloody Germans. We were certainly paying a heavy price for the "goal that never was" in 1966, and it came as no consolation when my Italian colleagues went out of their way to say how England-West Germany had been the most entertaining game of the tournament. I knew fine well that they were taking the Pizzul, for deep down they didn't think much of English football, what with our kick-and-rush style and our hooligans. I also knew that the only time they ever found nice things to say about us was when we were beaten – they'd been equally magnanimous the day after we lost to Maradona's hand (and left foot) of God in 1986. Personally, I would have much preferred winning the final with the whole world hating our guts.

The way the Germans did. They went on to beat the Argentinians in possibly the worst final of all time, in which the South Americans spent the whole match rolling across the floor, while their European opponents played pass-back-to-the-keeper (which, incredible as it may now seem, was allowed in those days). It was such an unfitting finale to what had been, despite England's semi-final exit, a wonderful, topsy-turvy festival of football: Cameroon had beaten Argentina, Argentina had beaten Italy, Italy had beaten England, and England had beaten Cameroon.

And good old West Germany had beaten them all. As Gary Lineker once put it, "Football is a simple game: twenty-two men chase a ball for ninety minutes and, at the end, the Germans win"

England 1   West Germany 1
(after extra time; West Germany won 4-3 on penalties)

Poletti & Lanfranconi vs. Bar Sport
Mosana, Lake Como, Italy
3 October 1990

Limelight

> *El lâch de Com l'è cume un om*
> *Un pè a Lecch e un pè a Com*
> *El cô a Dumâs e i cujun a Belâs*
> *(Lake Como is shaped like a man,*
> *One foot at Lecco, the other foot at Como,*
> *Its head at Domaso, its balls at Bellagio)*

Abbadia Lariana is a little village of three thousand inhabitants on the eastern shore of Lake Como. A site of outstanding natural beauty, it is there that I moved when the change in job forced me away from the fog and hubbub of Milan. Whichever window of my apartment I looked out from, the views were breathtaking: to the front was the tranquillity of the lake set against deep green hills; out back was *La Grignetta*, "Little Grigna", a mountain small by local standards but nevertheless twice the size of Snowdon; and off to the right were the Alps and Switzerland, three minutes by helicopter, three days by car.

The people of Abbadia were among the nicest people you could ever wish to meet. They were also among the oddest-looking, for very few had arms and legs where the rest of us have them. I couldn't work this out until one thoroughly exciting Saturday afternoon I decided to do a bit of tourism and visit the local cemetery, high up in the hills overlooking the village. Now it is customary in Italy to stick a photo of the deceased on his tombstone – presumably so that we can remember how ugly he was when he was alive – and the first thing I noticed was that the local peculiarity of three-fingered hands and an arm growing from the forehead wasn't just a recent evolutionary development, it had been like that for years (if I told you where the other arm was you wouldn't believe me). One other thing that struck me was that as few as three surnames accounted for ninety-five per cent of the dead population. It didn't take major brain -surgery to conclude that before they'd started cutting roads and railways into the steep rock face, Abbadia Lariana must have been so inaccessible that the three families who lived there had had no choice but to keep giving it to each other, generation after generation ("I'll marry your sister if you'll marry mine"). The result of all those centuries of inter-breeding was today's Daleks.

Then there was the language problem. I'd sweated long and hard to master Italian during my time in Milan, but up on Lake Como many people spoke in a dialect I'd never previously known existed, a curious mixture of Italian, French, German, and Mountain Goat. It was also disappearing fast. My mate Giuseppe, for example, is one of the last generation able to speak both dialect and Italian, and by the time his grandchildren come along the dialect will have disappeared for ever. This is a pity, not because I believe in preserving old languages just for the sake of it, but because of its entertainment value; little rhymes like the one at the beginning of this chapter, the learning of which brought me local acceptance and helped break the ice at parties.

Or would have done had there been any parties to go to. In moving to Abbadia I became a boring old fart overnight. I said goodbye to nights out with the lads, goodbye to going everywhere by bike (I'd just bought my first ever car, a Fiat, a sure sign that I was going downhill); and, more importantly, I said goodbye to my chances of ever getting fixed up with an Italian woman – well into my mid-twenties, by local standards I was already way over the hill, since the single ambition of every girl from the Italian sticks was to get paired off in her teens. All I was left with were the Daleks, and the Daleks were left with me.

I didn't know a soul in the early days, and other than the occasional trip to the cemetery, I spent the best part of my weekends gazing at the lake from my armchair, dozing off, gazing at the lake again, and so on until Monday morning came to the rescue. Six months went by without my kicking a ball, going to the cinema, or even just laughing. All the sitting and gazing started to take its toll on my physical appearance, too, so much so that one morning I looked in the mirror to find that not only had my neck muscles disappeared, but my head was beginning to merge with the right shoulder. For fear of ending up in Abbadia cemetery with a photograph showing an arm sticking out of my forehead, I decided it was time I got up off my backside.

It was Giuseppe who saved me from the Daleks. He started by inviting me to his house for Sunday lunch and the wonderful cuisine of his lovely wife, Paula. Then he introduced me to the coach of his local football team, and I knew immediately that my lake-gazing days were over.

One of the great joys of football in Italy is that, other than the month of August when everybody rushes off to the beach, it's an all-year-round sport. There is practically no such thing as the "close season". This is possibly because the Italians are very fortunate not to have cricket. I did try explaining the rules once or twice, but all those bats, balls and bails confused the life out of them, and they had a particularly hard time grasping the precise role of the *stupidello mediano avanzato* (silly mid-on). Their take-out of all my explanations and gestures was invariably something along the lines of "seems like a stupid game, no?" – which I suppose showed they'd at least got the gist of it!

Even for us minor league players there was no let-up. The final whistle that signalled the end of the last game of the season had hardly been blown when the phone started ringing, and with it invitations to play in the hundreds of five-a-side tournaments that were about to take place in the *oratori* (church playgrounds) of the villages scattered around Lake Como.

The nice thing about these competitions was that they were open to all levels. One evening you might find yourself being given the run-around by players from as high a level as Inter-regionale standard, and that was when you realised just how crap a player you really were. These guys out-dribbled, out-tackled and out-ran us, and refused to shoot at goal unless it was on the volley from thirty yards, preferably from next to the corner-flag to make it extra difficult. Then the next day you would come across a motley bunch and you knew immediately the points were in the bag from the thick glasses, boxer shorts and Hush Puppies – and that's just what they played in! These were lads who stopped play to point at passing aeroplanes, had considerably more spots than friends, and almost invariably worked in computer departments.

The Billy Elliots disappeared early on under a barrage of goals, leaving the more serious teams to battle it out over the next weeks. Tensions were often high, but all in all the mood was good. Goals were celebrated by high fives (or in the case of the players from Abbadia, high threes), and the friendly atmosphere was helped by the large and generally non-partisan crowds who turned up to watch – at Abbadia, which staged one of the better tournaments, sometimes they'd be standing as much as three deep along the touchline.

The only problem with the five-a-sides was that they seriously interfered with my evening routine of calling in at a local restaurant for a five-course meal after work. Sometimes the game you were due to play in wouldn't start until well after ten o'clock, so it wasn't unusual to start tucking into your first of three pizzas at around midnight. One tournament where I made an exception to this play-first-eat-later rule, however, was the one my pal Luca invited me to, in his home village of Verano Brianza. It's not that I intended to eat and drink myself stupid before playing, but

Luca's mother – Signora Pina – gave you no other option. It has to be said that her cooking was the meaning of life itself, and the delicious aromas coming from her kitchen just about sucked you into the place. But it is equally true that there should have been a government health warning outside their home, since from the moment you crossed its doorstep there was no let-up. Before you knew it your legs had found their own way under the table, and a combination of cold meats and red wine (both from the family farm in the south) were busy pulverising your taste buds. Then in quick succession came my favourite dish of all time, Pizzoccheri (wholemeal pasta mixed with potatoes, cabbage and melted cheese), a main course (yes, you read that correctly), followed by cheese and coffee. As if all of that wasn't enough to have you spewing up five minutes after kick-off, last but not least the bottle of grappa was brought out. Not good for my football, I protested half-heartedly. Good for the digestion, replied Pina convincingly, and I was only too pleased to help her force the stuff down my throat. The five-a-sides didn't quite seem so important after that.

The last tournament I ever played in in Italy turned out to be my most memorable. Yet it was a fairly low key affair by local standards, partly because it attracted none of the dream teams (the football season proper had already restarted), partly because it took place in a tiny village hidden away in the rocky hills above Lake Como. As the crow flies, Mosana couldn't have been more than a couple of miles from where I lived, but despite many an Italian's attempts to prove the contrary, Fiats don't fly, and I had to leave home at lunchtime to have any chance at all of making the early evening kick-offs. With no signposts to guide the way, it was only after guessing the correct lakeside turn-off, then zigzagging up a seemingly never-ending series of one-in-three climbs, that I finally made it. Welcome to Mosana – twinned with Hillbillybuggery, Montana. Or something like that.

With the streets designed to take nothing wider than a *Cinquecento,* I abandoned my car and went in search of the ground. It wasn't long before I came across a group of locals, whose bowls of fruit for faces made the people of Abbadia Lariana look positively multi-ethnic. They stopped grunting at each other in order to concentrate their stares on the new arrival – as if I was the one sporting a strawberry in place of a nose – and I knew that I'd better play my cards pretty accurately if I didn't want to end up in a field with my trousers down. I'll find the ground all by myself, thank you very much.

The mini-football pitch was right next to the village church, and had literally been carved out of the mountain. The lower touchline was a ten-foot high fence, this to prevent the players from falling to their certain deaths in Lake Como half a mile below; and the upper touchline wasn't a touchline at all, but an eight-foot high wall on which the spectators sat to watch the game, and from where they were able to swing kicks at your head as you were flying down the wing.

We easily made it through to the final, and there, funnily enough, we came across a team of lads from my very own Bar Sport. We were one-nil down at half-time, and had been severely under the cosh, so it was all over bar the grunting. Knowing as I then did that I would soon be leaving Italy, it was looking increasingly likely that I would be doing so having won nothing at all in seven and a half years. But at the start of the second half I managed to bag a couple of goals, and it was (literally) backs to the wall after that. In the last seconds, Bar Sport scored what looked to be a perfectly valid equaliser, but somehow the referee, instead of choosing to end the evening in front of the telly with his wife, opted instead to spend it in the next field with his trousers down. He disallowed the goal for a handball that only he had seen, then, with our opponents waiting to rip into him like lions to a zebra, spent the last seconds of the match standing next to the exit, before quickly peeping at his whistle and running for it. The photo of the missing referee was in the Giornale di Lecco for weeks after.

If I was disappointed not to win the trophy for

"Tournament Best Player", I was however delighted to learn afterwards that someone had recorded the whole match on video. At last, I thought, I would have something to show the grandchildren, to back up all those lies about how great a footballer I was when I was a lad. On it would be the two goals, of course, but just as important was the "up and over". This was a trick I'd been practising in my front garden for ages, but had never before dared try in a competitive match. It basically involves starting out with the ball between your ankles, then sending it in a loop over yours and the heads of your astonished opponent, and collecting it on the drop while he picks himself up from the floor. If it comes off, which it did to perfection that night, you are so chuffed you really don't give a damn how the rest of the game pans out, and the grunts of appreciation from the wall were a sure sign that the people of Mosana had never seen anything like it. Even Jonnie Wales's grandkids would have been impressed.

Many years after leaving Italy, I came home from work one evening to find Dad "the VHS maestro" in very enthusiastic mood. "Come and have a look at this, man, I've taped it for you." As always when Dad was excited about showing me something, I feigned total disinterest, as any self-respecting son would, before going off to fetch a beer from the fridge. Then, just I was leaving the room, I casually asked, "By the way, Dad, which tape did you use?"

"Oh, I just took one of yours."

"Yes, but which one?"

Guess. Thanks Dad. My grandchildren will never believe me now.

Poletti & Lanfranconi 2   Bar Sport 1

Hail-Stone

Why on earth, after seven and a half years in what is still my favourite country, did I leave Italy? Was it because I'd begun to take a dangerous interest in Italian pop music and wanted to get out before it was too late? Or because the girls in the accounts department no longer laughed at my monkey impressions? Naaaaaa. The fact of the matter is, I didn't so much give up Italy as grab a hold of France, the country of my boyhood dreams. France was in my blood. France was my destiny. France was la crème de la crème. As Dad put it, "Ye can't get tomatoes like that in Gateshead, man!"

Italy wasn't going to be an easy act to follow, though. Especially if the comments of the French teacher of a friend of mine were anything to go by. He said, "French is a beautiful language, and France is a beautiful country. But the French are shit."

Now most British people would no doubt wholeheartedly agree with that statement. There again, they would also agree that the average Frenchman wears a beret, rides a bike and smells of garlic. So from the very moment I climbed into the taxi at Paris Charles de Gaulle airport on the day of my first interview, I decided I was going to put these ancient prejudices to bed.

My first inkling that France wasn't everything I'd built it up to be came within seconds of jumping into the cab.

Having been in a Milanese taxi just a couple of hours before, what immediately struck me was that whereas the Italians drove their cars aggressively in order to win some sort of an imaginary race, these motorists did so because they were basically out to kill each other. Incredible but true, more people die on those beautifully-kept French roads than on the grubby Italian equivalent. This image of a nation of psychopaths was further reinforced when I got out at probably the world's most dangerous roundabout, the Place de l'Etoile. There I almost got myself killed when mistaking some black and white stripes stretched across the road for a zebra crossing (it was in fact a Voluntary Euthanasia Zone). Mon Dieu! I'd come to admire the Arc de Triomphe, not put my name on the Tomb of the Unknown Pedestrian! Welcome to the country of human rights. Liberté, Egalité, Get out the way!

Paris is definitely not for the faint-hearted. Newcomers, unsuspecting tourists, pregnant women, the old and the weak, they all suffer like crazy. They find themselves apologising to taxi-drivers for asking to be taken somewhere that will cost less than ten quid; being attacked by shop-owners for daring to enter their boutique, or by waiters for requesting the inclusion of a smile in the standard fifteen per cent service charge – say what you like about the Americans, but I much prefer the not-so-sincere, have-a-nice-day of the Californians to the highly sincere, what-le-Fouquet-do-you-want? of your average Parisian shopkeeper. It seemed that about the only time the Parisians turned on the charm was when they were after something, like sex or your parking spot.

Good old English chauvinism working its way through the pores? Well, let me tell you this: my job brought me into frequent contact with just about every European trait you can think of, from the Spaniard's ability to laugh as long as it is not at himself, to the Scandinavian's inability to laugh under any circumstances. Yet, be they gangly and ruddy like the Dutch (pity their wives) or podgy and hairy like the Portuguese (pity their husbands), they were all somehow endearing for what they were. I therefore feel able to state quite categorically that your regular Parisian is one of the most temperamental, unfathomable human beings you are ever likely to come across: be careful how you say bonjour, and don't forget to kiss him at least twice a day, otherwise he will feel unloved. What a contrast to the universally friendly, no-nonsense Italians!

Was living in Paris really all that bad? Of course not. Few would disagree that it is one of the most beautiful cities in the world, and if one good thing came out of all the surrounding hostility, it bashed off a few of my rougher edges. Sophistication-wise, after six years by a golden lake I had some catching up to do. The white socks that had been all the rage in Abbadia Lariana for the previous fifty years had to go for a start. But unquestionably the rudest awakening came on my first visit to a Parisian unisex salon. Apart from being greeted by a puzzled *Oui?* when I walked in (as if you could do other things at the barber's than simply have your hair cut, like buy a baguette or book a theatre ticket), I was then told that despite having washed each one of my four hairs individually that very morning, for reasons of hygiene they were obliged to wash them all again.

Now I'd never in my life had my hair washed at a hairdresser's, so when the girl said *installez-vous* before going off to see to another client, for a moment I was stumped. There before me stood a row of wash-basins, and just in front of that a line of what looked to me like raised prayer cushions. *Que faire?* Then I remembered how I used to wash my hair (when I had hair) in my pigsty of a bedsit in Sheffield – bending forwards over the basin and dipping my head in and out – and simply assumed that in Paris it must be the same thing, only here they gave you something to rest your knees on. Confidently, then, I moved into position and waited. And waited. And waited. Then my back started to ache a little and with it came the sneaky feeling that there was something not quite right about sticking my derrière out like that in a public place. I mean, what if she were to take advantage and stroke my thigh? I was just beginning to wonder whether there wasn't a more suitable approach when there came a sudden shriek from behind…

"*Monsieur*! What are you doing?" Never have I felt like such an uncultured tosser in my whole life. I meekly turned round to sit the way I should have been sitting from the off, then spent the next half-hour watching on, bright red, as the girl's face muscles struggled to contain her howls of delight at the mere thought of telling her mates when she got home.

Paris was also an eye-opener on the matter of sex. The French are refreshingly open and liberal about it, unlike – in their minds, at least – the no sex please, I haven't had six pints and a curry yet, British. They are astounded by the holier-than-thou manner in which our gutter press hounds public figures for hints of homosexual, adulterous or otherwise non-missionary behaviour. In France, having a mistress, for example, is considered no worse than having two cars. Indeed it is such a customary practice for the President to have one (or two, or three) that nobody bats an eyelid.

Another nice thing is that not only do French women love to be flirted with, there isn't the same risk of being looked at as if you had a cabbage patch up your nose that used to greet my rare chat-up attempts in England. My boss recounted how a former female prime minister (and possibly the country's first case of mad cow) once famously accused British men of all being homosexuals, since they never turn their heads to admire a passing woman. I politely explained that apart from the fact that the lady in question had a face like a badly baked croissant, we British are a discreet race – we only turn our heads when the woman has safely passed – but the French simply dismiss this as typically English, *faux-cul* (false-arse) behaviour.

Now. Leave Paris aside as I did one day, then wipe the slate clean of everything I have just said about the French. That's right. Wipe it clean. For if it is true that an essay on the merits of the average Parisian wouldn't get past the title, in coming across people from *la province* I realised that the

French teacher had got it wrong. Not all French people were shit after all. Indeed the real French and the real France are why so many of us – me included – become unashamed francophiles. Paris is not France, and France is not Paris. Other than sharing the same civil rights of going through red lights and smoking in non-smoking areas, they might as well be two separate countries. Which is strange, when you think that most of those living in the capital actually originate from the provinces. The thing is they, like me – well-meaning Crocodile Dundees all of us – arrived in Paris full of good intentions about being ourselves, smiling on the metro for today is a beautiful day, and saying polite things like "hello" to people living in the same building – in other words acting in exactly the opposite manner to all those around us. It's just a matter of time (three days, to be exact) before we are all sucked under the great Parisian wheel, and our relaxed, quaint, country ways are thrown out with the white socks, in exchange for a Marie Antoinette attitude towards all those peasants we left behind. Our job it is to sit in offices with fat salaries, theirs it is to produce wine and foie gras for our consumption. And if they don't like it let them eat cake. Or storm a refinery. Or block the motorways.

This Parisian sense of superiority, not just versus the rest of France but the world in general, is evident in the huge numbers of *tricolore* flags that seem to be flying everywhere, in celebration of the one or two half-decent moments in the country's history. And yet under this nose-up, *maîtres du monde* exterior lies a growing sense of inferiority. For deep down the powers that be are actually scared stiff. Scared that their whole culture is in danger of disappearing under a mountain of McDonald's hamburgers, which more and more of their kids are (perhaps understandably) preferring to snails. Frightened silly to see that the snorting, inflexible, ancient tongue that is the French language is each day being further invaded by its anglo-saxon enemy. Incredible but true, a three hundred and sixty-odd year old organisation called the Académie Française spends ridiculous amounts of energy trying to make it illegal for football commentators (for example) to use words like "penalty" and "corner" instead of their three-times-as-long French equivalent. Get it wrong and it's off with your head.

Whether the word "pudding" comes from the French *boudin* or vice versa, whether Cheddar is tastier than Roquefort, whether the Brits drove on the left before the French drove on the right, these were all potential bones of contention that brought many a Parisian dinner party to near blows, and which were totally pointless subjects into the bargain. For one thing remains absolutely clear: despite the very few miles of water that separate the "frogs" from the "rosbifs," the huge divide in our cultures and customs will take millenniums to bridge. They will never figure out why we put vinegar on our chips, nor why we spend so little time eating them, this despite my efforts to explain that, apart from the fact that British food is on the whole terrible, we have better things to do with our time, like waiting patiently in queues and being polite to each other – practices completely foreign to the true Parisian.

One subject on which there is growing Anglo-French concorde, at least, is in the superiority of the English Premier League over its French equivalent – if only because it is the best French players who have crossed the Channel to make it that way! To me, watching French league football was like watching a doornail die. And the French on the whole probably agreed; at the start of the nineties, other than a handful of clubs headed by Chris Waddle's Olympique de Marseille, if you pulled together all those who went to watch the weekend's other league matches you could just about fit them into Saint James' Park. So with the Alps no longer in the way of the radio waves, and Sir John Hall and Kevin Keegan in the process of rescuing Newcastle from the brink of eternal oblivion, this was a pretty good time to become a fervent Magpie again, as well as reconnect with English football generally.

Every Saturday afternoon, then, while other equally lonely people train-spotted or visited cemeteries, I drove my swish, black company Audi up to the vast Parc de Saint-Cloud, whose dominating position over Paris offered the best place from which to pick up BBC Radio Five's Saturday afternoon football programme. The trouble was, as high up as the Parc de Saint-Cloud might be, the reception wasn't always that good, and often, just when I thought I'd found a Radio Five friendly spot and could at last put my feet up on the dashboard, all of a sudden the sound would begin to fade. And I'd have to switch the engine back on, then drive slowly around the park in search of the lost voices of Alan Green and Mike Ingham.

Parks such as this were the nearest most Parisians ever came to the countryside, and on weekends the place was swarming with little kids running after fresh air, stopping occasionally to ask what that green thing over there was. Now imagine for a moment what must have been going on in the minds of watching mothers as along strolled this black Audi, its windows all steamed up from the wicked mixture of zzzziiiiipps, doiiiinggggggs and whooopppppeees coming from inside.

"*Maman*, what's that black thing over there?" A dirty old kerb-crawler! *Attention*!

Not so old if you don't mind. Ah well, at least I had the park to myself now.

This brain-debilitating, football-following routine continued into Sunday morning, when I would nip down to the Place de la Porte de Saint-Cloud (a huge square next to the Parc des Princes stadium) to buy the Sunday papers. After double-parking like everyone else, I aimed straight for the news kiosk, oblivious of the events around me. Beggars, oyster-sellers, mothers pushing their babies, people queuing up for their baguettes, they were all bustled aside, for I was a man with a mission. I always bought the same three newspapers, the Sunday Times, the Corriere della Sera, and the Journal du Dimanche, this to impress onlookers that I was a right clever bugger who spoke three languages. In reality, the French newspaper remained untouched, and the picture of someone lying on the ground in a pool of blood was enough to put anyone off looking inside the Italian paper at that time of morning. Even the thick wad of paper that was the Sunday Times contained far too few pictures for someone like me to take an interest in, and the only reason I bought it in the first place was for its excellent sports section.

Newspapers in hand, I raced off to the nearby Brasserie les Fontaines, found a quiet place where I could spread out Times Sport in front of me, nodded bonjour to the little old lady sitting tied to her dog opposite, ordered a *grand café crème et un croissant, s'il vous plaît*, and got stuck in. With so much football to take in, like a kid sitting down to fish fingers, chips and ice cream, I just didn't know where to start. It would be an hour before, good time over, I pulled up my flies, paid up and sneaked out. In that time I'd have studied all sorts of the most irrelevant information imaginable, like the exact time of Bristol City's goal in their one-one draw at Preston, and how many watched East Fife go top of the third division in Scotland. I would get so lost in my own little world that once I even managed to set the newspaper alight, in the flame of a candle some stupid waiter had put on my table.

Now it so happened that this particular weekend Newcastle weren't playing until the Sunday, so on the Saturday afternoon I left the kids of the Parc de Saint-Cloud in peace and visited cemeteries instead. I nevertheless kept up my Sunday morning rendezvous with the little old lady at the Brasserie les Fontaines, sent the waiter off for the traditional coffee and croissant, laid the Sunday Times sports section out in front of me, and let my eyes do the walking.

With our Steven still at Forest, and despite it looking as if he'd never get beyond the reserves, after Newcastle they were the team I took the most interest in. My eyes instinctively found their way to the Premier League section, and fell upon :

Middlesbrough (0) 1	Nottingham Forest (0) 2
Phillips 61	Clough 60, Stone 69
	Att. 15,639

What's that? Stone 69? My heart raced.

I blinked and tried again.

Stone 69! Stone 69!

Yes! Yeeeeessssss! Yeeeeeeeeessssssssssssssssss!

My arms punched the air, tears streamed uncontrollably down my cheeks, and the little old lady nearly filled her bloomers.

"Excusez-moi madame! It's my nephew! Steve Stone! Vous connaissez? He's finally made his debut! Not only that, he's gone and scored the winner! C'est incroyable!"

Yes! Yeeeeessssss! Yeeeeeeeeessssssssssssssssss!

The next thing I remember is not so much driving as floating across Paris, windows rolled down, singing *Stevie Stevie bang-bang we love you*. The only time I came back down to earth was to buy a newspaper stand out of its entire English stock, and on every inside back page there he was, my little nephew, arms aloft and a big smile across his face as he ran to the crowd shouting Yeeeeeeeeessssssssssssssssss!

The story goes that Brian Clough didn't tell Steven he was playing until the team coach was well on its way to Middlesbrough on the Saturday morning. Thanks to a quick call through to his mother on a borrowed mobile, a few hours later half of Gateshead had made the forty-mile trip to Middlesbrough to see him make his first full appearance, get his first touch and score his first goal, a diving, glancing header from just inside the area. After the game, his proud granddad – my Dad – sighed that he could now die happily. He didn't of course – he went to the Black Horse to celebrate instead – but I knew exactly what he meant. You see, to us it didn't matter whether Steven would ever make another appearance. As far as our football-daft family was concerned, he'd fulfilled our wildest Roy of the Rovers dreams. He'd played alongside greats like Roy Keane and Stuart Pearce. He'd scored the winner. He'd been on telly. Most importantly, he'd showed he was up to it. "Playing confidently," said the Sunday Times. "Yet another Brian Clough wonderkid," said The Sun on Monday. And so on. In short, he'd made it.

I have had some golden moments in my life. Passing exams, falling in love, being there when my kids popped out, that kind of thing. But I feel no shame at all in admitting that the greatest moment of them all was when I read "Stone 69". In fact I couldn't have been happier had I scored the goal myself. Anyway, I did score it. Our John scored it. The whole family scored it. All my mates, Bri Dixon, Robbo, Paul, Geoff, Simon, Giuseppe, Luca, Cesare, Ivan, Charlie, Mark, John, Nicola, Fatboy, Alvyn, they scored it. And then there were all those other people whom Steven had never met nor heard of, yet who, whenever I spoke to them on the phone, always asked how he was getting on at Forest before asking how I was doing myself: they all scored it.

It took me an hour to get into work the next day. My angry, obnoxious fellow Parisians were up to their usual tricks, hooting and tooting and huffing and puffing and generally trying to get me into a fight; but to their consternation one after the other I just kept letting them in. And smiling. For today I was unquestionably the happiest man in the world, and no Parisian, however psychopathic, was going to take that away from me.

Yes! Yeeeeesssss! Yeeeeeeeessssssssssssssssss!

Middlesbrough 1   Nottingham Forest 2

Footballers vs. Accountants
Nottingham, England
22 August, 1994

Grey Day For Some

Millions of kids dream of playing in the Premiership. But with just one vacancy for every five thousand applicants, most end up having to look for another activity to pay the bills instead. Take me. When I was a lad I had football on the brain. Never in my wildest nightmares did I imagine that some day my black and white stripes would be of the pin-striped variety, yet look at me now! A chartered accountant!

When you compare "a day at the office" of the professional accountant with that of the professional footballer, it's easy to see why I originally set my heart on the latter. John Cleese was dead right in portraying accountants as grey and boring, and surely it is highly unlikely that we will ever pick up the Sunday Times to read about Mr. Debit balancing his books in front of a forty thousand crowd. When accountants become famous it is usually for the wrong reasons (remember Cecil Parkinson?), yet every housewife in the country knows who David Beckham is. That's because football is a glamorous sport played by glamorous people who get off with glamorous women like Posh Spice.

But just how glamorous is it? Having had the opportunity to observe the life of one professional footballer from pretty close in, I have discovered that maybe it's not quite as wonderful as it's made out to be. That being a grey old accountant does have its perks. As an example, take a typical match-day viewed through the eyes of both Robert Henry Rowell, chartered accountant, and Steven Brian Stone, professional footballer. The occasion is Nottingham Forest's first home game of the 1994-95 season, against none other than Manchester United – and they don't come more glamorous than that.

A match-day in the life of Robert Henry Rowell, Chartered Accountant

I travel up to Nottingham from London on the eve of the match (I always try to organise my meetings in London around Forest fixtures, that way the company ends up subsidising my trip – clever, eh?), and we all go out for a few beers to the local pub. The only person not out enjoying himself is our Steven. That's because he isn't allowed to touch alcohol during the forty-eight hours before a game, and in any case he has to be in bed by ten.

There are about six of us squatting at Steven's house, so we make sure we are extra careful not to wake him up when we come home, quietly finishing the evening off with a few cans from the fridge. Judith – that's Steven's missus – is the first to retire, and we can tell from all the laughing coming from their bedroom that Steven must have been awake all along. He had probably been reading. It's nice to see he's so relaxed ahead of the big game.

Since it's an evening kick-off, I have all of match day to chat to Steven about football. I quiz him about what's going on at Forest, dressing room gossip, that sort of thing. Mind you, it's not easy keeping up with him! He's constantly on the move, keeping his limbs supple. I note that he also spends a lot of time in the loo. Hah! Got a touch of the runs, have we? It's only natural, I suppose. After all, they *are* playing Manchester United.

After another Steven-less session at the pub at lunchtime, I grab one of the last remaining cans from the fridge – Steven won't mind, he's a professional footballer so he can afford it – and pour Steven an orange juice. He's looking a bit off-colour, so I do my perfect uncle bit, helping him concentrate on the game ahead by going through the strengths of the United players, Giggs, Hughes, Ince and Kanchelskis. To raise his self-belief, I convince him that Man. United are crap, that their finishing champions the season before was a pure fluke. I think this does the trick because all of a sudden he takes on a really mean look. If I didn't know our Steven I swear I'd be scared stiff. He's up for it now allright!

Job done, I reward myself with another can while Steven goes out to the garden to loosen up, and that's the last we see of him before setting off. The great thing about Steven is, despite all the success, he's still such a considerate lad. For example, he's bought this car the size of a bus so that he can take us all to the ground. Good job, too, since we're probably over the limit anyway! Mind you, Steven's driving sobers you up in no time. I spend the whole journey concentrating on the road, pointing out hazards he hasn't seen. Ah, these young'uns nowadays, they've no sense!

As we approach the City Ground, the traffic intensifies so we say our "have a good games" and jump out. Steven's mam then remembers she's forgotten something, and shouts after him, "Don't forget to look for space, son!" That's our Audrey for you, always full of useful little tips like that. Should have been a manager if you ask me. But does he listen? Does he hell!

I break away from the others to look for a good old, rock solid cheeseburger. I tell you what, though, these Nottingham folk can be pretty thick at times. It takes me ages to convince the young lass selling hamburgers that I'm on expenses and need a receipt (I've got this French boss who'd sign a chunk of Camembert if you put it in front of him), and as for the programme-seller, the way he looks at me you'd think I was asking for a snog. Don't get me wrong, it's a thrill coming to watch Steven play and all that, but if you're not careful it can work out very expensive.

Last but not least, I nip into the supporters' shop to pick up a few photos of Steven that I must remember to have him sign later on – it's not easy, you know, what with all these requests for dedications. Then it's off to the ticket pick-up point. Steven always makes sure there are enough tickets for all of us, which is very kind of the lad, especially when he usually ends up having to pay for half of them out of his own pocket. "It's for your birthday," he always insists. Blimey, it's my birthday every week with our Steven! I know he's a professional footballer, and I know he's not short of a bob or two, but one of these days I'm going to have to put my foot down.

In the little brown envelope with the tickets is a voucher to get us into the players wives' lounge. Good lad! It's like gold, that voucher is, since the beer and sandwiches in there are all free. But when I get there, this obnoxious man wearing a Nottingham Forest blazer tells me it doesn't matter whose uncle I am, he's not letting me in without a tie. With kick-off just half an hour away, the situation is pretty desperate, but just when I'm about to storm off our Steven happens to wander past and all of a sudden it's like me and this bloke have been mates since school.

We take our seats just as the teams are coming out. Since we always sit in the same part of the ground, I have this little routine where I jump up and down, waving my arms about, and sing my favourite Newcastle songs to attract Steven's attention. A few louts sitting right behind me tell me to "siddown!" in no uncertain terms. So I do. But then Steven comes across to give us a wave and just you watch, they'll be asking for my autograph in a minute!

The game gets under way, and my eyes are like a Sky player-cam, following Steven all over the pitch. It would be great if he could score a hat-trick tonight, since I've a meeting in London tomorrow and, well, it would be great if he scored a hat-trick, that's all. As it happens, he doesn't even get on the scoresheet in the first half, and at half-time, with the score one-one (Kanchelskis and Collymore), it's back to the players' wives' lounge for some refreshment. There, while everyone else concentrates on Sky Television's Andy Gray's half-time analysis, I take the opportunity to concentrate on some of the longest, loveliest legs in Britain. Isn't it amazing how even the ugliest of footballers end up with the most gorgeous of blondes!

Steven doesn't score in the second half, either, but he plays well and I am a happy uncle. It's back to the lounge to cool off with a last drink, but the bad news is the wives have finished off all the free beer while the rest of us were out there egging on the team. Steven doesn't half take ages to get showered and dressed, but thankfully I have my calculator with me, so to pass the time I do some quick sums, just to keep the old fingers in trim.

When Steven finally surfaces, he tells us he has been voted Forest's "man of the match" by the people in the boxes opposite, so we all follow him across the now empty stadium to pick up his award. He's the centre of attention, of course, but the first thing he does is make sure someone goes off to fetch us all a drink. That's my boy! I then find myself holding his pint of lager while he is being presented with a bottle of champagne, photographed with fans, that sort of thing, and it goes on for so long that I think if I don't drink it, it will go flat. So I do.

Steven enjoys letting his hair down after the match, so once back at the house we all get dolled up to go out to the Black Ostrich nightclub. While Judith books taxis, I ask Steven if he has a shirt he can lend me, since I don't have any designer clothes with me (to tell the truth, I don't have any designer clothes full stop!). He points me towards a drawer full of his cast-offs, and since it all looks like pretty good stuff to me, I do him a favour and empty half its contents directly into my suitcase.

Steven is well-known by the bouncers, so we are ushered through without paying. Many people recognise him immediately and pat him on the back – "good game Stoney" – as we make our way upstairs. Being a few yards behind,

I overhear several girls make him some highly interesting propositions. I tell them that unfortunately Steven is unavailable, but have they ever been to Paris? They just giggle and run off. It must be this daft shirt I'm wearing.

A couple of pints of expensive lager later, it's my turn to get the drinks in, so I nip off to the toilet, and this young lad comes and stands next to me and asks, "Stoney's Dad?". What the hell, I think, and answer, "Yes, that's right, taught him everything, I did". And before I know it he's pulled out a pen and I'm scribbling "Best wishes to Darren from Steve Stone's Dad" across the palm of his hand – while accidentally peeing on his shoes. He leaves the loos without washing his hands. So, for that matter, do I.

The rest's a bit of a blur, really. Early the next morning I'm up and away before everyone else in order to catch my train to London. As we pull out of Nottingham, I look for my beloved calculator in my jacket pocket and come across the fifty photographs of Steven. Blast, I forgot to ask him to sign them! Oh, but wait a minute, he *has* signed them – if a little untidily. Funny, I can't remember him doing that. One of the photos is even dedicated to me. It says "To Uncle Robert, silly bugger." Hah! Good sense of humour, our Steven. I spend the rest of the journey counting my money and totting up all the receipts I've picked up over the previous couple of days. By the time we pull into St. Pancras I am able to conclude that two days in Nottingham and a one-all draw with Manchester United are a pretty good return on my net investment of £13.59. Ah, the accountant's lot is indeed a happy one. When's the next game, I wonder?

A match-day in the life of Steven Brian Stone, Professional Footballer

It's hell when my family and friends come to see me play. I get no peace whatsoever. On the night before the game I'll be tucked up in bed and just nodding off when they come rolling in from the pub, screaming at the tops of their voices, clattering fridge doors and unleashing ring-pulls. The next thing I know Jude comes into the bedroom and jumps on top of me, giggling her bloody head off. I try telling her from under the quilt that I've got Man. United the next day, but I might as well be talking to a brick wall.

I spend the day trying to avoid people like our Robert, who starts by promising not to talk to me about football, and then spends all day doing nothing else. He asks really stupid questions, like who's peg is next to mine in the dressing room, and whether I've ever spoken to Stuart Pearce. No of course I've never spoken to him, he only plays in the same team, doesn't he! He follows me about everywhere, and about the only safe place is the loo.

I get some peace when they all go off to the pub at lunchtime, but things get even worse in the afternoon. There I am drinking orange juice while they empty my fridge of all the lager, and they don't even have the decency to ask! Uncle Robert insists on telling me how good the Manchester United players are, one by one. Bloody hell, I know they are good, thank you very much, the last thing I need is to be reminded about it. If I was a tad apprehensive when I woke up this morning, I'm a nervous wreck now. Robert then makes a pathetic attempt to retrieve the situation by saying that Man. United are crap really and should have been relegated last year. You could have fooled me.

The way they all circle like vultures waiting for scraps of wisdom drives me crazy. The last straw comes when I'm sitting out in the back garden trying to relax, and Jude comes up and asks me to make her a cup of tea. Doesn't even she realise that I'm playing Man. United in two hours time? "Be like that then, I'll make it myself," she says before storming off in the huff. I promise myself that next time I'll stay in a hotel.

I'm due to leave for the ground when all of a sudden everyone becomes interested in a lift, so I wait a full fifteen minutes by the front door as drinks get finished, clothes get ironed, hair gets brushed and flasks of tea get prepared. I end up having to drive faster than usual to make up time, and about the only laugh I get all day is watching Uncle Robert put his foot flat down on the imaginary brake pedal – he's not used to doing more than thirty.

What happens next is unbelievable. We're just approaching the ground when Robert lowers his window and shouts, "Make way for Steve Stone, please". And in no time at all I've got half the noses of Nottingham squashed up against my car windows. We are now reduced to a snail's pace, which apparently isn't quick enough for my passengers, and they all decide to jump out and leave me on my tod. Thanks a million. My mam has forgotten something, though, so she catches up and I roll down the window to see what she wants. "Don't forget to look for space, son!" she says. With a straight face too! Bloody hell, how I made it as a professional footballer with two parents who know sod all about the game I'll never know.

I get a rollicking off the manager for turning up late. I try telling him that I've spent the last half-hour running around looking for tickets for the family, but he doesn't want to know. I've even had to fork out fifty quid to pay for some of the tickets myself, and you can bet your bottom dollar there's fifty quid I won't be seeing again. Free tickets, free beer, free phone calls, they eat me out of house and home. They must think I'm made of money.

I am just getting ready to go out for the pre-match warm-up when someone comes running up saying that a guy claiming to have taught me everything I know is trying to sneak into the wives' lounge without a tie. Uncle Robert. I'll kill him. I just about break a leg as my studs skid across the stone steps, and get there just as poor old Ted is explaining to Robert that no, his leather belt wrapped round his neck like that doesn't qualify as a tie. I smooth things over and dash downstairs again just in time for the team-talk.

I'm knackered after all the running around but once I'm out on the pitch I feel that there at least I will get some peace. I wave to the folks in the stand – you can't miss our Robert, he's the one jumping up and down like a monkey – get into position, the referee blows his whistle, a loose ball bounces in my direction, and the next thing I know I'm being kicked into the crowd with the ball. Who are we playing again? It's about time I stopped worrying about whether they all got their tickets and got on with it.

Game over, I shower quickly and dodge the reporters so that I can go and greet the family waiting for me upstairs. The box-holders have voted me best player, but the first thing my Dad says when I reach the wives' lounge is "hey, what kind of a pass do you call the one you gave Collymore in the thirty-fifth minute?" Dad's got this thing in his head that if he doesn't slate me off after every game I'll get all big-headed and go off the rails. To keep my feet on the ground, he says. He'd be after me even if I scored a hat-trick in the World Cup Final so I don't take any notice nowadays. What pass, anyway?

They all follow me across the pitch to the box-holders' lounge where I am due to pick up my man-of-the-match bottle of champagne, stopping briefly on the way so that our Robert can take an imaginary penalty at the Trent End (you'd think he'd be past that at thirty-five). Five minutes later I've finished with the photos and the autographs, and I go across to drink my first beer in three days. I can't wait, but neither by the look of him could our Robert. The greedy blighter's supped the lot!

Back home, while we are getting changed to go out to the Black Orchid, I watch on in amazement as two middle-aged men – Dad and Uncle Robert – fight over my expensive, trendy shirts. Just because I said I didn't want to be seen out with people wearing seventies gear. I search the whole house for the brand new shirt I bought last week, only to find that Robert's wearing it. Not only that, he's spilt what looks like beer down the front. Cheers, mate!

At two in the morning it's time to go home, and when I wake up our Robert (who's been curled up in a corner for the last hour), he suddenly decides that now is the time for me to sign about a hundred photographs for the benefit of his French and Italian mates. He nods off halfway through spelling out G-i-u-s-e-p-p-e, so I take one of the photos, write "To Uncle Robert, silly bugger", sign it, then slip it with the rest of the pile into his jacket pocket.

On the way home, while the others are all snoring their heads off in the back, I'll give you three guesses who is left with the job of (a) keeping the taxi-driver awake by asking him silly questions like what time he gets off his shift; and (b) forking out the thirty quid fare when we get home. Steven Brian Stone, that's who. Our Robert then has the cheek to ask the driver for a receipt.

The next morning I sit there all alone, drinking my tea in the kitchen while everyone else is still tucked up in bed with their headaches. Everyone except Uncle Robert, that is. How he managed to get up this morning I don't know. Ah well, other than a little gift he's left us in the downstairs loo, the main thing is he's gone. Which reminds me, I must open all the windows before I go into training.

What a life. It'll be relative peace now for a few days, but come the next home game they'll all be back again, drinking my beer, eating my food, carrying on where they left off. Sometimes I really wonder whether I shouldn't have gone in for something less complicated than football. Accountancy, for example. Like Uncle Robert.

Just kidding. Had you going, though.

Footballers 1,500   Accountants 100,000

France Pub Espoirs vs. Equipeforte
Rueil-Malmaison, near Paris
November 1995

Showers

> *My belly lies over the ocean*
> *My belly lies over the sea*
> *It ebbs to and fro when in motion*
> *And blots out my view when I pee*

What am I doing here? I'm cold, I'm tired, I've had a bloody hard day at work, and we're eight-nil down. What's worse, it's me who scored the eighth – the first own goal of my entire life.

It is fair to say I didn't come to Paris to improve my football. The subject didn't even come up at the interview, despite it being there in black and white on the c.v. as my one and only outside interest. And when my boss-to-be, Monsieur Lafaye, asked me what my greatest achievement was in my previous job, I didn't even have the guts to admit that it was leading the Admin. department to victory in the company tournament – it doesn't always pay to tell the truth at job interviews!

It didn't take me long to realise that the people who worked in my new line of business – advertising (or rather adver-lying) – were quite different from those of the down-to-earth factory world I had left behind. I had moved from a corporation that made drills to one that made idiots out of all of us, and it still worries me to think that a thirty second spot showing a woman's boobs hanging out is likely to influence my choice of soap powder, car, dogfood, or whatever.

My initial thought was to stick it for six months, learn the language, then move back to the real world, but it took just a few days to see that, on the contrary, this new lifestyle suited me perfectly. For although we worked hard, we chose pretty much when and where we wanted to do so. Punctuality and rigour were dirty words, meetings never started on time, if at all, and we laughed all day long. Right up my street!

My headquarters' job saw me in Madrid one day, Stockholm the next, and I could no doubt be spotted a mile off as one of your typical, travelling British businessmen. You know the type, the ones with the give-away unpressed trousers and unpolished brogues, who hate having their bags handled for fear of having to leave a tip; and who threaten their air miles on hotel staff if they don't get what they want *tooda sweet.*

My role in the company was supposedly to go around our European offices asking them to do nice, simple things like increase profits, fire people, that kind of crap. And if that didn't work I told a few jokes and did some silly impressions instead. I'm not sure I ever became an expert in international financial management, but I was really good at shirt-folding and figuring out hotel shower fittings. As a measure of the high respect in which I came to be held throughout the group, my unofficial title was "Laughing Overhead".

My best footballing years might now have been behind me, but there was no way I was going to let my early thirties do what they had done to all my other old mates and call it a *jour.* In between foreign trips I managed to fit in a couple of office friendlies, was quickly "spotted", and invited to play for France Pub, the team sponsored by the French advertising industry.

France Pub had two teams: the first team went on exotic tours and played celebrity matches in the company of former internationals like Michel Platini. The "Espoirs" (Hopefuls), on the other hand, played all their football in a Monday evening league, in Parisian suburbs that made Gateshead look like Beverley Hills, and where Platini wouldn't have been seen dead. Guess which team I ended up with.

I was now into my fourth season, and frankly wasn't enjoying my football very much. In Sheffield, the main thing that helped the Sunday footballer get out of his bed on a frosty morning was the camaraderie and pint with the lads after the game. Here there was none of that. About all the other lads knew about me was that I was "Bob" and supported Newcastle United. This was mainly because the games started so late in the evening that the few of us who were still there when the last goal was conceded were much too tired to do anything other than go straight home to bed afterwards. In four years only twice did we go out for beers. I barely knew their names.

It didn't help that we weren't very good. The turnover of players was very high – such is the fickle nature of those in the advertising world – and we always insisted on recruiting lads who were just as unable to trap and pass a ball as those they replaced. I have never seen such a sorry sight as our dressing room before games. We looked more like a weight-watchers gathering than a soccer team; indeed some of the boobs on show were as big as the ones in the adverts I mentioned earlier. The manager-cum-captain-cum-secretary did his best, though. He solemnly read out the team formation (a total waste of time, since there were only nine of us, and once the referee blew his whistle everyone wanted to be centre-forward anyway). Then he told us how we should play. Now my football career has taken me into dressing rooms all over the world, and ever since the age of eleven the pre-match team talk has nearly always been the same: "Let's keep it simple lads, pass it around, ball to feet". Don't they realise that if any of us knew how to do those things – keep it simple, ball to feet – we'd be playing for Paris Saint-Germain, not freezing our nuts off on a Monday night!

We did at least start with the right intentions, though. At the blow of the ref's whistle, one forward tapped the ball sideways to another, he in turn rolled it back to the midfield, and from there it was shifted back to the centre-half. Centre-halves being centre-halves, he invariably made a mess of the straightforward pass out to the full-back, and by now the opposition's entire forward line was in our penalty area. Panic stations. Corner. Our simple, ball-to-feet passing game had lasted all of ten seconds, and from now on it would be strictly kick and rush.

The second half was always worse than the first, mainly because the sort of defensive resolve that had kept the ball out of our net for the first ten minutes of the game was seriously undermined by the half-time departure (without a word of explanation) of our two central defenders. And I swear I saw them holding hands as they walked through the front gates.

I suppose being on the end of a hiding each week did at least give me the opportunity to observe just how good the French could be when they played football. Some of the teams we faced actually played their serious football in good quality leagues on the weekend, and treated these Monday night games as training sessions. To the spectator – I might have been on the field but I felt like one that night – it was lovely to watch. Whereas every time one of our players had the ball we all screamed in pointless unison for a pass (the sole aim of the player in question being to boot it as far up the pitch as possible), by contrast when one of our opponents had it there came no collective shout, just a hissed "sch" from one or two of his team-mates to say, "here I am, I'm available if you want me". Quick passing, scintillating technique, it was a joy to watch. Our opponents went home to their proud wives that night with "hat-trick" written all over their faces, and I was left sulking over my first ever own goal and my worst ever defeat – and not even the chance of drowning my sorrows with my team-mates. In the quiet solitude of my car as I drove home, I reflected upon how pathetic we had been, how pathetic *I* had been, and, most pathetic of all, how I couldn't live without it. Football. Bloody hell.

France Pub Espoirs 0 Equipeforte 13

Olympique Lyonnais vs. Nottingham Forest
Lyon, France
5 December, 1995

Name-drops

It's great being the close relative of a famous footballer, it really is. Apart from the tremendous pride at seeing your own flesh and blood kick a ball about in front of thousands of adoring fans, newspaper journalists and television cameras, there is the added thrill of watching strangers' heads turn when you cleverly slip the family link into conversation. What? You're Steve Stone's uncle? Wow! What's it like?

If you've got two hours, I'll tell you.

At first I milked the Steve connection quite a lot. It was a way of becoming sort of famous myself without actually having to put any of the work in. Sitting with strangers on a train, for example, I would gently coax the conversation along a set of rails whose destination was known only to me. It would usually start with some casual mention of Nottingham (got friends there, have you?), no, that's where my nephew lives (what's he doing there?), he's a footballer (what, a professional?), yes, with Nottingham Forest (really, what's his name?), oh, I don't suppose you'll have heard of him, (go on, try me), Steve Stone.

Steve Stone! The England player! And I had them eating out of my hands after that.

But I mellowed over the years. Amazingly, I found that some people weren't at all interested in knowing who my nephew was. And a lot of those who already did were getting fed up of me going on about him. Just jealous? Maybe, but I learned my lesson and shut up.

Which isn't something that can be said for Dad. At his age, life's too short to worry about what the other bloke thinks. Take the time he turned up for his first lesson at a French evening course just days after seeing Steven play for England. The teacher asked the students to tell the rest of the class, in their best French, what they had been up to during the previous week. Dad was champing at the bit, of course, and when his chance came, he casually recounted how, "Monday I am go library, Tuesday I am go Gateshead buy potatoes, Wednesday I am go Wembley watch my grandson make goal for England..." And he spent the rest of the lesson signing autographs.

Dad was unstoppable. The whole of Low Fell knew who his grandson was. They also knew that Steven had been born on the same day of the year as him (20th August), as if therein lay the secret to his success. Yet Dad didn't actually go to watch that many of Steven's matches. "Too cold, too far, can't be bothered", and Mam it was who usually grabbed the chance to go in his place.

One match Dad wouldn't have missed for the world, however, was the second leg of the third round of the UEFA Cup, in which, as luck would have it, Forest had been drawn against Olympique Lyonnais. Here was Dad's opportunity to return to the region in which he had been born three-quarters of a century before, as well as to show off his famous grandson to the whole branch of the family that still lived there.

Dad's only problem was going to be how to communicate all of this. For despite the French birth certificate and all those lessons, his French never got much past "the book is red" stage. This isn't to say that he didn't kid us on for years that he was totally fluent ("je parle très bien le français, like"). Speaking a foreign language is a bit like playing football – self-confidence is everything. So on rare get-togethers with our French cousins, we'd all watch on in admiration at the ease with which Dad switched from Geordie to French and back to Geordie again. It was only when I started learning the language myself that I realised he'd been talking a load of Balzac all along. I would cringe as he listened with great intent to his dear cousin Charles – with whom, until the latter passed away, he shared a cross-border weakness for anything alcoholic – only to completely miss the point and reply with total nonsense. About the only time Dad ever managed to complete a French sentence without mixing it with Geordie was in asking for special rates for pensioners, in which case his French was of the purest Molière. Curiously, though, neither he nor Charles ever seemed to mind not having a clue what the other was saying, no doubt because the Pastis bottle – the one language they did have in common – was always on hand to translate.

A couple of days before the game, I picked up Dad at Paris Charles de Gaulle airport, and he spent the whole of the drive down the A6 motorway to Lyon rehearsing – in French – his favourite stock phrases about Steven. Three hundred miles later he was fluent, and two days after that he'd bored the life out of half of Lyon. He built Steven up so much that anything less than a hat-trick on the night and we'd both look silly.

The game itself followed exactly the same course Forest's three other games against French opposition (Auxerre in the previous round, and the first leg against Lyon) had followed: the French played football the French way, the English played football the English way. In other words, neither Steven nor his Forest team-mates got a kick, yet somehow they managed to qualify for the next round.

Guy Roux, the renowned Auxerre coach, once commented that the English are only interested in what goes on in the penalty area. He was right, too. What he forgot to mention was that the French are only interested in what goes on *outside* the penalty area. In those days at least, they approached the game of football in rather the same way they approached eating food – by making a huge meal out of it: a lengthy entrée (Barthez to Desailly to Thuram to Desailly), an indescribably rich *plat de résistance* (Deschamps to Zidane to Zidane to Zidane), and far too much farting about over the *fromage* (whose turn to shoot today, Roquefort or Camembert?). The reward – just desserts if you like – was often nothing but indigestion. Such was the case for the frustrated fans of Auxerre and Lyon. After three hundred and sixty minutes of football, it was the beans-on-toast, shoot-on-sight philosophy of the English that won the day, despite match statistics that must have read something like this:

French teams, 99% of the ball, 0 goals.

Nottingham Forest, 1% of the ball, 2 goals.

For Dad, it was an emotional few days in Lyon, the highlight of which turned out to be neither Forest's going through nor seeing all the French family again. The BBC got wind that Steve Stone's granddad had been born in Lyon and wanted to interview the great Louis Henri Rowell himself. Dad, never one to shun the limelight, was more than happy to oblige. He treated his two minutes worth like Opportunity Knocks', telling a few funnies and slipping in the bit about Steven being born on his birthday. He was in a particularly jovial mood when we made it back to the hotel that night, so we nipped out for a last pint to celebrate his overnight stardom. Then the barman switched on the television and there was our Steven chasing this French player up and down the wing, and I could see from Dad's change in expression that he was busily organising whole French sentences in his mind, in readiness for the big name-drop.

"Dad, don't bother. He's not interested"

"I'm going to tell him."

"Dad…"

"Lui, c'est mon petit-fils. Steve Stone. Vous connaissez ?…"

Blank look.

"…Nous avons le même anniversaire, lui et moi…"

Another blank look.

" …Je suis born à Lyon, moi. Je suis parlé avec le BBC…"
Another blank look, plus a grunt.

"Bloody hell, what a miserable bloke. Haway, Robert, pay up and let's go somewhere else."

Olympique Lyonnais 0   Nottingham Forest 0

Newcastle United vs. Manchester United
Munich, Germany
4 March, 1996

Close

Question: what do the following football teams have in common?

  Arsenal
  Aston Villa
  Birmingham City
  Blackburn Rovers
  Burnley
  Chelsea
  Coventry City
  Derby County
  Everton
  Ipswich Town
  Leeds United
  Leicester City
  Liverpool
  Luton Town
  Manchester City
  Manchester United
  Middlesbrough
  Norwich City
  Nottingham Forest
  Oxford United
  Queen's Park Rangers
  Sheffield Wednesday

Southampton
Stoke City
Sunderland
Swindon Town
Tottenham Hotspur
West Bromwich Albion
West Ham United
Wimbledon
Wolverhampton Wanderers

Answer: they have all won at least one major domestic trophy (League, F.A. Cup or League Cup) in my life-time.

Question: what do the following football teams have in common?

Blyth Spartans
The Black Horse Pub
Hartlepool United
Kells Lane School
Newcastle United

Answer: they haven't.

Visitors shopping on Northumberland Street in Newcastle's town centre could be forgiven for thinking that the occasional cries of "The end is nigh" are coming from your usual High Street presence of Jehovah's Witnesses. But they'd be wrong. Were they to listen carefully, they would discover that it's not the end of the world that is being prophesied, but the end of misery for all Newcastle United supporters: "And so it is written that the Lads shall win something very soon. Honest."

Of course nobody on Geordieside buys that brainwash nowadays. But there was a time not so long ago – mid-January 1996, when Newcastle led the Premiership by as many as twelve points – when people began to think there might be something in it. "For so it is written that twelve points is too great a gap even for Manchester United to bridge." Certainly, looking at all the combinations of results possible up to the end of the season, there seemed to be no way we could be caught. The end really was nigh. We were about to win the holiest grail of them all – the league title – for the first time in seventy years.

Seventy years! It is as disgraceful as it is amazing. I mean, you'd think a football-daft town like Newcastle, with its massive local talent base (rivalled in England perhaps only by Merseyside) and huge supporter backing, would win the league a bit more often than that. But no. What's more, the team that was about to walk away with the championship hardly had a Geordie in it. A typical starting eleven that season included as many as eight "foreigners", most of whom had been paid for out of Sir John Hall's private fortune:

Newcastle United, 1995-96 season

Shaka Hislop
(Hackney)

Steve Watson Darren Peacock Steve Howey John Beresford
(Geordie)   (Bristol)   (Sunderland)   (Sheffield)

Keith Gillespie Robert Lee Lee Clark David Ginola
(Ireland)   (Hornchurch) (Geordie)   (France)

Les Ferdinand   Peter Beardsley
(London)   (Geordie)

If only Newcastle had a decent scouting system, plus the kind of glamour (i.e. chances of winning something) you need to keep local favourites at the club, we might not have needed any "foreigners" at all. Just for fun, have a look at the hypothetical "Local Lads Eleven" below (with incidentally over 250 England caps between them). As you will see, only five players were on Newcastle's books that year. It is up for debate whether they and the six "that got away" would have fared as well as Kevin Keegan's team above, but one thing is for sure: had Newcastle spotted them all first (and hung on to them), today Sir John Hall would be some thirty million quid better off!

Local Lads Eleven, 1995-96 season

Steve Harper
(Newcastle U.)

Steve Watson   Steve Bruce   Colin Cooper   Robbie Elliott
(Newcastle U.)   (Man. Utd.)   (Forest)   (Newcastle U.)

Steve Stone   Paul Gascoigne   Lee Clark   Chris Waddle
(Forest)   (Lazio)   (Newcastle U.)   (Sheff. Wed.)

Alan Shearer   Peter Beardsley
(Blackburn)   (Newcastle U.)

Of course nobody cared where United's players came from at the time. At the rate they were picking up points (a massive fifty-four from their first twenty-three games), they were all honorary Geordies to us. Even when our form dipped ever so slightly in February, and despite what was to be the start of a breath-taking run by Man. United, when the two teams met at Saint James' Park at the beginning of March we were still four points clear with a game in hand. Win and we'd be home and dry.

Circumstances dictated that I was in Germany at the time. Nottingham Forest were due to play their UEFA Cup quarter-final, first-leg game against Bayern Munich the day after the Man. United game, and the Steve Stone International Fan Club was there to see it. Bri Dixon, my oldest Newcastle United mate, came with his wife Angela. So too did our John, now living in Rome and by now a born-again Magpie (though never quite as credible as us "lifers", proof of which came when he chose to lay a kitchen floor instead of watching Man. United take us apart in the 1999 F.A. Cup Final). Other of Steven's fans in attendance were my old mates Paul, from Sheffield, Luca and Erika from Italy, and finally Volker, my firm's German Finance Director ("von and von is two"), himself a Bayern Munich supporter.

The Forest match was of course just an excuse, as Volker would put it, for a "couple of beers – the first and the last." After all, the game itself was only going to last an hour and a half, yet we arrived in Munich fully five days before! It turned out to be a fairly dull encounter, too (two-one to Bayern), played in front of a half-full Olympic Stadium that was impressive only for being totally void of atmosphere. Indeed the only highlight of the evening was my going back to the hotel wearing Jürgen Klinsmann's sweaty number nine shirt, which he had swapped with our Steven at the final whistle.

No, what really had our stomachs churning took place the previous evening, And it wasn't the heavy German food that was responsible, either. Bri, John and I tried very hard to laugh along to Luca's approximate translations of jokes that were already dreadful in his native Italian, but our minds were elsewhere. At half-time, John rang home and came back with heartening news from Saint James': Newcastle were on top and Man. United hadn't yet left their own half. Indeed were it not for goalkeeper Schmeichel we'd be six-nil up. "It's just a matter of time," John's wife had said.

It *was* just a matter of time, too. At full-time – while Luca was coming to the punchline of his all-time favourite – John returned from the phone box with the sort of glum expression that told it all. Eric Cantona, said John. Because zee frog hees baldy, quipped Luca. Ja ja ja, laughed Volker. Shut your gobs will you, said Brian. Time for bed, said Zebedee. The rest is history. Pity. The end had been nigh, very nigh.

Goodness knows what will happen if Newcastle ever do win the league. It really could be the end of the world. After a three-day long Geordie version of Armageddon – Armageddon smashed the neet, the morra neet and the neet after that – what I'm really afraid of is waking up on day four with an almighty hang-over and the understanding that suddenly there is nothing else worth living for. And then what? A nervous breakdown, perhaps? Suicide, even? God only knows. I tell you what, though – and this is a message for the management and players of Newcastle United Football Club – I think I'm willing to take the risk

Newcastle United 0   Manchester United 1

England vs. Germany
Wembley, London
26 June, 1996

Strong South-Easterly

> *This blessed plot, this earth,*
> *This realm, this England.*

Penalties against the Germans again. Five-each. All those about me were singing Football's Coming Home as if they really believed we were going to win. Then Gareth Southgate stepped up to take England's sixth and we all thought, What? Gareth Southgate?

I don't blame Southgate for taking that penalty. I blame everyone around him for letting him take it in the first place. For letting him think that – despite hardly having taken a penalty in his entire life, nor practised beforehand – he could just walk up and have an eighty per cent chance of beating Andreas Kopke in the German goal. I blame it on that amateurish, "have a go" side to the English make-up which takes pleasure in watching George take on the dragon. I blame it too on Agincourt, Waterloo, the Battle of Britain, and those other great landmarks in our history that, over time, have lulled us into a false sense of superiority over all those "greasy bloody foreigners".

As if we had something to feel superior about. Take football. For a nation of forty-odd million self-appointed masters of the beautiful game, England's record is rather like Newcastle's – mostly mid-table. And to think that we once deemed it below our station to participate in the first World Cups, only to lose to the U.S.A. when we did finally take part in 1950! That should have opened a few eyes, but it didn't. Even the one high point that was 1966 only served to wrap us in English-is-best blankets for another thirty years. In that time we failed to qualify for as many as three out of six World Cups.

French football guru Guy Roux once said, "the English invented the game, but they didn't change much between 1890 and 1990." He was no doubt referring to our good old-fashioned, get-it-in-the-box approach, but he was right only in part, since at international level we did at least try to change. Whatever justification successive England managers had for abandoning the quick-paced, in-their-faces, Saturday afternoon game that used to win us so many European trophies at club level, abandon it they did. For as long as I can remember, we have been trying to play the international game "their" way. The continental way. Only to get hopelessly lost somewhere in the middle. I mean, possession football and patient build-up play are as alien to our boys as kissing each other on both cheeks. I don't know about you but when I was a lad, retaining possession was considered fannying about and as often as not you got clobbered for it. It was a case of whatever you do, do it quickly. Maybe this is why the closest our national team ever comes to "playing the ball about" is the goalkeeper throwing it to the centre-half, who shoves it wide to the left-back, and HOOF! away it goes down the line. As the flying Dutchman Johann Cruyff once said, "When I played I always loved to go out against English teams because they always gave you the ball back if you lost it. They still do."

Some people blame the coaches. I reckon it's in our genes. The fact of the matter is that we Anglo-Saxons are quite different from everybody else. We neither possess the exuberant, festive ways of the Brazilians (at least not unless we're smashed out of our heads); nor do we know how to dive, kick, spit, tug and lean on opponents (in short, cheat) the way the Argentinians and Italians do; we don't have that confident, "we have ways of making you lose" attitude of the Germans; and we have nowhere near the same supplies of poise and grace that gush from the Dutch and French systems. For while it's true English league matches are probably the most fun to watch, were it not for foreign imports they would be seriously short of silk. No, grass-roots football in our country is not finesse, theatrics and cunning. It is get stuck in. Bulldog fighting spirit. Robust shoulder charges. Muddy pitches. Cold showers. No stars, only heroes – no wonder nobody's ever interested in the England manager's job.

And no Zinedine Zidanes, either. According to Alan Hudson, "Zidane would never have made the grade if he'd been born and raised in this country. Not because he would have been outshone by more skilful youngsters – quite the opposite. He would have lacked the ability of our kids to run all day and run around like headless chickens."

This peculiar preference we English have for brawn over brain can be seen, heard, felt at every football ground in the country; from the stands at Saint James' to the muddy centre circles of Sunday mornings. And although there are indications of an ever so slight shift in attitudes, our conservative island ways will no doubt ensure that nothing will change too quickly. In short, we are English. And proud of it.

Now if you'll just help me down from my high horse a second, I will be happy to concede that all is not gloom. From time to time, we do actually turn out an England team that, with a little bit of luck, looks as if it might go all the way. Take Euro '96, which could very well have been "the one". We had home soil advantage, a coach in Terry Venables who really seemed to know what he was doing, and players like Shearer, Sheringham, Gascoigne, Adams and Seaman all at the heights of their careers. After an unconvincing start, by the time we had reached the semi-finals we were so confident of our chances against the Germans that the Daily Mirror devoted whole pages to taunting the "hun" in one of the most embarrassing moments in the history of English xenophobia.

We just about deserved to win, too. Then Southgate stepped up to take that penalty. And missed. And suddenly it struck us that football wasn't coming home after all, it was going back to Germany and the continent, where it had been, and might well be staying, for years.

England 1 Germany 1
(after extra-time)
(Germany went through 6-5 on penalties)

WCJ Frankfurt vs. Dingsbumsmannschaft
Munich, Germany
13 July,1996

Sizzling

Sausages everywhere.

Sausages for breakfast,
Sausages for tea,
Sausages for you,
Sausages for me.

Bratwurst, Weißwurst
Curywurst too,
Ich bin having ein Berliner
What about you?

Sausages like the ones sitting half-finished in front of me. Next to a hardly touched bowl of dumpling soup Uri Geller would have been proud of for the mess it had made of my spoon.

I was of course back in Germany. Other than the contents of my plate and the fact that Munich was written on my plane ticket, it was clear just from glancing at the passers-by that the majority were German. The women were on the whole very, very attractive (lovely, long blonde hair, lovely, long blonde legs), and I could only wonder at what they ever saw in their other halves, who must rank among the most unstylish, badly-dressed men on our planet: the three hairs dangling like broken legs they dare call a moustache; the tuft of hair that mushrooms from a point just above the forehead; that angry, Teutonic Nein! Nein! Nein! frown you see on the faces of certain German soccer players (goalkeeper Kahn, midfielder Effenberg) – no wonder they always beat us. As for elegance, whereas the Italians can take three colours and look like a million dollars, give the same three colours to a German and you have a flower show: never have I seen so many purple jackets, and the airport was bedlam what with all those loud ties.

And behind the kaleidoscope exterior? Before I joined the company, I must say my image of the Germans was pretty much the "square heeds" version I'd got off Mrs. Carson during my Dean Street days, an opinion she held to be the absolute truth despite having been no closer to Germany than Dad's war wound. She was of course quite wrong. Other than a terribly annoying habit of thumping their fists on the table in order to get their own way, I found them to be a very pleasant, friendly people. Certainly on my business travels I was given as warm a reception in Frankfurt as I ever was in London.

Which brings me to why I was back in Munich in the first place. Every July, a train sets off from one end of the country (this year it was Hamburg) and makes its way to the other end (this year Munich), where the Advertising Agency Cup, a weekend football tournament, takes place. On its way, the train is boarded by the players, supporters and crates of beer from forty or so advertising agencies, and by journey's end everyone is sozzled.

Having flown in direct from Paris that same afternoon, I missed out on the cross-Germany bender, and finally met my new team-mates at a debriefing held in the hotel lobby that evening. As soon as the elevator doors opened, I could hear the heavy German laughter and animated *ja-ja-ja*-ing that told me everyone was in party mood. Until they saw me, that is, at which there was a great hush. You see, I shouldn't really have been there at all. Officially, "ringers" weren't allowed. More importantly, this lot had been training twice a week for months in order to build a team to take on the rest of Germany – about the only training I had put in was for a pie-eating contest. So what right did I have to just come along on the eve of match-day and spoil everything?

The answer was that I happened to work for the company's European headquarters, which gave me the right to pee in their waste-paper baskets if I felt like it. I was also a big mate of their boss, Volker. Wasn't I the one who had let Volker borrow my Jurgen "Klinsy" Klinsmann shirt to take into the office so that they could all sniff its armpits? That, I think, is what swung it.

I gingerly pulled up a chair to join the outside of the group, and their coach, Herr Grappatoni, explained the strategy for the following day. I never felt so out of place in all my life – I didn't even speak the language! Never mind, I said to myself, laugh wenn zey laugh, nod wenn zey nod. It was going to be one of those weekends.

Advertising people being advertising people, they had spent lavishly for the occasion. And Germans being Germans, it was immaculately organised. The tournament playing fields were in perfect condition, the goal-nets had all the holes in the right places, and the white lines were at perfect right-angles. On the Saturday morning we gathered in our private team tent (specially built for the occasion), brand new jerseys were brought out of brand new boxes, and there was even a change strip in the event of colour clashes. All those around me were pulling on pristine, shoot-straight Adidas Predators at a hundred and thirty quid a pair, with studs that were shiny bright and legal. And there was I, ashamed at my dirty old boots with rough, well-worn studs more suitable for ripping legs open to the bone than gripping the playing surface. The seriousness of it all brought home to me that at thirty-six, I was getting on a bit, and that the stone and a half I'd put on in the few months since I had last kicked a ball wouldn't last more than five minutes on a boiling hot day like this. In short they were fit, fresh, and German, I was fat, fading, and English. They were winners, I was a loser. With Euro '96 still ringing in my ears, I struggled not to cry.

Grappatoni gathered us round a huge notepad on which he had drawn a football pitch, and placed in their respective positions the names of the eleven players who would be starting the first match. He then instructed each player on his role, showing him with the help of three or four arrows the positions he was to take up depending on who had the ball and where. I understood none of it, of course, but I'd seen arrows like that in the Italian sports newspapers and was greatly impressed. Privately, I was also immensely relieved that my own name was nowhere to be seen, since I had no intention of putting my country to shame on German soil.

During the brief warm-up I watched on as fantastic shots were blasted at goal from all angles, then took my place on the sidelines with the girl supporters, who were all dressed up as cheerleaders and chanting songs that they'd clearly been rehearsing for weeks. It was all so professional, all so organised, and I prepared myself for a lesson in power-play football.

The game kicked off and I couldn't believe my eyes as the ball bounced off one guy's knee – the one who had smashed in a stunning thirty-yard volley in the pre-match warm-up – before sliding under the boot of another. Twenty-two players completely ignored the pre-match game plans and raced after the ball like a bunch of five-year-olds. They tripped over their pony tails, complained at being shoulder-charged, dodged out of the way of headers, and play had to be stopped at one stage so that our centre-half could search for his missing earring. Effen Berg! They were crap! Crap like the advertising people I'd played with in France. Crap like advertising people the world over. Let me on!

It wasn't until we were two-nil down with ten seconds to go that Grappatoni, seeing the opportunity to clear his conscience, decided he'd better bring old baldy on and get it over with. That way he wouldn't have to play me again and I'd be free to get changed and fly back to France. As soon as I ran onto the pitch the referee blew his final whistle, I shook hands with the opponent standing closest to me and thought wow, thanks a million for the game.

Lunch came as a welcome break. I knew that I probably wouldn't be kicking another ball all weekend, so I thought what the hell, tucked into sausage of the day and had a beer or two. I was still bringing up wind one hour later when our left midfielder was forced to come off with two suspected wrong feet, and Grappatoni was left with no choice. My wobbling kilos took to the field to the distinct sound of sniggers, and ambulances began rolling towards our pitch in the hope of some violent vomiting or, you never know, a heart attack. Unfold the stretchers and prepare the oxygen, boys!

Being the obvious weak link in the team, our opponents immediately swung the ball out to their winger, who came happily tip-tapping his way down the touchline, la-di-da-di-da, oh vot a beautiful Tag, almost as if the sweaty, wheezing egg-head coming towards him wasn't even there. He was no doubt thinking ahead to the cross he was going to put in once he'd reached the byline when I thought stuff this lark and came lunging in with probably the best slide tackle of my whole life. In text-book fashion, the ball stuck to the inside of my outstretched boot, and my startled opponent landed like a bunch of Allen keys ten yards up the line.

To the disappointment of the ambulance men and surprise of everyone else, I picked myself up, laid the ball off, and there was no looking back. By the time the first half had ended several minutes later, Grappatoni had turned to a fresh page in his notepad and stuck "Robert" bang in the middle of it, with more arrows sticking out than a medieval court jester going into battle.

The twenty minutes of the second half were of the rare sort that I have already burdened you with in this book, where everything came off, and which culminated in a loopy dribble that led to our second goal. By the final whistle they were singing my name, and I was all but carried off the pitch shoulder-high.

At the huge party held for all the participants that evening I was made to feel like a superstar. People who had previously snubbed me by talking in German were now coming up to me to compliment me in English on how well I'd played. They didn't need to speak English, though, since with all the free drinks I could have spoken Bavarian. There were even some girls hanging around, too, and I thought *ja ja ja*, my chances are looking good. But this was at about that time in the evening when you take the one fatal sip that suddenly has you thinking you can drink all the beer in the world and still be witty and charming – before going into lager overload and the rest is a blur. For sure the only stiffness I ended up experiencing that weekend was in my legs, which I quietly and painfully accompanied back to Paris the next afternoon.

WCJ Frankfurt 2   Dingsbumsmannschaft 0

Thirteen Men vs. Twelve Men And A Girl
Bois de Boulogne, Paris, France
August 1996

Sultry

The Bois de Boulogne in Paris is a huge, wooded park which part-time joggers, cyclists and footballers happily share with full-time prostitutes. Stunning Brazilians, transvestites, lorry-drivers (and that's just the footballers!), it is a veritable drive-in brothel that mostly caters for slackened neck-ties in spacious German cars. Needless to say I went there every night after work – if only because it was the quickest route home.

On one occasion, just one (honest, officer!), did I actually get out of the car and expose my nether regions. I regret that I sank lower that day than I had ever sunk before, this in accepting to join in, sin of all sins... a kickabout with a bunch of computer geeks – imagine the scandal if anyone from the office ever found out!

The soccer pitches at the Bois were out of shape and all overgrown at the sides, in perfect keeping with those who played on them. I will spare you the sordid details of the game itself, except to say that after spending the customary French half-hour trying to persuade everyone to stop chasing footballs about so we could form two teams, I then spent the rest of the evening watching on as if the two teams had never been formed at all. While others frolicked about in the long grass in search of the goal that would win the World Cup Final, I stayed at the back, arms folded, watching how football was played at the wrong end of life. Every five minutes the ball would come bouncing my way, at which I would lay it off and fold my arms again. I had all the time in the world to reflect upon my day at work, the agenda for tomorrow's trip to Lisbon or wherever, and my football career to date, which the Rothmans Guide to Everyday Football (were such a book to exist) might have summed up as follows:

Robert Henry Rowell   Midfield
Born: Gateshead   7-8-59
Height: 5' 11"
Weight: 13st 1lb
Source: Dean Street Rovers

Season(s)	Apps	Goals
Kells Lane Primary School 1969-70	6	2
School House tournaments 1972-77	9	5
Dryden Senior High School 1974-75	5	1
Charterac (Sheffield) 1978-82	65	15
Friendlies (Sheffield) 1980-83	6	1
Bradkirk (Sheffield) 1982-83	22	2
Friendlies/tournaments (Milan) 1983-86	15	2
Solese (Milan) 1984-86	11	2
Derviese (Como) 1986-87	6	0
Bar Sport (Como) 1987-91	75	9
Various tournaments (Como) 1988-90	5	2
Friendlies/tournaments (Paris) 1991-96	19	1
France Pub Espoirs (Paris) 1992-96	33	7
Munich tournament 1996	2	0
TOTAL	**279**	**49**

So there I was, the sweetest right foot in the universe, and all I had to show for it were a twenty-six year career that some players get through in a fifth of that time. Not to mention a miserable average of just two goals a season!

It is fair to say that a trophy room will never be on the list of priorities in my house. In fact the only thing remarkable about my football career is that I had the cheek to write a book about it. Imagine: not once in a quarter of a century did I do any of the following in eleven-a-side competition:

* captain my team
* give away a penalty
* take a penalty
* foul anyone on purpose
* punch the referee
* get sent off

The other thing I'd never done on a football pitch, nor come close to doing since my Sheffield days, was score three goals in a match. Which brings me conveniently back to the game at the Bois. There was this girl in their team, who ran around doggy-paddle the way girls do, and who held up play for ten seconds every time she measured up to kick the ball. She spent most of the time standing very close to, sometimes even on, our goal-line, ignored by all except our goalkeeper and a cigarette-smoking defender who, in trying to chat her up, also happened to play her onside – not that any of those present knew exactly what the offside rule was.

Three times the ball chanced the girl's way, and three times she somehow helped it over the line. Not the greatest hat-trick I'd ever seen, but you ask Alan Shearer if he cares how they go in. There I was, I'd never scored a hat-trick in my whole life and now, shame of all shames, I was being shown how to by a girl.

Thirteen Men 15   Twelve Men And A Girl 11

England vs. Italy
Hotel Weiberhoefe, Aschaffenberg, Germany
Late summer 1996

Waterlogged

Corner to England. Our John takes it, Italy's Paolo Maldini makes a complete hash of clearing his lines, the ball drops to me and my fumbled left-foot effort somehow works its way through the crowd of players and into the bottom corner. Goal! One-nil to England!

Franco Baresi robs our Steven but his pass back to the 'keeper stops short in the mud. I pounce on it, take the ball forward, unchallenged, and find myself one-on-one with Walter Zenga. I notice there is a big gap to his right, so I smash the ball past him and he doesn't even dive for it. Goal! Two-nil!

Free-kick thirty yards out on the right. I take my place on the corner of the eighteen-yard box, our Gloria steps up to take it, the ball is floated over, here it comes, here it comes…

…hold on a second, if this is the World Cup Final, what is our Gloria doing taking free-kicks for England? And why are we using coats for goalposts? Why are Maldini and Baresi shouting instructions in Geordie? What's this toy train set doing in the middle of the penalty area? And why is there beer all down the front of my shirt and tie?

Shirt and tie? The television screen in my head goes all fuzzy and I gradually come to my senses. It was, of course, a dream. For a start, I'm not a professional footballer, I'm a financial something-or-other. And I'm not at Wembley, I'm lying on a sofa in a dark and unfamiliar room. A hotel? Yes, now I remember. I'm in Germany on business. And oh bloody hell, I'm soaked to the skin – I must have dozed off while drinking that last can.

It's the same old dream. The same one as last night, only we were playing Brazil and I was in Madrid. The same one as the night before, back home in France against the Germans – I know they were German because they all wore purple jackets. And always the same theme: there I am playing in the World Cup Final, and just as I am about to score my third goal the picture fades and I come round. How I would love, just once, to complete that elusive hat-trick, lift the World Cup, drink champagne in the dressing room with the lads, smile and joke at the press and television interviews, and take my pick among the beautiful girls waiting for me outside – and all that *before* waking up.

That dream tells me a lot about myself. First, despite the fact that I am now in my late thirties and "past it", the dreamer in me still craves for glory in football, the sort of easy glory you don't have to work too hard for (this is why, in the fantasies of my mind at least, defenders miskick their clearances, goalkeepers never move, and I'm the one who gets to score all the goals). Second – just in case you hadn't already worked it out – I'm a spineless weed for never having transformed those dreams into reality. Someone once asked legendary Liverpool manager Bill Shankly whether he thought the "This Is Anfield" sign above the tunnel leading out onto the pitch ever put the fear up the away team's players. His clever answer, "Only the bad ones", referred to easily-intimidated people like me. Not that I ever played at Liverpool, you understand. It's just that at each major Anfield of my own career, somehow I always bottled it.

Finally, that dream is a nightly reminder that I have never, ever scored a hat-trick. Imagine the conversations with my grandkids: "Aye, yer granddad was a hell of a player. Could turn on a sixpence, dribble through the opposition as if they weren't there, hit the top corner from forty yards every time. Could have walked into any team in the Premiership, yer granddad could, and scored hat-tricks every week."

"Granddad, what's a hat-trick?"

"A hat-trick? Oh, it's when one player scores three goals in the same game, son."

"Oh, I see. So you being such a marvellous footballer, then, you must have scored loads of hat-tricks, right? How many did you get, granddad?"

"Oh, my fair share. I could shoot with either foot, me, you know! Now do us a favour and go and fetch my slippers like a good lad."

"Yes, in a minute, but how many hat-tricks did you score?"

"Erm, well, I was a midfielder, you know. I was a hell of a passer of a ball. I could hit a door-handle from forty yards, son, I could."

"How many exactly, granddad?"

"Erm, well… none son."

"Here, granddad, take your cod liver oil and I'll go and get those slippers."

How am I ever going to get around admitting to my grandkids that the greatest footballer that ever lived never, ever scored a hat-trick? Not in a World Cup Final. Not on a park pitch. Not even in my dreams. I must get a hat-trick, any old hat-trick. Just one, before it's too late.

In the meantime, back to reality. Meeting starts in one hour and I still don't have a clue what I'm going to do with these soaking wet clothes.

England 2   Italy 0
(abandoned due to waterlogged pitch)

Standard Athletic Club vs. Londoners Disunited
Bois de Meudon, near Paris
Not so very long ago

Twilight

On successive days in September 1996 two things occurred that would change my life: I made my debut for a new football team and I met a new girlfriend. The first was love at first sight, the second would take a little longer. Both, I hoped, would be for ever.

And I thought my career was coming to an end! Our captain is fifty and one of the fittest of the lot. This admittedly doesn't say much for the rest of us, but all these old guys have given me new hope. They are the living evidence that, knees willing, there are another ten years in me yet.

And what a place to do it! The Standard Athletic Club is the oldest surviving football club in France. Founded in 1890 by a group of British engineers who had originally come to Paris to build the Eiffel Tower, it went on to win five French football championships, including the first ever held in 1894. A century later, the twisted moustaches and plus-fours may have long since disappeared but I doubt whether the approach to the game has changed much. Considerable amounts of energy are devoted to shaking the hands of team-mates after a "rather honourable shoulder-charge, my man", or a "frightfully menacing shot, old fellow". And the quality of play is probably just as good as it was then, the only problem being that the rest of the world has long since overtaken us – about the only time we take on the likes of Paris Saint-Germain nowadays is when their over-sixties team comes to play us.

But who cares? I love it, we all love it. After all those years I'm again back with a group of people who understand the real meaning of Sunday life: a kick-about in the morning and a few beers at lunchtime – with lads who don't faint at the sight of a pint! And I'm a happy man. I know I'm happy because I'm doing things I haven't done since my Dean Street days. Like kicking out at invisible footballs in the street, curling them into the top corner of imaginary Big Blue Garage Doors. Oh and muttering running commentaries to myself: IT'S ROWELL…HE SHOOTS…GOAL! Am I the only person in the world who does this?

I can't wait for weekends. When I go up to the club on Sunday mornings I feel at home. To the right on entering the lounge, a painting of the Queen stands majestically over the hearth to commemorate the day she came to open our new clubhouse in 1958. And over on the left, just as British and ten times as important, is our raison d'être. The bar. One that sells salt and vinegar crisps, and Newcastle Brown Ale that sends you just as ding-dong as the Newcastle Brown Ale back home. From there, nice and warm and glass in hand, we look out onto our lush, well-drained, slightly sloping football pitch, reflect upon our morning's glorious achievements, tell manly jokes and drink too much…

…time is running out…Rowell makes one last break from deep…he's got options left and right but he chooses to go straight down the middle…he's past the last man, there's surely no stopping him now…it's one on one…he must, he must…

"Pint of bitter and a packet of salt-and-vinegar crisps, please."

…and he has! Rowell has been served!

All this while my naïve, football-ignorant (and by now) wife is back at the flat thinking the reason I leave home at ten and come back at three is because we play two hours each way. Surely this is what the club's founders had intended the game of football to be all about.

Our team is that usual mixed bag of lawyers, bankers and accountants that tend to make up most F.A. Cup giant-killing sides. Which is where the comparison ends. The fact of the matter is that not many of these lawyers, bankers or accountants played much football when they were kids. Or if they did, it certainly doesn't show. The dressing room talk isn't Shearer and Owen, it's stocks and shares, and the closest any of us ever came to stardom was Jack playing for Ireland – at cricket.

Commitment to turning up isn't exactly one hundred per cent, either. Of the twenty of us promising to be there when Sunday comes, several will drop out during the week due to a dodgy ankle or one of the wife's dodgy mood-swings, one or two will overdo it on Saturday night and simply not turn up, and a couple more will burst a pipe while getting changed before the match. If we're lucky there'll be eleven of us at kick-off time.

The club admits French members nowadays, and on the playing field this makes for an interesting concoction. At some time during the match the French will start bitching with each other ("you haven't passed the ball to me once, not once!") and for a fifteen minute spell we'll effectively be down to seven (British) men. Then there is the range in ages, from the very young (fifteen) to the very old, some of whom are rumoured to have featured in the 1894 championship-winning side. The young whippets charge around in search of lost causes while the oldies take their time, look up, lay the ball off and have a well-earned rest. Every time they kick out at something (the ball usually, but it might be an opponent's leg or thin air) you hear all sorts of clanging and snapping noises, and each match produces more discarded bandages, broken screws and bone fragments than your average hip operation.

I have a foot in both the young and the old camps. For ten minutes of each game I pretend I can still do it by running around and getting stuck in, then spend the rest of the time plodding along with the mobility and elegance of a combine harvester – my turns on the ball nowadays are of the three-point variety. Then there are the knees, the only bones in my body not to have stood the test of time, and which would crumble to dust were I ever to crouch down to look for something under the wardrobe. Every time they creak I know they are telling me, "Hey, enjoy it while you can!" In a nutshell, I now fit into that category old pros refer to of "doing a job", which basically means scything down those younger and quicker than myself, and saying stupid things like my brain knows what to do but my legs can't follow.

Actually, we are not a bad side. OK, we don't play in a league or anything, but we do play some decent football: passes that reach their man, balls played below Eiffel Tower level, that kind of stuff. Pure p-l-e-a-s-u-r-e. Oh how I love this game. We also win far more matches than we lose. Admittedly, our opponents are generally of the plimsoll-wearing kind that play two matches a year (both against us), and don't own a full set of strips. They come, they play, they admire the full-blooded British approach, drink their lemonades and go home. Most importantly, they let us win (by six goals to four, on average), otherwise we don't invite them back. In short, I have found the ideal stage on which to end my football career.

And the elusive hat-trick, I hear you ask? For a couple of seasons it remained as remote a possibility as ever. Of all the things I'd become good at over the previous thirty years, scoring goals wasn't one of them. It's strange. Like Ray Wilkins I could ping a thirty-yard pass with either foot to within a yard or two of a team-mate, yet when it came to hitting any one of the 192 (yes, that's one hundred and ninety-two) square feet that make up the regulation goal, whether I be outside the penalty area or standing under the crossbar, nine times out of ten I would fluff it. I used to put this down to the 'keeper's green jersey (green being a bad luck colour in our family), but they stopped wearing green years ago. No, the real cause was the dreaded blood rushes: my God, I'm through, I'm going to score, just wait until I tell the missus! Every red blood cell in my body would receive an urgent message to rush to the brain and join in the coming celebrations, while the calls from that tiny corner of my mind of "hey, keep your head steady and body over the ball!" were completely drowned out. To onlookers it must have looked comical – pathetic even – to see the ball fly off, high, wide and into the trees. Nice legs, shame about the finish.

Don't get me wrong. I have no regrets. There comes a time in life when you accept that you simply weren't good enough anyway, when you start thanking your lucky stars that you're still playing the game at all. But there were odd moments when I just wished there was a touch of the Alan Shearers or Michael Owens in me. These guys make a living out of scoring goals, it is their bread and butter. As soon as they get a sniff, not for a moment do they consider passing the ball to a better placed team-mate (as Sky's Andy Gray, a former centre-forward himself, often says, "he's a striker so he *has* to shoot"). Their approach to the whole shooting event is very clinical, it is purely a question of percentages: stay calm and concentrate on hitting the ball cleanly, and eight times out of ten it will hit the back of the net. Only then – never before – do they allow their arms, face muscles and inner emotions to get the better of them. My bet is that most top strikers would happily exchange their own mother for a goal, whether it be a stunning volley, a tap-in on the line when it was going in anyway, or the last in six when it simply didn't matter any more. That's because in their league table, that of top scorers, every goal is worth a total of exactly one, no more no less. They know too that in fifty years time nobody will care how many of Alan Shearer's 34 league goals in the 1994-95 season came from the penalty spot. "Alan Shearer – 34", that's all that matters.

Similarly, when I come home on a Sunday afternoon having played a blinder, my wife doesn't show the slightest interest in how many goal assists, correct passes or tackles I've donated to our victory. All she wants to know is how many goals I've scored. And once she has her answer (none), she spends the rest of the day wondering what, other than a secret mistress, can possibly justify the smug look on my face.

It wasn't until late on in life that I finally got it into my thick head that, as obvious as it should have been all along, in football it's goals that count. So I set out to show my wife and everyone else that if it was goals they wanted, it was goals they were going to get. I went up for corners, made runs from deep, got in amongst it. Like Alan Shearer and Michael Owen I stopped passing to better placed team-mates, and to my surprise every so often I'd fluke one in. So what if (as several of my team-mates dared comment) my overall performances were on the slide? What mattered was that I could feel the hat-trick coming. And when it did, no one at home was going to need to know the final score was 13-7!

Then one day, it was the last Sunday before Christmas, a team from London came across to France to play us. They went out to get drunk on the Saturday night, and by the time they'd managed to pull themselves out of their beds we were already two-nil up. What's more, I'd scored both. For the first time in fifteen years I was on a hat-trick!

I didn't want to rush things, though. I wanted to earn the hat-trick, savour it when it came. For the next hour I stayed back, let others have a go, and it wasn't until late on – the very last minute, in fact – that my chance finally came...

...Athletic make one last break out of defence, the ball is played to Plummer down on this right-hand side...

As a contest the game was long since over: all their players were hanging around waiting for opening time, while all of ours were rushing forward to get onto the score sheet. Including me. From the very moment I set off from just inside my own half, I sensed that this was the big one.

...Plummer plays a neat one-two with Hellawell, he's got bodies waiting in the penalty area...

Sure enough, here came the ball, the sticky conditions bringing it to a dead stop just inches away from my right boot.

...it reaches Rowell eight yards out...

For once in my life I didn't get the blood rushes. There was no need. The nearest defender was several yards in front, legs crossed and hands over his privates as if he were desperate for the loo, and clearly in no mood to come and spoil my fun. As for the goalkeeper, he was hiding somewhere behind, no doubt praying he wouldn't have to make a dive and get all dirty this late in the game. From my left I could hear Charlie, the Scottish lad, calling "Rob! Rob! Over here! Over here!" No way. In front of goal Charlie was worse than me – he it was who invented the "Loch Ness Monster" shot, the one that bobbles up and down across the surface before disappearing below the murky waters. Finally, just a few yards ahead and slightly to the left were what must have been a thousand four-by-four-inch squares of empty netting, all screaming out, "ROB! ROB! OVER HERE! OVER HERE!"

...surely he can't miss from there...

Part of me wanted to blast the ball into the gaping net and get the drinks in, but another, more philosophical side started asking disturbing questions like whether there wasn't more to life than the cheap thrill of scoring an easy hat-trick against a bunch of hung-over donkeys.

...he'd better hurry though, the referee's about to blow for time...

Then in a flash of inspiration I thought back to the first time I ever saw Jonnie Wales, the day he scored three goals for Lumley against Hilton. What would Jonnie have done in my position? Inwardly, I smiled at the answer. Jonnie Wales wouldn't have looked this or any other gift horse in the mouth. He would simply have walloped it. Buried the bugger. And raced off Alan Shearer-style in celebration.

So I walloped it. Skied the bugger. And raced off Robert
Rowell-style to be first in the showers.

Stuff the hat-trick. See you in the bar, lads.

Standard Athletic Club 6   Londoners Disunited 2

Rain Or Shine

Once upon a time, there was this little boy who had two feet and a ball. His Mam said get yourself out to play...

...and my life has been one, long football match ever since: the warm-ups with my mates in the back lanes of Gateshead; the muddy first-half in Sheffield that often had me pleading to the bench to bring me off; the brighter second-half that was Italy. Overall, probably a draw. And so to France and extra-time.

Have I ever thought of hanging my boots up? Yes, many times. Like when my body aches for days after a match. Or when it's freezing cold. Or at the sight of two middle-aged men shaping up to punch each other after a petty foul. But then there are all the positives. Football keeps me alert and fit. It gets me into an almost embarrassing state of euphoria after we have all played well. And I just love the you-must-be-mental looks people give me when I tell them I'm still kicking a ball about.

I came across some "canny" players over the years, but ask me to name my "most difficult opponent ever" and I'd have to plump for the one I now face every week when I pull my boots on: Father Time. I used to have Time on my side, but at some stage in my life he changed colours without my even noticing. Now, in football terms, he is all over me. Time flies by as if I weren't there, pegs me back into my own half, has me chasing shadows. I defend doggedly, spring the occasional counter-attack, but know full well I can't go on for ever. My only hope is that when Time does, inevitably, score the "golden goal" that puts me out to grass, I will be big enough to shake hands and swap shirts. When exactly that moment will be, only Time can tell, so don't type up your match reports just yet. Meanwhile...free-kick to Rowell... OOOOOOOOoooooohhhhh...

Robert Rowell 0   Father Time 0
(latest score)

Desiderata *(Or How To Play The Game Of Football)*

Go placidly amid the noise and haste and remember what peace there may be in stopping for a moment to put your foot on the ball. As far as possible, without surrender, be on good terms with all your team-mates. Tie your boot-laces quietly and neatly, and listen to others, even the dull and ignorant, for they are generally the ones who pick the team. Avoid getting involved with loud-mouthed, aggressive opponents, they are vexations to the spirit of the game. If you train regularly with others, you will get better and better, for all the great players started out as lesser players like yourself. Enjoy your achievements as well as your plans. Keep confident in your own ability, however humble, it is a real possession in the changing fortunes of a football career. Exercise caution in your penalty area, for the game is full of diving Italians. But let this not blind you to what virtue there is in just hoofing it. Many defenders strive for the highest rows in the stand, and every ground in the country is full of mediocre players being paid a fortune for doing the simple things well. Be yourself. Especially do not feign to go one way if you're then incapable of going the other. Neither be cynical about good ball control, for in the face of many a tricky situation it is as perennial as the grass you play on. Take kindly to the two-touch game of later years, gracefully surrendering the pointless dribbles of youth. Nurture strength of spirit to shield you in sudden fifty-fifty balls. But do not distress yourself with imaginings, many wayward passes are born of fatigue and thinking there is someone up your backside. Beyond a wholesome diet, be gentle with the booze. You are a child of the youth system, no less than the stars and the trees. You have a right to be here, and whether or not it is clear to you, no doubt your career is unfolding as it should. Therefore keep your peace with the referee, whatever you conceive his father's shortcomings to be. And whatever your goal-scoring aspirations, in the noisy confusion of the shooting moment keep your head over the ball. With all its play-acting, thugs and broken dreams, it is still THE beautiful game. Play often. Get in the first tackle.

For further information about Zymurgy Publishing and other independent publishers please access the following web site http://www.ipg.uk.com. All Zymurgy titles may be ordered from all good book shops.

Natural North
by Allan Potts
Foreword by the Duke of Northumberland

A photographic celebration of flora and fauna in the North of England. Supporting text provides background information. Sections cover; high fells, upland, woodland, agricultural, coastal and urban areas.
ISBN 1 903506 00X hb 160pp £16.99

Bent Not Broken
by Lauren Roche

Lauren Roche's autobiography; an abused child, stowaway, stripper, prostitute, drug abuser. She turned her life around to become a doctor. An international best seller. Lauren has been interviewed by Lorraine Kelly, Esther Rantzen, Johnny Walker, Simon Mayo and others.
ISBN 1 903506 026 pb 272pp + 8pp plate section £6.99

A Lang Way To The Pawnshop
by Thomas Callaghan
Introduction by Sid Chaplin

An autobiographical account of growing up in 1930s urban Britain; a family of ten, two bedrooms, no wage earner. An amusing insight into a period of history still in living memory.
ISBN 1 903506 018 pb 144pp £6.99

The Krays: The Geordie Connection

by Steve Wraith and Stuart Wheatman
Foreword by Dave Courtney

After seeing the Krays at a funeral on the news (aged ten) Steve writes letters, meets the brothers and eventually becomes one of 'the chaps'. The book is about the Krays final years and how they ran things on the outside.
ISBN 1 903506 042 pb 240pp + 8pp plate section£6.99

The River Tyne From Sea to Source

by Ron Thornton
Foreword by Robson Green

A collection of nearly eighty water colours and hundreds of pencil drawings following the River Tyne from outside the harbour to the source of the North and South Tyne rivers. Supporting text provides a wealth of information on the history surrounding the Tyne.
ISBN 1 903506 034 hb 160pp £16.99

Life On The Line

by Lauren Roche

Following on from Bent Not Broken the book covers Lauren's life once she becomes a doctor. Bankruptcy, depression, a suicide attempt - and the shock revelation that her son was a sex offender. What can a mother do when she suspects that one of her children is being abused? What happens when you discover that the abused child has become an abuser?
ISBN 1 903506 050 pb 192pp + 8pp plate section £6.99

A Memoir of The Spanish Civil War
by George Wheeler
Foreword by Jack Jones
Edited by David Leach

Thousands from across the world went to Spain to form the International Brigades; many did not return. Through George Wheeler's experience and memories of the Spanish Civil War you will discover what the war was really like. What were they fighing for? Why did the Spanish people fail in their fight against facism?
1 903506 077 pb 192pp + 8pp plate section £8.99

Alcatraz Island Memoirs of a Rock Doc
by Milton Daniel Beacher, M.D
Edited by Dianne Beacher Perfit

MiltonDaniel Beacher, M.D. arrived on Alcatraz Island a naive and compassionate young doctor. One year later he left with a journal.It chronicled the suicides, discipline problems, force feedings, and details of a long strike and successful escape.

He also penned conversations with famous prisoners like Al Capone, Alvin Karpis and Machine Gun Kelly. Dr Beacher later worve the journal into a vivid acoount of life on the Rock.
1 903506 085 pb240 pp + 8pp plate section £6.99